ONE MAN'S FREEDOM

EDWARD BENNETT WILLIAMS

ONE MAN'S FREEDOM

INTRODUCTION BY EUGENE V. ROSTOW
DEAN, YALE LAW SCHOOL

ATHENEUM NEW YORK
1962

Library of Congress card catalog number 62–11689
Published simultaneously in Canada by McClelland & Stewart Ltd
Manufactured in the United States of America by H. Wolff, New York
Designed by Harry Ford
First Printing April 1962
Second Printing May 1962
Third Printing May 1962
Fourth Printing June 1962
Fifth Printing August 1962

ISBN: 978-1-4391-9686-1

Where the mind is without fear and
the head is held high;
Where knowledge is free;
Where the world has not been broken
up into fragments by narrow domestic walls;
Where words come out from the
depth of truth;
Where tireless striving stretches its
arms towards perfection;
Where the clear stream of reason has
not lost its way into the dreary desert
sand of dead habit;
Where the mind is led forward by
Thee into ever-widening thought and
action—
Into that heaven of freedom, my
Father, let my country awake.

RABINDRANATH TAGORE

ACKNOWLEDGMENT

I acknowledge gratefully the advice and help I received in selecting, researching and organizing some of the materials in this book. James E. Clayton rendered invaluable assistance in this area. So, too, did my law partners and associates. John Charles Daly read the first draft and made some wonderfully constructive suggestions.

INTRODUCTION

DURING a conversation two or three years ago with a Russian law professor, I realized that despite all obstacles the idea of the lawyer—the classical, central idea, that is, of the lawyer battling in the criminal courts—corresponds to a universal trait in the human family. Certain kinds of people are irresistibly attracted to the lawyer's role, in that ultimate sense. Like some newspapermen, they prefer to be somewhat withdrawn from the daily work of society, leading lives of independence, even of isolation. They know that things are seldom what they seem, and that many Great Men are stuffed shirts, hypocrites, or the possessors of skeletons in their closets. Lawyers of this stripe are both cynics and idealists. No frailty surprises them; indeed, their surprise is reserved for their occasional confrontations of virtue. Nothing gives them more pleasure and satisfaction than to win a difficult case against the pressure of inflamed opinion, vindicating the stirring principles of the legal tradition against all odds. They have the blood of Don Quixote in their veins. Heaven help a society which lacks men of their breed.

Edward Bennett Williams, though still young, is already a legend in the line that includes Clarence Darrow, John Adams, William H. Seward, Rufus Choate, and many another tough, worldly (and usually soft-hearted) knight-errant of the bar. Once asked why he represented a man of unsavory reputation, he is reported to have said that "no one would think of reproaching a doctor for removing Earl Browder's appendix. Why is there any difference when a lawyer stands up to defend his legal rights?" An able law teacher and practitioner, Mr. Williams is already a notable figure in the profession. At a time when many, perhaps most, young lawyers go into large firms, train as specialists, and become busy, useful, highly organized but restricted participants in one phase of the life of the law, he has demonstrated that an honorable lawyer can have an exciting life representing persons accused of crime.

It is not an easy career. In many places, the criminal practice is riddled with corruption and near-corruption. A sizeable minority of police officers, judges, and others in or near the judicial process are said to be addicted to disgraceful habits, difficult to prove and rarely brought to book. A lawyer, when he meets such problems, faces an almost impossible choice: to expose the scandal, and imperil his client; or to get by as best he can without personal involvement. Mr. Williams has been among the leaders in a refreshing movement to make the defense of criminal cases once more a respectable branch of the modern profession.

There is another barrier for lawyers who prefer to practice as Mr. Williams does. Public opinion still tends to identify the lawyer with his client, and not with the courts and the law. And many lawyers accept this view, or feel inhibited in fighting it. The labor lawyer whose clients are unions fears, with reason, that his practice may vanish if he represents an employer in a labor dispute. In the highly charged atmosphere of labor relations, with its vivid memory of "turncoats," the lawyer tends to be caught up on one side or the other. The situation is thought to be the same, or nearly the same, in many parts of the practice. Corporate lawyers often refuse to represent stockholders in management fights; those who represent plaintiffs in accident cases almost never represent insurance companies, and so on.

The resulting pattern presents society with a grave problem. Winston Churchill, talking to an Italian audience in the middle of the war, remarked that the distinction between civilization and tyranny could be summed up in two words —"habeas corpus." The quality of a civilization is largely determined by the fairness of its criminal trials, and of its other proceedings in which men may lose their liberty, their reputation, or their right to pursue callings of their choice. Our notions of fairness in the conduct of such enterprises have a long history, and are constantly developing. But these tenacious ideas about the protection of the individual before the massive power of the state are meaningless without independent and courageous lawyers to defend them, and to defend them without fear of reprisal. Lawyers involved in the affairs of one client, or one class of clients, normally accomplish useful work for society. But they have lost a large part of their freedom to represent the Tom Paines of this world. Such occasions do not arise often, and not all lawyers face tests of this order even once in a lifetime. But they do arise, and in the United States they arise too frequently for complacency. When they come, they measure the difference between life and death. For such trials are the ultimate moral test of a culture. It is a tribute to the France of the Third Republic that the country was riven by the controversy over the fairness of the Dreyfus case, and that there was no peace there until that miscarriage of justice was cured.

Mr. Williams is one of the rising generation of lawyers who lives his creed. He is a very old-fashioned lawyer, whose skill is available to all comers. As his book testifies, he loves the fight, and he loves the law. And in *One Man's Freedom,* he eloquently explains the principal ideas which animate our criminal law, and deals also with some of the leading modern problems of civil rights—censorship, wire-tapping, the scope and conduct of congressional committee hearings, the right of the press to comment on criminal trials, and the realization of the promise of equality in the Fourteenth Amendment. Often illuminated by his own experiences at the bar, his chapters are lucid and cogent. Addressed to a popular audience, they undertake to expound and defend some of the major precepts of the Constitution dealing with the rights of the individual, and to urge Mr. Williams' own views as to the lines along which they should develop. It is a valuable book, which articulates the faith of a lawyer—a faith as needed in our day as it was in the time of Peter Zenger's trial, or Tom Paine's, or that of the Scottsboro boys.

For we live in a time when constitutional rights are often challenged, a time too when they are evolving rapidly, and in the main, along lines which should fortify our pride. Constitutional rights are rarely invoked save in situations which stir strong and hostile feelings. It was precisely for this reason that the makers of our Constitution entrusted a major part of the task of enforcing it to the courts. They thoroughly understood both the capacity of the American people for political turbulence and their overriding respect for law. We need lawyers to represent these claims, or the healthy development of our constitutional law of civil rights will wither away. In many parts of the country, north and south, many lawyers avoid these cases, for reasons which are all too often real—the risk of personal ruin.

Mr. Williams' book, and his example, are a call to action on one of the fronts where we must never cease to battle—the perpetual struggle for constitutional liberty through law.

It is a privilege to commend his work to the public.

EUGENE V. ROSTOW

New Haven, Connecticut
March 7, 1962

CONTENTS

ONE MAN'S FREEDOM

CHAPTER I

THE STRONGEST LINK

". . . law is the strongest link between man and freedom . . ."

PRESIDENT JOHN F. KENNEDY
Law Day Proclamation, May 1, 1961

THE headlines of a New York tabloid caught my eye at La Guardia Terminal in the very early morning hours of May 3, 1957, after an uneventful flight from Washington. There were only five words on the front page:

MC CARTHY DEAD
FRANK COSTELLO SHOT

I bought a paper, hailed a cab and started into the city. When I turned the first page of the paper, I saw the headline for the third feature story of the day:

DAVE BECK RECALLED BEFORE
SENATE RACKETS COMMITTEE

At six o'clock on the previous evening Senator Joseph R. McCarthy of Wisconsin had died in the United States Naval Hospital at Bethesda, Maryland. I had known him for about ten years and had represented him in three cases—a libel suit brought against him by Drew Pearson, the famous Senate censure case and a tax case.

Later the same night a shot had been fired at the head of

Frank Costello, the New York gambler, as he entered the lobby of his apartment at 72nd Street and Central Park West. He had been wounded slightly. It was a narrow escape.

The year before, Costello had sent a New York lawyer to seek my services in the defense of a case brought against him by the government and designed to strip him of his citizenship. After meeting Costello I had agreed to take the case and it was still in litigation at this time.

Beck, too, was a client. He had asked me to represent him in his reappearance before the McClellan Committee and I had agreed.

It would have been a startling experience for any lawyer to read about three clients, each with a name familiar to a whole nation, who had been catapulted to the top of the news on the same day—one by death, one by a would-be assassin's bullet, one by a committee subpoena.

In retrospect, it should have been even more startling to me, for the first years of my professional life were spent in the representation of corporate clients involved in purely civil matters. I had started with a big firm, a fine, well-established and greatly respected Washington firm. It had many large companies on its roster of clients, and its volume of court work was tremendous. I was assigned to work with the lawyers who tried jury cases. They were superb craftsmen, experienced, skilled and resourceful. For five years I was in court every day, representing the local streetcar company, a galaxy of insurance companies and other corporate interests, usually defending them against damage suits. It was invaluable and unusual experience for a young lawyer.

But this was not the part of the law which had first excited my interest and attracted me to law school. It was the law in its relationship to human rights as distinguished from property rights which had first captured my attention and concern. With this firm, or with any other large firm representing major corporate interests, I knew that I would rarely deal with problems of human rights, of individual freedom, of personal liberty.

I decided to put my name on a list of lawyers who were willing to defend people without fee—people who were accused of a crime and had no money to hire a lawyer. On six or seven occasions during my last two years with the firm I was assigned by the court to represent an indigent defendant charged with a major crime. Some of these were capital cases—cases in which the punishment could be death in the electric chair. In all of them the punishment could have been imprisonment. This was a new world for a lawyer steeped in a civil corporate practice. I was dealing with people's liberty, reputations and sometimes with their very lives. Most of these clients were not only penniless but also friendless. What was at stake was far more important to them than the money damages involved in a civil suit. I have come to know since that it was also more important to society as a whole.

Ultimately I severed my connection with the firm and opened a small office of my own. My practice turned more and more to the facet of the law concerned with constitutional issues and questions of civil liberties on both the civil and the criminal sides of the court. Some of the people whose cases presented problems in this area were controversial and some had already been prejudged by society and sentenced to obloquy. I soon discovered that this sentence is sometimes extended to their counsel as well. My representation of the men whose names were in the headlines of May 3, 1957, had provoked, each for different reasons, scores of querulous questions from strangers and friends alike.

When the cab reached my destination, a small boy was standing on the corner selling the next edition of the same tabloid I had bought at the airport. For the second time the front page caught my eye. The same two headlines covered it, only in reverse order:

FRANK COSTELLO SHOT
MC CARTHY DEAD

In just the time it takes to get out a new edition of a tabloid the Senator who had rattled his saber through the nation had taken second billing to a gambler. I still have both papers. I shall always remember standing on the street, with the dawn just breaking over Manhattan, looking at them—one in each hand. Here was a graphic illustration of a basic premise of my profession. If what we lawyers do professionally has any meaning and if it makes any real contribution to the universal welfare, it must of necessity transcend the identities of the individuals involved. The individuals come and go and are forgotten. But the principles which are the very matrix of our American system of justice live on so long as the system lives on. I don't suggest for a moment that principles are more important than people, but I do say that they are more important than the specific identities of the people to whom they apply.

It was on that day that the idea of this book was born. I had a powerful impulse to sit down and write about what I regard as some of the most basic principles of individual liberty guaranteed by our Constitution. I wanted to write of the right to counsel, of fair procedure in congressional hearings, of the right to privacy, of the Fifth Amendment, of lawless law enforcement, of the right of everyone to a fair trial, of censorship, of civil rights, and of the whole concept of rule of law. I wanted to write of the transcendent importance of safeguarding and preserving intact all of our civil liberties, and of my deep conviction that whenever government infringes on any of these rights it begins with the weak and the friendless, or the scorned and the degraded, or the nonconformist and the unorthodox. It never begins with the strong, the rich, the popular, or the orthodox. I wanted to document my conviction that most of the history of civil liberties in this country has been written in its criminal courtrooms. For four years I resisted the impulse because of a feeling of inadequacy to the task. That feeling has perdured, but it has yielded to an increasing concern over the inroads that I believe are being made into these areas of individual freedom.

In the spirit that principles are more important than the identity of the individual to whom they apply, I have undertaken to lay out this lawyer's credo. Where I have spoken of specific persons in specific cases in which I have appeared as counsel, I have done so only because their cases seemed to illustrate a principle. At no place is a story told for the sake of the story, nor is this book intended in any sense to be a professional autobiography. For the most part the materials included are available from court records accessible to all. Where I have gone beyond the record, permission has been expressly given.

This book is premised on the old and simple proposition that ours is a government of rules—laws—not of men. The rules and laws are applicable alike to rich and poor, strong and weak, guilty and innocent. And they are just as applicable to the state as to the private citizen. The difference between our system and the system of which Mr. Khrushchev is so proud is that in his system the police are the law. In ours they are under the law—a difference dramatically symbolized by the fact that in Moscow the corpse of Lenin is kept on display under glass. In Washington we keep on display under glass the Constitution of the United States with its Bill of Rights.

A few years ago one of the great universities in the midwest conducted a poll among its students majoring in political science. The cardinal principles of the Bill of Rights were listed seriatim and the students were asked to indicate on the page whether or not they believed in each individual principle. To the amazement and the chagrin of the professors, about half of the students indicated they did not believe in the right of all Americans to peaceable assembly. They did not believe in the right of every accused to meet his accuser face to face and subject him to cross-examination, and they did not believe in the privilege against self-incrimination. But all of them, 100 per cent strong, said they believed in the Bill of Rights, though their answers demonstrated that they did not know what the Bill of Rights is.

In the past three years I have visited and lectured at more than twenty-five American law schools, and I have found disturbing signs of apathy and indifference to some of the freedoms guaranteed by the Bill.

Chief Justice Warren in a speech delivered at Washington University in St. Louis, Missouri, on February 19, 1955, said that if the Bill of Rights were offered as a piece of new legislation he had grave doubts that it would pass the Congress. I think he understated the case. I am doubtful that it would get out of committee and onto the floor for a vote.

I am concerned that all of this is reflective of a national mood. We have allowed an erosion of individual liberty and freedom to take place in the last three decades—not as the result of the overreaching of big government, nor as the result of the calculated assaults made upon liberties and freedoms in the last decade, but rather because of collective lethargy and a cavalier attitude of unconcern.

I think we have made a substitution in our national ranking of values—an evolutionary substitution that is only now reaching its culmination. We have placed security in a position of primacy and subordinated individual liberty to it.

I am afraid that, if the test could be made, the majority of Americans would trade away the right to speak in public assembly, the privilege against self-incrimination, the right to a jury trial, the right to be secure from unreasonable police searches, the right to indictment by grand jury, the right to confront an accuser and the right to counsel—would trade these rights for a guarantee of total economic security until death.

The fires once blazing for freedom in the minds and hearts of Americans everywhere have been carefully banked. They need new kindling if we are to compete successfully for the ideological adherence of the uncommitted world.

I am sure that there are dark and difficult days ahead for our country. The concept of government by consent is boldly challenged by the concept of government by compulsion. We are directing much of our national energy and talent into the efforts of the free world to prevent the spread of global Communism—all to the end that the liberty, freedom and dignity of the individual as we have known them will be preserved.

It would be a tragic paradox if we should surrender any part of our heritage in the name of this effort, for we should then have done to ourselves from within what we fear most from without. I believe that the prevention of this surrender is the real responsibility of the American bar today. That responsibility demands the bar retain an intellectual sensitivity to and an emotional concern about any encroachment on personal freedom and individual liberty, regardless of whose they may be. This is rendered difficult indeed when the overriding issues of our time are peace and security.

It sometimes seems that we lawyers are out of the main stream, and that our spectrum is narrow and our horizons limited when we debate problems of individual liberty while our collective freedom is imperiled. We appear to be polishing the brass while the ship is sinking.

But when the storms brewing about us distract us from the task at hand I like to recall a story that Alistair Cooke tells in his book *One Man's America,* a story to which President Kennedy made frequent allusion during the 1960 presidential campaign. On the 19th of May, 1790, in Hartford. Connecticut, the skies at noon turned from blue to gray. By midafternoon they had blackened so densely that in that religious age men fell on their knees and begged a final blessing before the end should come. The Connecticut House of Representatives was in session, and as some men knelt down in the darkened chambers and others clamored for adjournment, the Speaker of the House, one Colonel Davenport, came to his feet and silenced the din with these words:

> The day of judgment is either approaching or it is not. If it is not, there is no cause for adjournment. If it is, I choose to be found doing my duty. I wish, therefore, that candles be brought.

In the following pages I have tried to bring some new candles and to relight some old ones that have been burned before in the same kind of darkness.

CHAPTER II

GUILT BY CLIENT

In 1960 Igor Melekh, a Russian employee of the United Nations, was indicted in federal court in Chicago for espionage against the United States. The American lawyer for the Soviet Embassy in Washington came to see me and asked me to represent Melekh in the criminal trial. Defending an alleged Soviet spy in an American courtroom is an open invitation to be widely misunderstood. But popular misunderstanding is often the license fee the criminal trial lawyer must pay to ply his trade.

I asked from Melekh only three things—total candor, total control over the case and what I regarded as fair compensation. Two of my associates were opposed to my taking the case, not because the cause was necessarily bound to be an unpopular one, but rather because they feared we would not get the candor and control every lawyer must demand from his client. They feared that Melekh's government rather than his lawyer would be in charge. As I shall develop at some length later on, it turned out they were wrong.

But I did feel the lash of stinging criticism when I took on this defense. I had expected it. Every time I have assumed the defense of a case in which the crime charged is a heinous one or the defendant is a social or political outcast, the criticism has come. But expecting it and being insensitive to it are very different. I am sure that it is sensitivity to misunderstanding and criticism that has kept many lawyers from taking on an unpopular cause and is, in fact, driving some able young lawyers of impeccable integrity from the criminal courtrooms.

Not long ago I listened sadly as a man whom I regard as one of the better trial lawyers in America told me of his decision to give up the trial of criminal cases. He had built a splendid reputation as district attorney in one of our larger cities. When the local election brought about a change of administration, he was replaced, and he went into private practice. He quickly learned that glory and esteem are generally reserved for the prosecutor. When he appeared as defense counsel for a labor leader who was in disrepute locally, he found that, solely because of his representation of his client, some of the client's local disrepute flowed over onto him. He was politically ambitious and quickly decided that the fulfillment of the trial lawyer's commitment not to turn anyone away because of the unpopularity of his cause might end his hopes of elective office.

It was shortly after I entered the Melekh case that the columnist John Crosby, a critic of American morals, slandered me during a television interview. (Later, the station and the producer of the show apologized and repudiated Crosby's statement.) I had never met Mr. Crosby or had any dealings with him directly or indirectly. He made a moral judgment on me solely on the basis of his distaste for the people whose cases I had tried in court. Although the sting was not lessened by this fact, I'm sure that in the frame of reference in which he spoke he lacked information and understanding. He had the same kind of misinformation and misunderstanding that many other bright and articulate Americans have about the administration of criminal justice. He did not understand the right to counsel guaranteed by the Constitution and the role of the advocate in Anglo-Saxon jurisprudence. He did not understand that for the trial lawyer the unpopular cause is often a post of honor. Like other lawyers who try criminal cases, I have taken on many difficult cases for unpopular clients, not because of my own wishes, but because of the unwritten law that I might not refuse.

The concept of guilt by client is not new. Trial lawyers defending the rights of people condemned in the court of public opinion have always suffered the ostracism of the uninformed. Many better informed Americans could remind Mr. Crosby of an episode of American history peculiarly important to newspapermen. In 1734 a poor New York printer named John Peter Zenger was thrown into prison for publishing articles critical of the despotic royal governor. Bail was set at an exorbitant sum far beyond his means, and his lawyers were disbarred for their efforts on his behalf. Andrew Hamilton of Philadelphia then agreed to take the case. Hamilton was nearly eighty years old and suffered from severe gout, but his argument, later printed by his grateful client, shows why he was still regarded as the ablest advocate in America. Hamilton risked severe reprisals for espousing a cause politically so obnoxious. On account of his age and his eminence, the court did not dare to treat him as contumeliously as it had his predecessors. With great courage and eloquence he argued that Zenger should be acquitted because his criticism of the governor was justified. The jury agreed and returned a verdict of not guilty, in plain defiance of the court's instructions. This verdict has long been regarded as a milestone in the struggle for freedom of the press.

Even more celebrated is the defense of Captain Preston and his soldiers by John Adams and Josiah Quincy, Jr. Against a background of rising tension between the Sons of

Liberty and British troops garrisoned in Boston, Preston's men shot into a mob of colonists on March 5, 1770. Five men were killed, and the entire city of Boston was thirsty for the blood of the culprits. Adams and Quincy were both ardent patriots, but they were also lawyers. So they agreed to defend the captain and his soldiers. They at once became the targets of a vituperative public attack. Their patriotism was challenged and their reputations were sullied.

Quincy's father promptly wrote to his son, explaining that he was "under great affliction at hearing the bitterest reproaches uttered against you, for becoming an advocate for those criminals who are charged with the murder of their fellow citizens." He continued that he would not believe his son had done so "unless it be confirmed by your own mouth, or under your own hand."

Young Quincy replied to his father in a classic letter which read in part:

> Let such be told, Sir, that these criminals, charged with murder *are not yet legally proved guilty,* and therefore, however criminal, are entitled, by the laws of God and man, to all legal counsel and aid; that my duty as a man obliged me to undertake it; that my duty as a lawyer strengthened the obligation; that from abundant caution, I at first declined being engaged; that after the best advice, and most mature deliberation had determined my judgment, I waited on Captain Preston and told him that I would afford him my assistance; but, prior to this, in presence of two of his friends I made the most explicit declaration to him of my real opinion on the contests (as I expressed it to him) of the times, and that my heart and hand were indissolubly attached to the cause of my country; and finally that I refused all engagement, until advised and

> urged to undertake it, by an Adams, a Hancock, a Molineux, a Cushing, a Henshaw, a Pemberton, a Warren, a Cooper and a Phillips. This and much more might be told with great truth; and I dare affirm that you and this whole people will one day REJOICE that I became an advocate for the aforesaid "criminals" *charged* with the murder of our fellow-citizens.

Subsequently Preston and six of the soldiers were acquitted. Two others were acquitted of murder but convicted of a lesser offense. The courage of Adams and Quincy prevented a judicial lynching of innocent men.

Another justly celebrated example of courage at the bar is found in the biography of William H. Seward. Seward had already served two terms as governor of New York when he agreed to defend one Wyatt, a convict accused of murdering a fellow convict. The jury was unable to reach a verdict, and Seward remarked in a letter that the world was angry with him because he had defended Wyatt too faithfully.

Shortly after the Wyatt trial a Negro named Freeman, who had just been released from the penitentiary, murdered an entire family with no apparent motive. The public had pronounced it a wanton and wicked misuse of Seward's intellectual powers when he tried to save Wyatt from the gallows. When it was rumored that, besides continuing his defense of Wyatt, he also intended to defend Freeman, threats of personal violence were forthcoming. Despite the remonstrances of his friends, however, Seward remained firm in his determination to take the case. He wrote to one of his friends that he expected a storm of passion and prejudice, but that he intended to do his duty and he did not care whether he was ever forgiven for it.

Freeman was ultimately convicted, despite almost overwhelming evidence that he was insane and despite Seward's stirring plea on his behalf. In the course of this plea Seward referred to the feeling which had been aroused against him for his fidelity in a case where he was doomed to defeat.

> In due time, gentlemen of the jury, when I shall have paid the debt of Nature, my remains will rest here in your midst, with those of my kindred and neighbors. It is very possible they may be unhonored, neglected, spurned! But, perhaps, years hence, when the passion and excitement which now agitate this community shall have passed away, some wandering stranger, some lone exile, some Indian, some negro, may erect over them an humble stone, and thereon this epitaph, "He was faithful!"

Many years later, after Seward's distinguished career as a Senator and as Secretary of State, these simple words were chosen as his epitaph.

Clarence Darrow encountered similar hostility when he defended twenty members of the Communist Labor Party in 1920. Darrow answered his critics in the course of his summation to the jury.

> I shall not argue to you whether the defendants' ideas are right or wrong. I am not bound to believe them right in order to take their case, and you are not bound to believe them right in order to find them not guilty. I don't know whether they are right or wrong and you don't know whether they are right or wrong. But I do know this—I know that the humblest and the meanest man who lives, I know that the idlest and the silliest man who lives, should have his say. I know he ought to speak his mind. And I know that the Constitution is a delusion and a snare if the weakest and the humblest man in the land cannot be defended in

> his right to speak and his right to think as much as the greatest and the strongest in the land. I am not here to defend their opinions. I am here to defend their right to express their opinions.

Our own times have seen many distinguished advocates defy public opinion in the defense of unpopular causes. During World War II Harold R. Medina was appointed to defend Anthony Cramer, who was charged with treason on account of certain dealings with saboteurs who came to the United States from Germany by submarine. Judge Medina later wrote:

> I can honestly say that I worked harder on that case than I did on any other in my whole professional experience. One reason for this perhaps was that after I had undertaken Cramer's defense I noticed that people generally and my friends in particular, especially the wives, began to treat me with a certain coolness. . . . The general public which thronged the courtroom every day of the trial indicated to us very plainly that they thought perhaps we were in some way involved. . . . After a recess one day I was walking up the aisle of the courtroom to the counsel table when a spectator stood up and spat in my face. I think this is the worst thing that ever happened to me in my whole life.

Judge Medina did a very courageous thing when the trial judge praised him in front of the jury for defending Cramer as assigned counsel without compensation. He did not want the jury to think that perhaps he believed Cramer was guilty and was defending the case only because he had been assigned by the court to do it. And so, instead of thanking the judge for his praise, Judge Medina objected to it. Later he wrote: "Can you imagine how difficult it was for me to say those words? . . . But I had to do it, if I was to remain true to my trust."

Finally Judge Medina's courage and hard work won a reversal of Cramer's conviction by the Supreme Court. The majority concluded that the government had not produced sufficient evidence to support a conviction of treason.

But, unfortunately, this kind of courage and independence is not always shown by trial advocates in similar situations. In 1959 a Negro was sentenced to death by an all-white jury in North Carolina for raping a white woman. No defense whatsoever was presented. At the conclusion of the case the Negro attorney who had been appointed to defend him stated:

> I want the court to know that in all my years I've never been treated more cordially than I have here. No one uttered any word to make me feel uncomfortable. I hope to God I'm never again called to try this type of case. I think I would offer my license before undertaking such an ordeal again. All Alamance County citizens, and Mrs. Starnes in particular, have my deepest sympathy for this act, especially since it was perpetrated by one of my own race.

This statement doubtless increased the lawyer's status among some of the white citizens of North Carolina and saved him from any public criticism or worse for representing an unpopular defendant. But it was a breach of his obligation to his client. It was diametrically opposite to what Judge Medina had done in the Cramer case. Unless the confidential relationship of lawyer and client is to become a travesty, no lawyer can thus express his personal belief in his client's guilt.

Wendell L. Willkie defied public opinion during World

War II by defending the citizenship of William Schneiderman before the Supreme Court. Schneiderman was admittedly an upper-echelon Communist, and Willkie's political enemies made the most of it. SAYS WILLKIE FAVORS REDS OVER G.O.P., ran one headline. Willkie's courage and hard work, like Judge Medina's, brought about a Supreme Court decision in favor of his client. I have always admired Willkie for taking this case at a time when he still hoped to be the Republican candidate for President in 1944.

As these cases show, a full and fair defense is especially important to the defendant already condemned by society. Popular prejudice can all too easily take the place of evidence in such cases. Unfortunately, the conviction of the innocent has not yet become a mere myth. Judge Curtis Bok, a veteran of many years on the Pennsylvania bench, recently expressed the view that the convictions of the innocent far outnumber the acquittals of the guilty. This view is dramatized in Judge Jerome Frank's fascinating and fully documented study of thirty-six cases in which wholly innocent defendants were convicted and imprisoned for other men's crimes.

I am sure that these cases represent only a small fraction of the miscarriages which occur each year in our courts. I am equally sure that the best weapon against such miscarriages is to restore the defense of personal liberty to the position of prestige now reserved for the defense of property rights.

There is, however, another and perhaps even more important reason why the most unpopular defendant should have the best defense he can possibly get. Justice Frankfurter once observed, "It is a fair summary of history to say that the safeguards of liberty have frequently been forged in cases involving not very nice people." Freedom of religion, freedom of the press, freedom of speech, security from unreasonable search and seizure, the right to bail, the right to counsel, the right to trial by jury—all have been forged and reforged through the years in the cases of men already condemned by society. During the past ten years almost every important civil-liberties case in the Supreme Court has involved a scorned and degraded defendant. These defendants have been accused of murder, rape, arson, narcotics offenses, bootlegging, and membership in the Communist Party. It is such cases as these which have, in a very real sense, given shape and substance to the Bill of Rights.

In 1956 I participated in three cases which convinced me that society is often the winner when the prosecutor loses: *United States* v. *Aldo Icardi, United States* v. *Frank Costello* and *Confidential* v. *Arthur Summerfield*. All three of these cases came to me after the court of public opinion had already returned a verdict of guilty. Each of them, however, raised an issue of fundamental American freedoms.

Icardi was accused of one of the most heinous murders of the century. Eleven years after this alleged murder took place, a special committee of the House of Representatives called him as a witness for the purpose of setting up a perjury case against him when he proclaimed his innocence. I suppose that it is of some importance to the country as a whole whether Icardi was guilty of this murder or not, but it is far more important that Congress not transgress its constitutional powers and conduct investigations completely unrelated to any legitimate legislative purpose.

After Costello's celebrated appearance before the Kefauver Committee, the Attorney General instituted proceedings to denaturalize and ultimately to deport him. I discovered that the government's case was built upon extensive wiretapping. It doesn't make a great difference to the country as a whole whether Costello is in jail, in exile or in his

New York apartment. But it does make a great difference whether a policeman can be a silent third party to any telephone conversation in the United States.

Confidential Magazine specialized in exposing the private lives of celebrities with a degree of intimacy and detail unknown to the so-called movie magazines. The Postmaster General proceeded to bar it from the mails before giving it any kind of hearing. Whatever the literary merits of this magazine—and I make no brief for them—the power to bar any publication from the mails without a hearing raises the very gravest questions about freedom of the press.

These three cases, which I shall later discuss in detail, involved far more than the fate of two men and a magazine already condemned by society. To say that a lawyer must be in favor of murder, perjury, organized gambling, undesirable citizens and salacious literature because he is willing to defend cases of this character is worse than absurd. If Icardi, Costello and *Confidential* had been denied a full and fair defense because the bar was afraid of society's opinion, issues of real importance to society would not have been raised and the resulting principles would not have been forged.

Today the voice of condemnation is almost universal when a lawyer dares to undertake the defense of a "Fifth Amendment Communist," a "labor racketeer" or a "dope peddler." This growing insistence upon tarring the lawyer with the client's brush finds no parallel in the other professions. The fact deserves elaboration.

All the problems of humanity can be broadly divided into three categories—physical, spiritual and social. The physician, the clergyman and the lawyer devote their lives to the solution of these problems. No physician worthy of the name turns away a patient because he suffers from a loathsome disease or is incurable. No clergyman worthy of the name turns away a suppliant sinner because his sins are too heinous or his soul is too black. Only the lawyer is expected to turn away a client because society regards him as socially, morally or politically obnoxious. Only the lawyer is expected to withhold his help from those who need it most.

Perhaps the explanation lies in the fact that the physician and the clergyman extend their help in the privacy of office, hospital or confessional, whereas the lawyer—or, at least, the trial lawyer—must act in the public arena. Whatever the reason, this thinking is at war with the basic tenets of democratic justice.

When I represented the late Senator McCarthy in his censure case, I received a large amount of mail excoriating me for being a "McCarthyite" and a "fascist." At about the same time I agreed to represent some motion-picture writers who were accused of contumacious conduct in refusing to answer questions about alleged Communist activities. The tenor of the mail shifted. Now I was a "red." On the same day in 1954 I was referred to in a west-coast paper as the "right-wing mouthpiece for the McCarthy fringe" and in a New York paper as the "courtroom apologist for left-wing groups." I was bewildered. Up to that time I had tried twenty-three criminal homicide cases and no one had ever asked me if I believed in murder.

Morris Ernst, the nationally famed civil-liberties lawyer, tells in a law-review article of his efforts to aid Frank Costello in procuring trial counsel for his denaturalization case:

> For example, it is clearly a detriment to our judicial system when a man can't get reputable counsel in a city as large as New York simply because his name happens to be Frank Costello. And yet such was the

> case. The issues upon which Costello needed representation were of the highest Constitutional significance and included the admissibility of evidence procured through use of wire-tap, the bugging of mail and the examination by the Government of the tax returns of jurors. After being turned down by leaders of the Bar in this City, Costello finally retained Edward Bennett Williams of Washington. And even here the irony of guilt by association was present. Costello himself was at first reluctant to accept Williams as counsel because, as he put it, "Didn't he (Williams) represent Senator McCarthy?"

Unfortunately, these attitudes lead many lawyers to decline the defense of controversial clients or causes. A recent survey conducted at an eastern law school reflects just what one might expect. Virtually all of the participating students believed that the most unpopular of prospective clients, the Communist, was entitled to counsel. Almost half of them, however, stated that they would refuse to represent a Communist. The principal reason assigned for declining was the desire to avoid unfavorable publicity associating the lawyer with Communism and possible professional, social and economic reprisals.

The law schools themselves must take much of the responsibility for this attitude. A cursory examination of the curricula of the leading law schools shows that the student's attention is focused upon subjects dealing with property rights—contracts, damages, real estate, corporations, partnerships, wills and estates, taxation, trusts—almost to the exclusion of human rights. The student leaves school thinking that the *ne plus ultra* for launching his professional life is to become a junior associate in a Wall Street firm, and that there is something professionally déclassé about standing at the bar of justice with some socially ostracized figure whom organized society is trying to put in a cage.

In order to understand why these assaults on the right to counsel are so unjustifiable, it is essential to understand something of the history behind the Sixth Amendment. Early English common law subscribed to the theory that a man should be denied counsel if he was too "guilty." In misdemeanor cases the accused was entitled to the full assistance of counsel, but in treason and felony cases the accused was expected to conduct his own defense save as to questions of law. We are told that even deaf-and-dumb defendants were compelled to "plead" their own cases. Trials for capital offenses were frequently nothing better than judicial murder. It was not until 1836, however, that Parliament finally allowed the full right of counsel in all criminal cases. The colonies rejected from the beginning the barbarous rule of the mother country. By the time of the American Revolution no less than twelve of the thirteen colonies guaranteed the right to counsel in virtually all criminal prosecutions.

It was not surprising, therefore, that the Sixth Amendment gave *every* accused the right to have the assistance of counsel for his defense. The framers did not say every accused except gamblers, thieves and robbers. They did not say every accused except Communists, labor racketeers and narcotics offenders. They had seen the English system, where counsel was denied to those who needed it most, and they determined that this system must be rejected for all time in the United States.

The right to counsel is thus an absolute right which extends to every person charged with crime, no matter how socially or politically obnoxious he may be, no matter how unorthodox his thinking or his conduct, how unpopular his cause or how strongly the finger of guilt may point at him. Of course, this right would be an empty sham if the members of the bar did not have a corresponding duty to defend all those who seek representation within the limits of honesty and integrity. To this extent, the Bill of Rights is a bill of obligations for the members of my profession.

These obligations find full recognition in the Canons of Professional Ethics of the American Bar Association. Canon 5 states unequivocally that it is "the right of the lawyer to undertake the defense of a person accused of crime, regardless of his personal opinion as to the guilt of the accused; otherwise innocent persons, victims only of suspicious circumstances, might be denied a proper defense." At its 1953 meeting the American Bar Association adopted a resolution reaffirming the principle "that the right of defendants to the benefit of assistance of counsel and the duty of the bar to provide such aid even to the most unpopular defendants involves public acceptance of the correlative right of a lawyer to represent and defend, in accordance with the standards of the legal profession, any client without being penalized by having imputed to him his client's reputation, views or character."

Several years earlier President Truman also reaffirmed this principle in a letter to the American Bar Association, which read in part:

> The bar has a notable tradition of willingness to protect the rights of the accused. It seems to me that if this tradition is to be meaningful today, it must extend to all defendants, including persons accused of such abhorrent crimes as conspiracy to overthrow the Government by force, espionage, and sabotage. Undoubtedly, some uninformed persons will always identify the lawyer with the client. But I believe that most

> Americans recognize how important it is to our tradition of fair trial that there be adequate representation by competent counsel. Lawyers in the past have risked the obloquy of the uninformed to protect the rights of the most degraded. Unless they continue to do so in the future, an important part of our rights will be gone.

It should go without saying that counsel's obligation to defend his client does not import any obligation to defend his client's crimes. Competent counsel does not defend an accused murderer by arguing that his client's victim deserved to die. A lawyer who defends a case brought under the Smith Act is not expected to extol the merits of Communism. In short, it is the client and not the crime which counsel must defend.

It should also go without saying that no lawyer is ever justified in defending his client with weapons of fraud and falsehood. On the other hand, he can never excuse himself for accepting a defendant's confidence and then betraying it by a halfhearted defense. Project yourself for a moment into the position of a defendant. If you should one day find yourself accused of crime, you would expect your lawyer to raise every defense authorized by the law of the land. Even if you were guilty, you would expect your lawyer to make sure that the government did not secure your conviction by unlawful means. You would be justifiably outraged if he sat silent while the prosecution deprived you of your liberty—or your life—on the basis of a defective indictment, perjured testimony or a coerced confession. You would scarcely want him to decide that these things were "technicalities" and that society would be better off if you were in prison—or in the electric chair. The most unpopular defendant in America has the right to expect the same kind of defense you would want for yourself, even if it means public criticism and worse for his lawyer.

No discussion of the right to counsel would be complete without laying to rest the perennial question: "How can you represent a guilty man?" This is a question that is posed often by laymen, sometimes by law students and, sad to relate, occasionally by some lawyers. There is, of course, a quick, simple and complete answer. Our whole system of criminal justice is built on the basic premise that every man is presumed innocent until he is proven guilty beyond a reasonable doubt. His guilt must be shown by evidence produced by the prosecutor in a courtroom—not in a tabloid or a news broadcast. "Guilty" in this frame of reference is not a moral term. It is a legal term. No one is legally guilty until a judgment of guilt has been made by a court. The lawyer is neither expected nor qualified to make a moral judgment on the person seeking his help. Moral guilt or innocence is no more within the province of the lawyer than within the jurisdiction of the court.

So long as representation is asked for within the limits of integrity and total honesty, the accused is entitled to the same rights as every citizen. He is entitled to have a trial and to have his legal guilt proven beyond a reasonable doubt by evidence tested in the crucible of cross-examination. He is not entitled to produce perjured evidence in court or to testify falsely himself. But he is entitled to sit silent and force the proof of guilt.

Trial lawyers quickly learn the wisdom of this rule. Moral judgments by the lawyer are frequently wrong, and he learns not to make them. In the first murder case to which I was assigned by the court, I concluded that the accused had committed the crime, notwithstanding his emotional protestations of innocence. This judgment was exploded in my face by conclusive proof of innocence that was developed before trial. Two eyewitnesses had been mistaken in their identification of the accused. The case taught me a valuable lesson at an early professional age.

Like other human institutions, our system of justice fails on occasion. Sometimes the truly guilty go free. This is the price that a democratic society must pay to safeguard the liberty of the innocent. But when the system fails in this direction there is still the majestic vengeance of God, in whose exclusive jurisdiction moral judgments must remain. Clarence Darrow nicely articulated the basic philosophy of the defense lawyer in the area of moral judgments when he paraphrased Omar Khayyám:

> Every son of man travels an unbeaten path—a road beset with dangers and temptations that no other wanderer meets. His footsteps can be judged only in the full knowledge of the strength and light he had, the burden he carried, the obstacles and temptations he met, and a thorough knowledge of every open and secret motive that impelled him.

In 1792 Lord Erskine insisted upon undertaking the defense of Tom Paine despite the warning that if he took the case he would lose an honorable and lucrative position as Attorney General to the Prince of Wales. He won the case and was promptly discharged from his position. But he summed up the whole concept of the right to counsel with an eloquence and clarity seldom matched:

> From the moment that any advocate can be permitted to say that he will or will not stand between the Crown and the subject arraigned in the court where he daily sits to practice, from that moment the liberties of England are at an end. If the advocate refuses to defend from what he may think of the charge or of the

defense, he assumes the character of the judge; nay, he assumes it before the hour of judgment, and in proportion to his rank and reputation puts the heavy influence of perhaps a mistaken opinion into the scale against the accused, in whose favor the benevolent principles of the English law makes all presumptions, and which commands the very judge to be his counsel.

CHAPTER III

TRIAL BY CONGRESS—ICARDI

"THE rights you have are the rights given you by this committee. We will determine what rights you have and what rights you have not got before the committee."

This is former Representative Parnell Thomas, then chairman of the House Committee on Un-American Activities, speaking to a lawyer who had appeared as counsel for a witness and was thereafter ordered to take the stand as a witness himself. During the past decade this concept of congressional investigatory power has been accepted with alarming apathy and applied with alarming abandon.

The congressional spotlight has been focused in turn upon racketeers, subversives and organized labor. In each of these probes there were the professional informers, rejoicing in their newly found virtue. There were the inevitable props—the microphones, the klieg lights, the cameras, the tape recorders and, finally, the curious crowds. There was the monotonous invocation of the privilege against self-incrimination by witnesses whose very intonations betrayed that they did not understand what they were saying.

Far too often the interrogation bore no relationship to a legitimate legislative purpose. It was exposure for the sake of exposure. The victims stood friendless before the country. They were, for the most part, incontestably "bad." Few observers dared to point out that the Bill of Rights was designed to protect the "bad" as well as the "good." Although the privilege against self-incrimination was constantly invoked, few remembered another and even more important part of the Fifth Amendment which provides: "No person shall be held to answer for a capital or otherwise infamous crime unless on a presentment or an indictment of a grand jury."

There was little sympathy for the leaders of organized crime who testified before the Kefauver Committee. The country was vastly entertained by their discomfort and wholly unconcerned about any violation of their constitutional rights. There were no outcries from the liberals for the unhappy victims of this investigation—and then it was the liberals' turn, and the public was almost indifferent to the violation of their rights. Next came organized labor, which had evidenced little concern when the rights of alleged racketeers and liberals were disregarded. As in the prior probes, the rights of witnesses before the McClellan Committee met with widespread public indifference. No one except those on the witness stand and their counsel was concerned with the rights of the witnesses. The general reaction seemed to be that legislative lynching was none too good for the likes of them. Finally, and inevitably, the spotlight swung to big business. As the leaders of the drug and electrical industries paraded to the stand, they experienced the same public indifference that they had shown to the victims who had gone before.

In 1956 I tried a case which forcibly illustrates the dangers of unbridled congressional investigatory power. Aldo Icardi of Pittsburgh, Pennsylvania, came to see me in the late summer of 1955. A short, bespectacled, bald-headed man, he looked anything but the central figure of the most widely publicized spy melodrama of World War II. He was under indictment by the United States government for eight counts of perjury allegedly committed in 1953 before a subcommittee of the Committee on Armed Services of the House of Representatives.

Icardi was a desperate and despondent man when I first saw him. And no wonder. He had been convicted *in absentia* by the Italian courts of murdering his commanding officer behind enemy lines during World War II while on a secret mission for the Office of Strategic Services. Extradition of Icardi for trial in Italy had not been and was not possible because the alleged crime had taken place in no man's land in the Italian Alps in 1944, a time when there was no valid extradition treaty in existence. But, worse than the Italian conviction, his own government had accused him of the same crime in a release issued through the Defense Department.

Years of living under the accusation of murder had obviously taken a heavy toll on him. When I first saw him it was four years to the day since the United States government had leveled an accusation of murder at him through the Defense Department release, which had been timed to come out just before a sensational story on the case in *True* Magazine. Icardi described that day in August, 1951, this way:

> It was a dull day. I came home from work, and while my wife Eleanor was clearing the table and the children were playing in the yard I was reading the paper. The radio was on, turned to a news program that we listened to regularly. All at once the radio was blaring. The announcer seemed to be shouting. He was talking about me. He was telling how I had masterminded the fantastic and brutal murder of my commanding officer

> in northern Italy in 1944. I sat paralyzed, unable to believe what I heard. Yet the announcer cited my name, Aldo Icardi, and Major Holohan, and Sergeant LoDolce, and Giuseppe Manini, Gualtiero Tozzini. The source of these lies was unbelievable. It was the Defense Department in Washington. It was the same Defense Department that had the documents, the reports, my investigations, their own investigations, the lie-detector examination. It was the same Defense Department that four years before had cleared me of the impossible charges after completely investigating the case on four separate occasions.

The Defense Department release and the Italian conviction provided a license for libel for every journal in the land. Headlines blazed across the country that Aldo Icardi had committed one of the most atrocious crimes of the decade—the cold-blooded murder of Major William V. Holohan. The press decried the fact that he could not be tried in this country. The military had lost jurisdiction over him by reason of his honorable discharge from the service, and the civil courts could not try him for an offense committed outside the territorial limits of the United States. He stood convicted in the court of public opinion and sentenced to infamy.

It was against this background that a congressional committee decided to investigate the death of Major Holohan. It was a bizarre story, replete with wartime espionage, alleged murder, treachery, larceny and even lust. It was a natural for headlines. No one cared whether such an investigation bore any relationship to the proper function of Congress and its committees. The fact is that the only conceivable legislative purpose that such an investigation could possibly have served had already been accomplished by the enactment of a law which gave the military the right to retain jurisdiction over its personnel even after discharge for crimes committed during service.

And so Icardi was "invited" to appear and defend what was left of his reputation. He did appear and he did testify fully and completely. He sought no protection in the Fifth Amendment. He forthrightly and unequivocally denied any part in the death of Major Holohan.

The subcommittee quickly turned the hearing into a legislative trial. Icardi was referred to as "the accused." His testimony was received with preconceived incredulity and a report was issued accusing him again of murder and referring the case to the Department of Justice for a perjury indictment. The subcommittee had sat as an open grand jury. It had artfully ensnared Icardi into testifying so that it could accomplish by indirection what could not be done directly. He could now be tried for the murder of Major Holohan under the guise of a perjury indictment and be sentenced to a term of imprisonment up to forty years.

I was greatly moved by the plight of this man. He stood charged by his government with a despicable murder—a murder that was already eleven years old. None of the witnesses was in the United States. They were scattered throughout Western Europe. Even if they could be found, they could not be subpoenaed to testify, because they were beyond the territorial limits of the United States. Against this one man was arrayed the majesty of the United States government.

I entered my appearance in the case on Icardi's behalf. I wrote a letter to the Attorney General of the United States setting forth in detail the problems confronting Icardi in the defense of his liberty. The government had spent a half-million dollars investigating the case for over a decade. Through four separate investigative agencies every witness who had the slightest knowledge of even peripheral facts had been interviewed. Arrangements had been made to fly such witnesses as the prosecution needed to Washington for the trial.

We had been able to conduct no investigation. We had no funds. Even if we had the money and could find the witnesses necessary to the defense, we couldn't subpoena them. Never to my knowledge, and certainly not within my experience, had a defendant been at worse disadvantage. Because of these factors I asked the head of the Department of Justice to afford to us, in the interest of justice, the benefits of the government's investigation so that Icardi could have a fighting chance to defend himself. The request was refused.

My sense of fair play was so offended by all this that I resolved to conduct on my own an all-out investigation into the facts. The odds were overwhelmingly against my being able to accomplish anything fruitful. I laid the facts before my old friend Robert Maheu, who had made a brilliant record as an FBI agent and had recently formed his own international investigative agency, staffed with former FBI agents. To the everlasting credit of his big heart, he agreed to help. He quickly enlisted the help of Giuseppe Dosi, formerly the Italian head of Interpol (the international police force in Europe).

Together Maheu and I traveled 12,500 miles in four countries. Our search took us in the dead of winter to tiny villages high in the Alps, to boarded-up villas on Lake Orta and Lake Maggiore, to Switzerland and England and France, and finally to the regal majesty of Rome. We came home ready for trial—so ready that I was certain the prosecution, if it were given another eleven years and another half-million dollars, could not prove us wrong.

It was estimated that the case would take two months to

try. A score of witnesses were flown here from Europe by the prosecution. On Monday, April 16, 1956, the trial began before Judge Richmond Keech and a jury in the United States District Court for the District of Columbia.

The prosecutor made a lengthy and detailed opening statement. He said he would prove that on the night of December 6, 1944, Icardi first tried to poison Major Holohan by putting potassium cyanide in his minestrone. When this did not work quickly enough, Icardi had him shot in the head as he lay in anguish from the poison. Then, contended the prosecutor, his body was dumped into Lake Orta, where it lay until it was recovered six years later. All this was done, he said, so that Lieutenant Icardi, as next-ranking officer, could take command of the mission.

When the prosecutor finished his opening statement to the jury, I did something that defense lawyers in criminal cases of this kind rarely do today. I made a full and complete opening statement to the jury, outlining precisely what we were prepared to prove by competent evidence. I could have waited until after the prosecution had called all of its witnesses and rested its case. This would have given us the advantage of surprising the prosecution later in the trial and shortening its time for gathering countervailing evidence. But I did not rely on surprise. Confident of our position, I exposed it to attack at the earliest moment.

A trial is not like a political campaign. A politician can get elected on the basis of his promises. He doesn't have to deliver until after the verdict of the electorate. In a trial a lawyer has to deliver competent, credible evidence to support what he promises to prove or he won't win the verdict.

I began my opening statement by outlining the political and military situation in Italy during the closing days of World War II, and then I detailed the movements of the secret mission of which Icardi was a part.

On July 18, 1943, Allied bombers struck at Rome for the first time. Italian troops were meeting with reverses and the morale of the Italian people was at low ebb. Against this background King Vittorio Emmanuele deposed Mussolini as Premier of Italy and placed in his stead the aged Marshal Pietro Badoglio. Mussolini, however, proceeded to set up in northern Italy a Fascist regime which was a puppet of the Nazis, with the result that Italy was divided roughly in half.

During 1944 Allied troops began to move up the Italian peninsula. Our military leaders believed that the Italian campaign was almost over. They were deeply concerned about the Po Valley, which was the heart of industrial Italy. A group of Italian partisans who called themselves the National Committee of Liberation had united in the Po Valley to fight the German Nazis and the Italian Fascists. Some of these partisans were Communists and others were violent anti-Communists. The Allies were fearful that civil war would break out between the partisan factions as soon as their common enemy was defeated. This would play havoc with Italy's industrial recovery.

The Allied answer to this problem was a mission to provide leadership for the partisans and keep the advancing Allied forces informed of developments. The OSS was called upon to form this mission, which was known as the Chrysler Mission. It had five members—Major William Holohan, Lieutenant Victor Giannino, Lieutenant Aldo Icardi, Sergeant Arthur Ciarmicola, and Sergeant Carl LoDolce. These men were intensively briefed on the political and geographical situation in northern Italy. They were given $16,000 in various currencies and in gold so that they could buy supplies and, more important, information behind enemy lines.

On a dark and moonless night in September of 1944

these five men took off from Maison Blanche Airfield in Algiers. They parachuted down on the slopes of Mount Mottarone between Lake Maggiore and Lake Orta in the Po Valley. Nazi and Fascist troops were garrisoned along the shores of both lakes. The Chrysler Mission was literally surrounded by the enemy.

Its members soon learned that the Po Valley partisans were divided into two groups. The Communist partisans were under the leadership of Vincenzo Moscatelli and the anti-Communist partisans were under the leadership of Alfredo Di Dio. Moscatelli, who had studied Marxism in Moscow, was a dedicated Communist and a future leader of the Communists in the Italian Chamber of Deputies. The other partisan leader, Di Dio, was killed by the Nazis. Lieutenant Giannino and Sergeant Ciarmicola were caught in the same Nazi attack and never rejoined the Chrysler Mission. The anti-Communist partisans were seriously weakened and the mission was reduced to three men.

The remaining members of the mission decided that they must go into hiding. They turned to a partisan named Aminta Migliari, better known as Giorgio. He had early offered to help the Americans, and they had come to depend upon him for information, food, clothing, and for many services. Giorgio finally found an empty house on the shore of Lake Orta known as the Villa Maria which could be used as a hiding place. He also found two men named Manini and Tozzini who agreed to act as guides and helpers to the mission.

While the mission was housed at the Villa Maria, word came that the Nazis were going to conduct a mop-up operation along the shores of Lake Orta. It was necessary to find a new hiding place. So on the night of October 30 the men hurriedly packed and rowed out to an island in the middle of the lake, where they were hidden in a monastery by two little Italian priests, Don Carletto Murzilli and Don Giovanni Vandoni. The Nazis did not overlook the monastery. The next day it was carefully searched, but the priests had hidden the men in a hollowed-out place in the altar and they were not found.

When the Nazis left, the five men rowed back to the western shore of Lake Orta and went into the mountains. All night they lay huddled together in a driving mountain rain. In the morning they came down into the village of Grassona, and once again they were helped by Don Giovanni Vandoni, who hid them this time in a tiny loft under the roof of the parish church. Again the Nazi troops were hot on the trail. They searched every house in Grassona, and for five days and nights forty of them were garrisoned in the church directly beneath the Americans.

Finally the Germans left and Holohan, Icardi, LoDolce and their two Italian guides, weak and weary, were able to come down from the loft. For two and a half weeks they managed to live in reasonable tranquillity in the Villa Maria, because the Nazis had temporarily discontinued their mop-up operation along the western shore of Lake Orta. During this lull Holohan and Icardi made radio contact with Allied forces and arranged for new supply drops for the partisans.

On November 25 the mission moved again, for the men dared not stay anywhere for as long as three weeks. This time they went to the Villa Castelnuevo, a quarter of a mile away. A large and splendid Italian summer home with twenty-two rooms, it had been boarded up since the beginning of the war. It was still boarded up when Robert Maheu and I visited it a dozen years later. The last persons to live in it were the members of the Chrysler Mission. The events of the last night it was inhabited have been the subject of thousands of pages of testimony and reports and will be debated as long as the history of the Italian campaign in World War II is recounted.

While the members of the mission were hiding in the basement of the Villa Castelnuevo, word came on November 30 that the Germans were coming back to the western shore of the lake. Word also came that one of the first men whom Holohan and Icardi had met when they landed on Mount Mottarone, a partisan named Cinquanta, had been a Fascist spy. He had been seen on the streets of Novara, resplendent in a Fascist officer's uniform. The Americans were sure now for the first time that the Fascists and the Germans were aware of their presence in the area.

I outlined all of these facts to the jury. Then I told them what we were prepared to prove about the fateful twenty-four hours immediately preceding Major Holohan's disappearance in these words:

> On December 5 of 1944 the same two priests, Don Carletto Murzilli and Don Giovanni Vandoni, came to the Villa Castelnuevo. They told Lieutenant Icardi and Major Holohan that the rumor was out all over the little town of Orta, across the lake, that the daring Americans were living at the Villa Castelnuevo. The priests implored them to move because they feared that this information would fall into the hands of the enemy. We will show you they decided to stay on the night of December 5, 1944, and they did stay. They slept with their eyes open and their guns out throughout that night, waiting for an attack on the villa.
>
> The next day, they sent word to Migliari to get them another place to live. We will show you that tentatively that day they planned to move, depending on whether Migliari could find them a place in which to live.

There was a message from Migliari that he was attempting to find a place for them to go. A light was to be flashed from the isle of San Giulio that night if he located a place.

The Americans waited. Manini and Tozzini were with them. After dinner a fog enveloped the lake. There wasn't a possibility of an exchange of signals between San Giulio Isle and the Villa Castelnuevo.

We will show you that in any event the decision was made to leave and preparations were made to leave. They determined that if they had to go back to the hills, they would do so. They prepared. About nine or ten o'clock that night they had their gear packed.

We will show you they had a rented boat which was on Lake Orta. It was probably 75 or 100 yards from the edge of the lake to the back of the villa. Perhaps the villa sat 50 to 75 feet above the level of the shore. There was a tremendous garden behind the Villa Castelnuevo, and a winding stone pathway through the garden up to the back of the villa.

We will show you they carried their equipment down and they put it in the boat. They were preparing to leave, and in accordance with their regular plan, one of the partisans was sent back to secure the villa. He was sent back to make sure that it was locked and that there was no evidence left of the fact that the Americans had been there.

Major Holohan, Aldo Icardi, and Carl LoDolce stood on the shore at Lake Orta in the fog under cover of dark, waiting to shove off. One of the partisans was on the path and one was closer to the villa.

Suddenly out of the night came the cry *"Chi va la,"* "Who goes there"!

There was a shot, followed by a blaze of gunfire.

The Americans, pursuant to OSS directives for a mission behind enemy lines, separated instinctively. Their practice was to separate so that all would not be captured and perhaps some could escape.

We will show you that guns blazed at the Villa Castelnuevo. Icardi drew out his .45 and fired. Then he ran along the lakeshore.

He ran along the side of Lake Orta for as long as his legs could sustain him and as long as he had any wind.

He ran under cover of dark and shrouded by a fog all the way to the village of Capella. He went to the home of Rizzoli, where Migliari was living. He burst into the Rizzoli home and poured out this story of the attack on the villa.

Members of the jury, we will show you that the last time Aldo Icardi saw Major William Holohan the Major was alive, standing at the edge of the water at Lake Orta.

At this point Judge Keech took the regular midafternoon ten-minute recess. When I walked out of the courtroom through a side door, there sat Manini and Tozzini waiting in the witness room. I had last seen them in very different surroundings. A month before, Robert Maheu, Giuseppe Dosi and I had interviewed them on successive days at their homes in northern Italy.

Manini lived with his wife and sons in abject poverty in the little town of Pettenasco. They had one room, where they all ate and slept. I remembered how cold it had been in the unheated room on the March day when I first saw him. He was terrified when we told him we had come to talk about the Holohan case, and at first he would say nothing. As far as he was concerned, the case was *"finito"*—he had suffered enough and would have no more to do with it. We asked him if he was going to testify at the trial. Only if he were paid enough money, he said. He had been given $25 a day for coming to the United States and giving evidence before the grand jury, and he wanted still more if he testified again. This, of course, was pretty good compensation for a factory worker who received the equivalent of $2 a day in wages.

He grew more and more excited as we talked. His excitement turned to anger when we showed him the conflicting statements concerning the events of December 6, 1944, which he had signed. It was apparent that he was a violent and unstable man. He sat before us flicking the blade of his switch-blade knife. Finally he exploded in a burst of profanity and shouted that Migliari and Tozzini were responsible for all of his trouble and that Tozzini was a *"Comunista."* When he ordered us from his home, we left. The switch-blade was very persuasive.

Tozzini had been less volatile and less unwilling to talk. But he claimed that he had been told by a representative of the CID not to discuss the case with us. Like Manini, he was poor and illiterate, and was attracted to the handsome witness fees being paid for his two trips to America. He heatedly denied that he was a Communist, and said we had confused him in this respect with Manini. Manini was the Communist, and, moreover, Manini had received a psychiatric discharge from the Italian Army, a fact which our investigation later confirmed. He refused to discuss the several contradictory statements which he had signed at various stages of the investigation, and he kept repeating that the "black beasts" in the whole affair were Migliari and Manini. In a second interview Tozzini admitted his membership in the Communist party, but sought to explain it away by professing his Catholicism.

Manini and Tozzini had vanished shortly after Holohan's disappearance and had not been heard from again until after the war. They had been interrogated exhaustively over a long period of time by various agents of the United States government. Gradually a pattern of inconsistencies had begun to develop in their stories. By the time of the Icardi trial each had given seven different versions of the events of December 6, 1944.

Aldo Icardi came out of the courtroom and interrupted my thoughts to tell me that the judge was about to come back onto the bench. His eyes shot to Manini and Tozzini —first to the short, fiery-tempered Manini and then to the tall, muscular Tozzini. This was the first time in a dozen years he had seen them. No words passed, and from the Italians there was no sign of recognition. I went back into the courtroom to conclude the opening statement. I resumed by recounting to the jury the details of the exhaustive post-war investigation of Holohan's disappearance. Then I told them exactly what we were prepared to prove regarding his disappearance and death:

> We will show you, ladies and gentlemen of the jury, when the evidence is in, that the United States government, acting through its duly authorized investigative agencies in 1947, was correct when it concluded, and I quote from the official CID report of its investigation, "The disappearance of Major Holohan was a political move engineered by the Communist group headed by Moscatelli, a man of few scruples who was capable of weakening the opposite party in order to enrich his group." We will show you before this case is completed that that conclusion, arrived at in an impartial investigation conducted immediately after the event, was right.

When the report was filed, the investigation was renewed. It was renewed for the purpose, members of the jury, of determining the specific individual responsible for the disappearance of the Major.

A man named Henry Manfredi, who is with the Criminal Investigation Division of the United States Army, was given the assignment to find out who it was, what individual it was, who was responsible for this act. We will show you that he marshaled all the information at his command. He examined all the reports that had ever been written on this bizarre episode of World War II history. Then he went back to the scene of the crime. He began, with the aid of those who were assigned to help him, a systematic investigation, going over all the steps that had been gone through before, from beginning to end, to double-check the conclusion previously arrived at.

We will show you that the emphasis of the investigation was on the Communist partisans. It was on Vincenzo Moscatelli and one of his executioners, a man named Davide Alessandro, better known as Lupo.

We will show you that emphasis was also on Manini and Tozzini.

We will show you that further inconsistencies developed in the stories of Manini and Tozzini.

We will show you that the involvement of the Communist partisans in North Italy in this matter became clear. And when Manini and Tozzini became suspects and the role of the Communist Party partisans became a hot subject of inquiry, a defense was conceived. A plot was hatched. The plot was to blame the Americans for the death of Major Holohan. The defense that was hatched to save Manini and Tozzini was that they acted under orders of the Americans.

So they were instructed, members of the jury, to change their stories, and in the spring of 1950 they did. Even when they changed them, they changed them so fast and under such pressure that they still did not fit together. They agreed in only one respect: The Americans were to blame.

They said that they were pawns in the hands of the Americans. They rowed out onto Lake Orta and they said to Mr. Manfredi who sat at this table yesterday, "We will show you. We dumped him in Lake Orta."

The body was taken out of Lake Orta, and lo and behold, there were bullets in the cadaver. The bullets were from the gun of Giuseppe Manini, a gun which he had carefully gotten rid of shortly after this event by selling it to one Edoardo Maulini.

We will show you, members of the jury, that Vincenzo Moscatelli, the leader of the Communist partisans, artfully devised this defense.

We will show you further that these men were then under the discipline of the Communist partisans, unknown to the American mission.

We will show you that Tozzini and Manini are members of the Communist Party under Vincenzo Moscatelli and that they were then.

We will show you, members of the jury, that as the first reports of the American investigative teams found, Major Holohan was liquidated after a meeting that he had with Vincenzo Moscatelli on December 2 of 1944. He was liquidated because Moscatelli belived that he constituted an obstruction to Moscatelli's plans after the war and during the concluding aspects of the war.

We will show you that the attack that was made on the Villa Castelnuevo was a simulated attack made by

> partisans under Moscatelli, with the knowledge and aid of Tozzini and Manini.
>
> We will show you that when the investigation grew warmer, and it was pointing at Moscatelli and his brigands, a defense was devised to shift responsibility for these actions to Aldo Icardi, the American.
>
> We will show you, members of the jury, that an official line of the Communist Party of Italy was promulgated to the effect that Major Holohan was killed on order of the United States Defense Department and the United States State Department. That line was devised to shift responsibility from the Communists. It was employed as a defense for Manini and Tozzini, who went to trial in Italy for this crime. It was planned and plotted in 1950.

The mere recitation of these facts held the rapt attention of the jury. I was telling them that before the trial was over we would show them not only that Icardi was not guilty of the charges against him, but also where the true guilt lay. This was a big commitment, but it was not idly made. We had begun the development of this line of proof a month before in an interview with Vincenzo Moscatelli. Robert Maheu and I had spent the better part of a day with him in Rome. We met him at the Italian Chamber of Deputies, where he served as one of the Communist members, and we began our talk at a small nearby restaurant known as Ristorante da Pancrazia.

Moscatelli was completely open and frank about the whole matter. As far as he was concerned, the incident was just another war story, and he could not understand how it could be the subject of a criminal case. He readily conceded that the Communist partisans had eliminated Holohan, and he defended it as a necessary act. He ridiculed the selection of a man who did not speak Italian as the head of a behind-the-lines mission in Italy. He told in dismay of Holohan's insistence on wearing his uniform at all times. Moscatelli's position was that Holohan was an obstructionist who had to be removed. There was no way to remove him except by murder. He absolved Icardi and LoDolce of any knowledge of or involvement in the killing, and was ready and willing to testify in court. He gave us details which checked out in every instance, and we were able to prepare a carefully documented line of proof, the very proof which I had just finished outlining before the jury.

The opening statement was almost over. There remained only an exposition of Icardi's willingness to cooperate in every phase of the postwar investigation. On that score, this is what we would have shown to the jury, and this is what I told them:

> We will show you that since 1944 this defendant, Aldo Icardi, has answered all questions propounded to him by any responsible official of the United States government concerning this matter.
>
> We will show you that he has voluntarily submitted to questioning by OSS agents and CID agents.
>
> We will show you that in 1947 at the request of the government, acting through the Criminal Investigation Division, Aldo Icardi voluntarily submitted to a polygraph test, more popularly known as a lie detector test, at the hands of the foremost expert in the United States military organization. He submitted to this for two full days and answered all questions propounded to him by a staff of interrogators from the CID.
>
> We will show you that he answered those questions truthfully and that this fact was so reported.
>
> We will show you that in 1953 he received a letter

from a Congressman named Sterling Cole, inviting him to give testimony on this subject—not subpoenaing him, not requiring him, but inviting him to come to Washington to testify.

We will show you that he voluntarily came to Washington, raised his hand, took an oath, all voluntarily, with no demand, no legal requirement that he do so, and testified concerning this whole matter from beginning to end.

We will show you that in all respects he testified truthfully. In all respects he answered the questions completely and candidly as he did before, and as he has done since 1944.

We expect to show you, members of the jury, that Lieutenant Aldo Icardi is not a murderer or a thief or a liar—the evidence will show that he was one of the real heroes of World War II. When we show you these things, we will ask, at your hands, at the conclusion of this case, a verdict of not guilty.

After the opening statements were concluded, the prosecution called members of the subcommittee to show that the hearings at which Icardi testified had a valid legislative purpose, that they were really looking for information and for a valid legislative purpose. Even the prosecution conceded that the existence of a valid legislative purpose was an essential element of its case. Further, it was necessary to show that the questions on which the indictment was based were pertinent to this purpose. To prove these things the government called Congressman Sterling Cole as its witness.

The atmosphere of the trial changed sharply. From a dramatic factual issue we turned to an important legal issue. On each phase the defense had to be prepared. I was convinced that we were right on the law as well as on the facts. I believed that the subcommittee had had no real legislative purpose in calling Icardi. The hole in the law which prevented the trial of discharged soldiers by military courts for offenses committed during their service had been plugged, and a congressional hearing on the subject was unnecessary. The factual issue was for the jury to decide. The legal issue presented a question for the judge. But before the prosecution could even get the factual issue to the jury, it had to win the legal argument.

Congressman Cole freely admitted that he was familiar with the Uniform Code of Military Justice and that he knew it covered the very situation presented by the Holohan case. He conceded that the law had been changed to permit prosecutions in cases like Icardi's, and that the changes had been made before Icardi was ever invited to testify.

Q. You knew, did you not, Mr. Cole, that in the 81st Congress, out of your very committee, there came legislation which made it possible to prosecute a member of the military service for a crime committed during the service after his discharge; isn't that so?

A. I made reference to that earlier, yes.

Q. You knew that, didn't you?

A. Yes.

* * *

Q. After you heard Mr. Stern and Mr. Manfredi on December 19, 1951, and January 10, 1952, respectively, you then knew from what they told you about this case that it was a case that fell squarely within the statute that you passed in the 81st Congress covering crimes committed by servicemen during their service, holding that they could be prosecuted in Army courts-martial after their service—did you not?

A. Yes.

Q. You knew that then, didn't you? You knew that existing law of January 10, 1952, covered the Holohan case?

A. Apparently covered it.

Cole first stated that he had "invited" Icardi to testify in order to afford him a forum in which to establish his innocence:

Q. But, in any event, the reason that the letter that Mr. Marony alluded to, the letter of March 19, 1953, went to Mr. Icardi from the subcommittee over your signature inviting him to appear was so as to give him an opportunity to rebut what you considered to be evidence against him?

A. Yes.

* * *

Q. Did you want his testimony sufficiently so that you would have subpoenaed him or were you simply giving him an opportunity to tell his story?

A. Principally the latter.

Q. Because the fact is you invited Carl LoDolce to come, too?

A. Yes, sir.

Q. And he did not come, did he?

A. No.

Q. You didn't subpoena him, did you?

A. No.

Q. You did not feel that his testimony was necessary to the work of the subcommittee, did you?

A. Not to the point of subpoenaing him, no.

Q. Nor would you have felt that Icardi's was necessary to the point of subpoenaing him, I take it?

A. Again I can't say what we would have done.

Then I broke the most elementary rule of good cross-examination. From the first day I had ever gone into court I had heard the lesson with which every young trial lawyer is deeply indoctrinated: "Never ask a question unless you know what the answer is going to be." Breaking this rule is almost always a mistake. This time it turned out to be a bonanza which electrified the courtroom. It went this way:

Q. Did you talk to anyone at all anywhere before Mr. Icardi was invited to testify with respect to a perjury case being set up against Mr. Icardi?

MR. MARONY: Objected to as beyond the scope of redirect examination.

THE COURT: Oh, I think I will permit him to answer.

THE WITNESS: Would you repeat it?

BY MR. WILLIAMS:

Q. Yes, sir. Did you talk to anyone, I say, anyone at all, sir, before Mr. Icardi was invited to testify with respect—did you talk to anyone with respect to setting up a perjury case against Mr. Icardi?

A. I cannot quite subscribe to setting up a perjury case. I can, in response, say that the question of perjury was a subject of discussion.

* * *

Q. Tell me the substance of what was said about perjury in relation to Icardi before he was called.

A. The substance of perjury is perjury itself.

Q. Tell me the substance of your conversation, sir.

A. It would only be repetition. The subject of swearing Mr. Icardi was discussed. It was determined to swear him. He offered no resistance to being sworn as a witness. It is my recollection that the question of prosecution for perjury was entered into in the discussion of the question of swearing him under oath. Now I cannot particularize beyond that.

Q. But this was all before he was invited to testify?

A. Well, it wasn't limited to that time.

Q. But you did have this discussion before he was invited to testify?

A. I can't swear positively that we did. I say it is my best recollection that we must have.

Q. Didn't you have a conversation with your counsel and with Mr. Kilday during which you discussed inviting Icardi to testify, during which you discussed that you would swear him if he accepted the invitation, and during which you discussed that a perjury case could be spelled out against him if he testified in accordance with the reports that you then had in your committee files obtained from the Army?

A. I cannot deny that that happened. On the other hand, I cannot swear that it did happen. I could very readily say that in all probability it did happen.

Q. And your best recollection here today is that it did happen?

A. It could very well have happened.

Q. And that is your best recollection here today?

A. I would not swear that it did, but it is my recollection.

Q. It is your recollection that it did, is that your answer, sir?

A. Yes, sir.

MR. WILLIAMS: I have no further questions.

When Cole finished his testimony I moved for a judgment of acquittal for Aldo Icardi. It had been made abundantly clear that the subcommittee in the Holohan inquiry was not seeking information that would be helpful to the

Congress in enacting or repealing or modifying any legislation. The Congress had long since undertaken to enact legislation to remove the loophole it felt existed in the Icardi case. The government had not shown that the Holohan inquiry had any valid legislative purpose. The investigation was exposure for the sake of exposure, a hearing for the sake of headlines. It was a show—and a bizarre show. But it was worse than that. It was a carefully laid perjury trap. It was a preconceived plan by members of the United States Congress to get Aldo Icardi. All this had come to light in what Congressman Cole had said.

I argued for hours before Judge Keech, tracing the whole history and purpose of congressional investigations. He was troubled and took the case under advisement overnight. I learned later that he worked the rest of the day and through the night.

The next morning, April 29, 1956, court reconvened at eleven A.M. Judge Keech read a long opinion acquitting Icardi on the ground that the subcommittee was not acting in furtherance of any legitimate legislative purpose. He scored the subcommittee report for referring to Icardi as the "accused" and for concluding that there was "probable cause" to charge both Icardi and LoDolce with murder and embezzlement. "The use of this language," Judge Keech wrote, "indicates the functioning of the subcommittee as a committing magistrate."

On Chairman Cole's testimony he had this to say:

> Chairman Cole testified that the subcommittee already had in its possession sufficient information on which to base its report to the Congress, including Icardi's prior statements on many occasions, and that the purpose of asking Icardi's appearance before the subcommittee was to give him an opportunity to tell

his side of the story. Chairman Cole further testified that, to the best of his recollection, before asking Icardi to testify, he discussed with his colleague and counsel for the subcommittee the calling of Icardi, putting him under oath, and the possibility of a perjury indictment as the result of Icardi's testimony. It is unnecessary for the court to determine for which purpose Icardi's testimony was sought or obtained, since neither affording an individual a forum in which to protest his innocence nor extracting testimony with a view to a perjury prosecution is a valid legislative purpose.

* * *

While a committee or subcommittee of the Congress has the right to inquire whether there is a likelihood that a crime has been committed touching upon a field within its general jurisdiction and also to ascertain whether an executive department charged with the prosecution of such crime has acted properly, this authority cannot be extended to sanction a legislative trial and conviction of the individual toward whom the evidence points the finger of suspicion.

On the basis of all the evidence before it, the court therefore finds, as a matter of law, that at the time the subcommittee questioned the defendant Icardi it was not functioning as a competent tribunal.

Judge Keech concluded his opinion by saying:

The facts sought to be elicited by the questions which are the subject of this indictment all dealt with the issue of Icardi's guilt of the crimes with which he had been charged. The court has not overlooked the government's argument that the matters sought to be elicited by these six questions were material because,

> if Icardi had impressed the subcommittee with his credibility and had produced substantial corroborative evidence, the subcommittee might have concluded that he was innocent. In the face of the evidence that, as of the time he was questioned, Icardi's answers could have no effect upon the subcommittee's conclusions in the field of legitimate congressional investigation, this slim conjecture cannot support a finding by this court, as a matter of law, that Icardi's answers related to a material matter. Whether Icardi denied or confessed guilt by his answers, his testimony could not have influenced the subcommittee's conclusion on subjects which might be legitimately under investigation, namely, whether existing law adequately covered the prosecution of crimes committed under the circumstances of the specific charge under investigation, and whether the Defense Department had functioned adequately in its investigation of the Holohan disappearance.
>
> Therefore . . . the court holds as a matter of law that the alleged false answers by Icardi were not material to the subcommittee's authorized investigation.

Under the authorities, Judge Keech was clearly right. The power to investigate is not mentioned in the Constitution at all. It exists for one reason, and one reason alone: because without it Congress could not intelligently perform the duties expressly entrusted to the legislative branch of government by the Constitution. Consequently, Congress may conduct investigations to aid it in passing laws, or confirming presidential appointments, or ratifying treaties, or conducting impeachment proceedings or deciding election contests.

What Congress may not do is to conduct an investigation for a purpose totally unrelated to its constitutional duties. It may not, for example, conduct investigations to punish crimes, influence public opinion or help the political fortunes of its members. Nor may it call a witness for the purpose of setting up a contempt case or a perjury case against him.

The Icardi decision was right because it recognized and reaffirmed these basic principles. This decision was vitally significant, moreover, because it was the first reported case in three quarters of a century to hold that a congressional committee had exceeded its constitutional powers.

While Judge Keech's opinion was virtually the first judicial curb upon such legislative trials since 1881, it was far from the last. The decision in the celebrated Watkins case, handed down by the Supreme Court just a year after the Icardi decision, set forth sorely needed ground rules for the conduct of congressional investigations. Chief Justice Warren took occasion to condemn precisely the kind of investigation revealed by the Icardi case: "Nor is the Congress a law enforcement or trial agency. These are functions of the executive and judicial departments of government. No inquiry is an end in itself; it must be related to and in furtherance of a legitimate task of the Congress. Investigations conducted solely for the personal aggrandizement of the investigators or to 'punish' those investigated are indefensible."

The Icardi case was both a triumph and a tragedy. For Aldo Icardi and his family the whole episode was a tragedy. It has caused them great suffering and torment, and not even the long passage of time will remove all the scars. On this score it was good that we were able at least to outline our position on the factual merits of the case in an American courtroom.

In its true significance, however, the case was a triumph.

It was a triumph on a matter of principle which transcends the particular individuals involved. When Judge Keech ruled that Congress has no power to conduct investigations for purposes of publicity or prosecution, he was saying something of vital importance to every American. We are all potential witnesses before some congressional committee. We all have a stake in ending "trial by Congress." What remains to be seen is whether the courts can compel contemporary congressional acceptance of the principles which were reaffirmed in the trial of Aldo Icardi.

CHAPTER IV

TRIAL BY CONGRESS— MC CARTHY

In contrast with the Aldo Icardi investigation, there has been one true legislative trial in recent years. That was the trial of Senator Joseph R. McCarthy of Wisconsin on charges that he had conducted himself in a manner unbecoming a member of the United States Senate. The Senate has the constitutional power to "punish its members for disorderly behavior," and the McCarthy case is one of the rare instances in which it undertook to use this power.

A select committee was named to conduct the initial investigation. It fashioned some *ad hoc* rules and, on the whole, tried to be fair and objective in the exercise of its wholly unfamiliar judicial function.

The censure charges against McCarthy were the climax of the rising opposition to him and to his methods of operation. Almost as soon as he took on the role of seeking out those he thought were Communists and subversives, complaints began about the way he ran investigations and about the character of the charges he often made. During those investigations he transgressed the rights of some witnesses in ways which I vigorously opposed. I had known Senator McCarthy for some time and we often argued about some of these practices. Our arguments, however, had little effect upon what he did. He believed, as did many of his colleagues in the Senate, that exposure for the sake of exposure was a proper objective for a congressional committee. His committee hearings were conducted on this premise.

In the spring of 1954 the furor he had raised reached its zenith when he attacked the security practices of the Department of the Army and sharply criticized General Ralph W. Zwicker. These attacks finally developed into what became known as the Army-McCarthy hearing, which was conducted by the other members of the committee McCarthy headed. McCarthy took a role in the hearing much like that of a prosecuting attorney. The Army employed Joseph N. Welch, a distinguished Boston lawyer, to present its case. Battle lines were quickly drawn. It was McCarthy versus the Army. For thirty-six days the hearing engrossed the attention of the nation. Television stations junked their regular schedules and devoted hours to direct broadcasts from the Senate caucus room. Newspapers devoted page after page to all the details. The hearing room was jammed day after day as the principals jabbed and parried under the hot camera lights.

Before the hearing the Senator had asked me to serve as his counsel in the case. But he wanted me for a role that no trial lawyer could accept. He was to conduct the cross-examination and retain ultimate control over the manner of presentation of his side of the case. I was to be present solely in an advisory capacity. Rule one for an advocate is that he have control commensurate with his responsibility—and if he is to be effective, this must be total. Moreover, this was not the kind of proceeding which brought into play the constitutional right to counsel and the obligation of the lawyer to assist. So I refused.

It seemed to me that on the merits the McCarthy side was

scoring more effectively than its opposition as the evidence began to unfold. McCarthy had charged that the Army had been negligent and remiss in its loyalty program. The Army was not putting forward a very convincing case that he was wrong. But the effect was being nullified by the Senator's constant interposition of objections and points of order and the endless wrangling between himself and members of the committee. It seemed to me he was dramatizing the old maxim about the foolishness of a lawyer who tries his own case. The country remained divided on the whole issue as the hearing approached its end.

Suddenly the atmosphere of the case underwent a dramatic change. Late one afternoon the Senator accused Joseph Welch of having brought to Washington a young assistant who had once been a member of the National Lawyers Guild, an organization charged with being sympathetic to Communism. Welch, a great courtroom lawyer, rose to the challenge. He made a stirring plea on behalf of his young man and won the sympathy of millions of Americans. When McCarthy had first approached me about representing him, he had told me in the presence of his committee counsel, Roy Cohn, of the evidence he proposed to use against this young lawyer. Cohn and I had extracted from the Senator a promise that he would never use it. We thought that, in the light of all the facts as we knew them, such an attack would be unfair, and we told McCarthy his case would be hurt by such a charge. But McCarthy was a man who could never resist the temptation to touch a sign which said WET PAINT, and he had to touch this one.

The hearing went on, but Welch's plea that afternoon had changed its tone and direction. The Senator's conduct had been a demonstration of the kind of procedure in a legislative investigation which I opposed. He had produced derogatory information in a public hearing without giving its victim an opportunity to be heard privately in advance to explain his position or giving him a chance to defend himself in the same public session in which the information was revealed. If it had not been for Welch's eloquent plea, the information might have seriously and unnecessarily damaged the career of that young lawyer. Few persons whose rights have been trampled by legislative committees have had the good fortune to have a Joseph Welch speak up for them.

A few days later I flew to Europe to fulfill a six weeks' teaching engagement at the University of Frankfurt Law School. While I was there, Senator Ralph Flanders introduced his motion calling for censure of Senator McCarthy. Early in August, 1954, a list of forty-six charges of misconduct was filed against McCarthy, and the select committee of six Senators, headed by Senator Arthur V. Watkins of Utah, was named to conduct an investigation. This committee decided to hold a hearing on charges which fell into five categories: (1) contempt of the Senate or of senatorial committees; (2) encouragement of federal employees to violate the law; (3) receipt or use of classified documents from executive files; (4) abuses of fellow Senators; and (5) abuse of General Ralph Zwicker.

When I returned from Europe on August 15, I read in the New York *Times* while I was going through customs that McCarthy had announced he was going to retain me to defend him against these charges. The Senate had passed a resolution providing specifically for his right to counsel in the hearing and authorizing payment of fees out of committee funds. When I arrived in Washington I received a call from him. He asked me to represent him and he quickly agreed to give me full charge of the case.

We met at my home and carefully spelled out our understanding. With the Army-McCarthy fiasco fresh in my mind, I was determined not to participate in a carnival of that character. So I insisted that he allow me to conduct the whole defense. I wanted the same authority I would get from any other person charged with specific acts of misconduct. He agreed that I should cross-examine the witnesses and put in the defense. He further agreed that he would say nothing throughout the hearing except when he was testifying. In short, I was given the power commensurate with the responsibility insofar as the hearing went. We shook hands on what I thought was a very carefully detailed understanding.

I notified the committee that I would represent Senator McCarthy, and that I would not accept compensation from committee funds. I felt that it was unwise for McCarthy's counsel to be on the payroll of the committee that was trying him.

The Senator stuck meticulously to our agreement. He let me conduct the entire hearing without any interference, and in the committee room he was a completely docile client. But I soon discovered I had been guilty of a tremendous oversight. I had not foreseen that under the terms of our agreement he would be free to make whatever comments he chose outside of the hearing room either about the hearing itself or about the committee members. He used that freedom to the fullest. From the opening gun he was holding press conferences and making statements over television networks. He attacked the committee members individually, and he attacked the manner in which they were conducting the inquiry. Needless to say, this did not make my role any easier. Day by day our relationship with the committee worsened, but I was unable to dissuade the Senator from continuing his verbal assaults on Senator Watkins and his associates.

Watkins and the committee had set out to establish rules

which would make the hearing as fair as a legislative trial could be. McCarthy had been informed specifically of what the charges against him were. He was allowed to make an opening statement, to testify and to be examined by his counsel. He was allowed to have counsel at every stage of the proceedings. His counsel was allowed to object to procedures and to specific questions and to cross-examine adverse witnesses, as well as to present evidence on McCarthy's behalf. There were no television cameras to distract the attention of witnesses and committee members. Although the press coverage was heavy and audiences were large, the publicity pressure which had surrounded the Army-McCarthy hearing was gone. Watkins kept the whole inquiry on such a dryly technical level that much of the excitement was drained out of the day-to-day proceedings. All in all, they were conducted with somewhat more decorum and calmness than usually surrounds a congressional hearing, although this one was as potentially explosive as any investigation had ever been.

After many days of testimony and deliberation the committee released its report on September 17, recommending that the Senate censure McCarthy on only two of the forty-six original charges. Many of the charges had lacked any substance. Others had melted away because the committee had given McCarthy a full opportunity to show how misleading they were. All that remained was McCarthy's actions in two cases. One was his failure to appear before the Gillette Subcommittee in 1952 and his leveling of severe criticism of its members. The Gillette Subcommittee had investigated certain aspects of McCarthy's private and political conduct in connection with a resolution for his expulsion from the Senate which had been introduced by Senator William Benton of Connecticut. The other count on which the Watkins Committee recommended censure was for what it termed "abuse" of General Zwicker. Zwicker had been a witness before McCarthy's committee and the Senator had severely tongue-lashed him for what McCarthy regarded as a failure to cooperate.

With the filing of the Watkins Committee report, the issue had been narrowed to these two specific incidents of alleged misconduct. The full Senate refused to censure McCarthy on the Zwicker incident. So the only one of the original charges in the case was the "contempt of the Gillette Subcommittee." Ultimately the Senate voted 67 to 22 to censure McCarthy on this ground and also on the ground that he was guilty of improper conduct toward the Watkins Committee itself.

On this last charge, which was filed after the committee had concluded its hearings, McCarthy was condemned for what he had done outside the hearing room. He had infuriated the members of the committee and the other members of the Senate by statements he made in newspaper and television interviews. But he never received an opportunity to defend himself in a judicial-type hearing on this charge. It was brought up, discussed and disposed of on the Senate floor—hardly the place for the type of cool and dispassionate inquiry which the select committee had conducted.

McCarthy's "contempt" of the Gillette Subcommittee was not a usual case of contempt. Normally a witness is cited for contempt if he is subpoenaed to testify and declines to appear or if he refuses to answer proper questions asked of him. The Watkins Committee report, however, charged that McCarthy declined the "invitation" of the Gillette Subcommittee to appear before it in 1952. Never in the history of the Senate had anyone been punished for declining an "invitation" to appear.

McCarthy had stated repeatedly in 1952 that if he were

ordered either verbally or by subpoena to appear before the subcommittee he would do so. He was never given either type of order. The only time he was even requested to appear was on November 21, 1952. This request was made in a telegram sent to Appleton, Wisconsin, which said he could appear on November 22, 24 or 25. At the time the wire was sent, McCarthy was deer-hunting in the woods of northern Wisconsin, and the subcommittee knew it. The Watkins Committee admitted in its report that this wire did not reach McCarthy until November 28, 1952, three days after the deadline set for his appearance by the subcommittee. At no time thereafter did that subcommittee either invite or request him to appear before it.

When the full Senate debated the merits of the Senator's conduct and finally voted to censure him for his failure to appear before the Gillette Subcommittee, we did not know the subcommittee's conduct toward McCarthy would certainly have justified his failure to appear even if the telegram had reached him in time. I knew that McCarthy had repeatedly attacked the motives and procedures of that subcommittee. I knew that two staff members and one Senator had resigned from the subcommittee in protest against what they regarded as unfair tactics. At the time of the hearings and of the debate, however, I did not know and could not have known the full extent of the improprieties perpetrated by that subcommittee.

Perhaps if I had known, or if the Watkins Committee had known, or if the Senate had known, the outcome might have been different. The subcommittee's conduct toward McCarthy was the type of conduct of which the Watkins Committee disapproved. It was also the type of conduct of which most Senators disapprove.

I say the outcome might have been different because the Senate came close to settling the charges against McCarthy without actually censuring him. I was still representing McCarthy's interests when the debate on the Watkins Committee report moved to the Senate floor. Although I was not allowed to speak in his behalf there, I was granted the privilege of sitting on the Senate floor and conferring with him and with others during that debate. As the debate wore on, it appeared that McCarthy could muster only twenty-two votes against censure of any type. Defeat seemed certain. But many other Republicans and some Democrats were not anxious to censure him if it could be avoided.

Senator Everett M. Dirksen, who supported McCarthy in the debate, worked diligently to arrange a compromise, and it appeared that he was succeeding. He drafted three versions of a resolution which probably would have won the votes of a majority of the Senate. The White House was anxious to have the issue settled as quickly as possible, and I met with Bernard Shanley, then counsel to President Eisenhower, to discuss compromise. The Dirksen proposal was a relatively mild resolution which was not censure. It said that the Senate did not condone what McCarthy had done, but that there had been no rules forbidding it. Therefore, it said, a committee should be appointed to draw up rules barring similar behavior. Anyone who violated these rules in the future would be censured. This seemed to me to be a victory for McCarthy and it appeared certain that there were enough votes to pass it.

Late one evening, Senator Barry Goldwater and I took the resolution to McCarthy. He was in Bethesda Naval Hospital suffering from a severe infection in his elbow, and the debate had been temporarily recessed. In a discussion lasting several hours, Senator Goldwater and I begged McCarthy to accept the resolution. We pleaded, but McCarthy was adamant. He said he would not ask his friends in the Senate to vote that they did not condone what he had done. He said he knew they did condone it and did approve it. If he could not win, he said, he wanted to lose with his twenty-two friends. Senator Goldwater and I came back to my home in the early hours of the morning convinced that McCarthy's judgment was bad and that he had rejected his only chance to stave off defeat. We went back to the Capitol that day, but the fight against censure was all but over. McCarthy was beaten.

Many times since it has been written that the Senator's censure marked the end of McCarthy, that it broke his spirit and left him a bitterly disappointed man. In my opinion, nothing could be more remote from the truth. He rejected a clear invitation to stave off censure. From the first he regarded it as inevitable, and when it came he wore it as a badge of courage. He showed no disappointment and no regret. I think I had a monopoly on the disappointment over the case. I felt all the disappointment of a lawyer who has lost a big case which he could have settled in a way favorable to his client.

But there was tremendous irony in this defeat—dramatic irony largely lost in the hue and cry that went up over the censure. The irony was that the man whose name became symbolic of objectionable congressional investigative practices was himself the victim of a lawless procedure.

The Watkins Committee recommendation of censure was sustained only insofar as it found McCarthy contemptuous of the Gillette Subcommittee. This was the only one of the forty-six charges against McCarthy which was finally validated by a Senate vote.

As I have said, I feel sure the charge would not have been sustained if we had had the evidence which came to us only after the censure vote had been taken. Not till then did we learn that the Gillette Subcommittee had put a "mail cover" on McCarthy during the time it was investigating him. Had this fact been brought out before the Watkins Committee, it might well have changed the result at the committee level.

A "mail cover" is a frequently used but little-known investigative technique employed by the Post Office Department at the request of other branches of the government. In McCarthy's case, at the request of the Gillette Subcommittee, all of McCarthy's personal mail was placed under surveillance. The Washington post office was asked to furnish the names and the addresses of all the addressors of mail to McCarthy's home. Each day this information was forwarded to the subcommittee. The surveillance was placed not only on McCarthy's home address but also on the residence of Miss Jean Kerr, who was later to become the Senator's wife, and on the residence of Donald Surine, a member of the Senator's staff.

The order purporting to authorize these mail covers bore the facsimile signature of the late Senator Thomas Hennings, then chairman of the subcommittee. Senator Hennings never signed such an order, nor was the mail cover imposed with his knowledge. He would never have brooked this kind of invasion of the privacy of McCarthy or of anyone else. It was done by an overzealous staff member who, in his desire to get McCarthy, ran roughshod over his rights.

In my view, a mail cover of this type is a lawless and illegal procedure. Its whole purpose is that everyone who has written to the person under investigation should be contacted and questioned about the contents of his letter and the reply he received. Of course the addressor is free to refuse to give any information, but few citizens hesitate to talk freely to federal officers who flash a badge of authority.

Over a century ago it was made a crime to open other people's mail and pry into their business. Our mores recoiled at such an invasion of privacy. The Fourth Amendment to the Constitution of the United States, as interpreted by the Supreme Court, forbids such opening of mail as an unlawful search and seizure.

In addition to the federal statutes which make it a crime to open mail, there are statutes which make it a crime to delay the mail for any purpose. Specifically, it is a crime to delay the mail for the purpose of prying into anyone else's business. These statutes apply to ordinary citizens, postal employees and law-enforcement officers alike. Obviously, it is not possible to impose a mail cover successfully without delaying the mail. First the mail must be taken out of regular channels and set aside. Then the information must be recorded before the mail is put back into its regular course.

When the requested information is turned over to the interested agency, the investigation into the contents of the mail begins. If the addressor is hailed before a grand jury or a committee of Congress and asked about his letter, he must reveal its contents, challenge the pertinency of the questioning or take refuge in the Fifth Amendment, unless his letter falls within the narrowly circumscribed area of privileged communications.

The mail cover is a technique employed by investigative agencies of the federal government with increasing frequency. It is used often in the development of income-tax cases. In this way the Internal Revenue Service can ascertain who is billing the taxpayer and can get fairly complete information on his expenditures.

When the McCarthy mail cover came to light, the Senate appointed a special committee to investigate the charge. The committee found that the charge was completely true: mail surveillance had been placed on the residences of McCarthy, Jean Kerr and Donald Surine. The committee unanimously agreed to refer the matter to the Department of

Justice for appropriate action. It was referred. There the matter ended.

But the censure had already been voted. The hearing was over. The debate was over. There was no chance to reopen. The Senate had had its fill of the whole matter. History must show in one of its more ironical paragraphs that McCarthy was himself a casualty of a congressional investigation that flouted the rules of fair play.

CHAPTER V

FAIR INVESTIGATIVE PROCEDURE

"THE constitutional guarantee against unwarranted search and seizure breaks down, the prohibition against what amounts to a Government charge of criminal action without the formal presentment of a grand jury is evaded, the rules of evidence which have been adopted for the protection of the innocent are ignored, the individual becomes the victim of vague, unformulated, and indefinite charges, and instead of a government of law we have a government of lawlessness. Against the continuation of such a condition I enter my solemn protest."

The speaker was none other than Calvin Coolidge. He was decrying abuse of the investigatory power in probes of big business during the 1920's. A quarter-century later we have come full cycle, and Coolidge's words have significance in showing that recognition of the need for reform is not the exclusive prerogative of the liberals any more than it is the exclusive prerogative of one political party. His words also highlight a fact of history: the investigators turn their direction. The forces of capitalism and conservatism and labor and liberalism all have their day in the witness chair.

Recent events demonstrate that the principle enunciated in the Icardi case and given the benediction of the Supreme Court in the Watkins case has not ended abuse of the investigatory powers. The apex of congressional inquiry today is apparently the calling of a witness who will invoke the privilege against self-incrimination in response to all questions on a subject about which the committee already has full information.

Just a few months after the Watkins decision said that congressional hearings must be clearly related to a legislative purpose Senator Barry Goldwater appeared on a television forum called *Youth Wants to Know*. He was questioned by four high-school students. During the preceding week the McClellan Committee, on which Senator Goldwater served, had called before it the notorious Johnny Dio. Dio was under indictment at the time for one of the most odious crimes of the past decade, the acid blinding of columnist Victor Riesel. It would have been the epitome of naïveté for the committee or its counsel to expect that Dio would do anything except take refuge in the Fifth Amendment and refuse to answer questions. This is precisely what he did for several hours while television cameras kept him in steady focus. The questions were like sticks poked at a caged animal, and the morbidly curious were entranced.

When the program opened, a little girl with braces on her teeth and freckles on her face asked Senator Goldwater an important question:

> QUESTION: Sir, why do you have people such as Johnny Dio on the McClellan Committee testifying when you know he isn't going to do anything but just plead the Fifth Amendment? Aren't you wasting your time and the taxpayers' money?
>
> SENATOR GOLDWATER: No, Jane, we are not. Re-

member, we just don't bring Mr. Dio down here cold. We have investigated him and his relationship to these rackets for many, many months and we have all the answers to questions we ask a man like Mr. Dio.

QUESTION: Then why have him?

To this question there was, of course, no reply. A high-school girl had deftly pinpointed the issue.

Many members of Congress still honestly believe that the scope of congressional inquiry is limited only by the scope of their own imaginations. When I appeared before the McClellan Committee in 1958 as counsel for James Hoffa, president of the Teamsters' Union, I had occasion to object that certain questions directed toward my client could have no real relationship to a legislative purpose. Senator Irving Ives replied. The colloquy, as transcribed by the Senate reporter, went like this:

MR. WILLIAMS: I feel there were areas of interrogation when it appeared to me, at least, as a lawyer looking over the record when the questions were designed more to humiliate the witness than they were to elicit information that would be helpful to this committee in proposing legislation to the United States Senate.

SENATOR IVES: Now, just a minute. I know of no question of that kind that could possibly have been asked him during the previous hearing a year ago this month, which in any way could humiliate him that wasn't brought on by himself.

Anybody that ducks questions the way he did is bound to bring on that kind of questioning, and he deserves it, and it does have a legislative purpose because that is almost contempt of the Senate, the way he acted here the last time. That definitely has a legislative purpose. You and I may not agree.

MR. WILLIAMS: We don't.

SENATOR IVES: Because I am very broad in this matter, and I don't think that there is a thing in kingdom come that doesn't come within the purview of legislative activity or scope. Even if it is outside of the Constitution, it is not outside because it calls for a constitutional amendment perhaps. So anything we do is within our limitations.

In June of 1959 Senator Everett Dirksen discussed current abuses of the investigatory process on a documentary television program presented by the American Broadcasting Company. He pointed out, "When it comes to a legislative inquiry there are no rules and actually the sky is the limit. I can ask a witness almost any question under the canopy of heaven and if one of my colleagues should intrude, I can say you mind your own business and I'll mind mine."

Exposure for the sake of exposure remains a goal of many investigators, despite the plain prohibition expressed by the Supreme Court in the Watkins case. A staff memorandum prepared two decades ago was being used by one congressional committee as recently as June, 1959. It urged the investigators:

> Decide what you want the newspapers to hit hardest and then shape each hearing so that the main point becomes the vortex of the testimony. Once that vortex is reached, adjourn.
>
> * * *
>
> Do not space hearings more than 24 or 48 hours apart when on a controversial subject. This gives the opposition too much opportunity to make all kinds of countercharges and replies by issuing statements to the newspapers.
>
> Don't ever be afraid to recess a hearing even for five

minutes so that you keep the proceedings completely in control so far as creating news is concerned.

A consistent offender on this score has been the House Committee on Un-American Activities. Numerous reports issued prior to the Watkins case admitted that exposure and publicity were primary functions of the committee. These admissions were reinforced by a report issued in February, 1959, which contained biographical sketches of thirty-nine lawyers who had been before the committee because they were accused of having Communist sympathies. It is difficult to see any purpose behind the issuance of this report other than exposure.

In June, 1959, four members of the Supreme Court concluded that in fact the principal purpose of the committee was "punishment by humiliation and public shame." The remaining members of the court did not indicate disagreement with this conclusion, but merely held that the judiciary could not scrutinize the motives behind congressional investigations.

It is fair to say that many members of Congress have not reciprocated this hands-off policy. Recent Supreme Court decisions in the field of subversive activities and criminal procedure have been answered with bills designed to strip the court of jurisdiction on many issues. While legislation of this nature was under consideration by Congress, the Senate Internal Security Subcommittee printed for the use of the full committee a "study" by the SPX Research Associates which contained the following questions and answers:

> QUESTION: Do Supreme Court patterns coincide with, or follow, established pressure patterns of the Communist global conquest by paralysis?
>
> ANSWER: Affirmative.

* * *

QUESTION: Do recent decisions of the Supreme Court follow pre-established Communist lines and contentions?

ANSWER: Affirmative.

* * *

QUESTION: Have recent decisions of the Supreme Court assumed a pattern of aid and comfort to the enemy?

ANSWER: Affirmative.

If congressional committees can attack the Supreme Court with impunity, it is obvious that no citizen is immune from the long arm of the investigators. Anyone who expresses an unpopular opinion is vulnerable. In May, 1958, a Cleveland industrialist named Cyrus Eaton made bold to criticize the FBI over a national television network. Representative Francis Walter, chairman of the House Committee on Un-American Activities, immediately signed a subpoena calling Eaton before the committee to explain himself. Apparently Eaton's Americanism became suspect as soon as he dared to criticize an American institution in public. Even in the most conservative quarters this type of "thought policing" was too much, and the celebrated subpoena was never served.

The subpoenas issued by congressional committees are often oppressive for other reasons. In the first place, a subpoena is valid at least as long as Congress is in session. I have had clients who were under subpoena, obligated to testify upon a few hours' notice, for almost a year. Neither the subpoena nor the notice to appear gives any idea of the subject currently under inquiry, so that a witness has no opportunity to refresh his recollection or to locate records which will enable him to answer honestly and fully. When the committee elects to subpoena the records themselves, its demands are sometimes incredible. On February 5, 1959, James R. Hoffa was subpoenaed to produce forthwith

> all books and records of the International Brotherhood of Teamsters, Chauffeurs, Warehousemen and Helpers of America for the period from January 1, 1945 to the present time, including cash receipts and disbursements, general ledgers, auditors' reports, all letters, communications, files, correspondence, interoffice communications, CPA reports, personal and confidential letters and memoranda, and any and all documents relating in any way to the operation of the International Headquarters or any of its associate Locals, Conferences and Joint Councils.

By the most conservative estimate, these materials would have filled one hundred freight cars. The demand was so unreasonable that it was eventually modified.

These examples—and I could cite many more—demonstrate beyond dispute that something is radically wrong with the congressional investigative process. A reckless minority is endangering the integrity of the entire Congress by persisting in investigations for the purpose of exposure or public punishment.

It is clear that reform cannot come from the judiciary. Chief Justice Warren's opinion in the Watkins case did everything which any court could conceivably do to curb legislative abuses. It brought the force of the nation's highest tribunal to bear upon errant investigators in a decision of sweeping breadth and stinging rebuke. The results have been unsatisfactory.

The trouble with judicial control of congressional investigations is that it comes too little and too late. The basic doctrine of separation of powers compels the courts to give congressional committees the benefit of every possible inference as to their procedures and purposes. Unfortunately, Congressman Sterling Cole stood on a lonely pinnacle of candor in the Icardi case. Most members of Congress are absolutely unwilling to admit that they subpoenaed a witness for purposes unrelated to any legitimate legislative objective. It is a case of good reasons and real reasons, with the investigators always asserting a good reason, and the witness always unable to establish the real reason by competent proof.

Not only is judicial control too little for proper protection of the witness; it also comes too late. The decisions are uniform that a witness must judge at his peril whether the committee has jurisdiction over the subject matter of his interrogation, whether the questions propounded to him are pertinent to this subject, whether the purpose of his interrogation is related to a legitimate legislative objective and, in short, whether he is legally obligated to testify. If he wrongly decides any of these complex legal questions he has committed a crime. Neither good faith nor honest reliance upon the advice of counsel constitutes any defense. Every witness is thus faced with a terrible decision. He can play it safe and submit to an interrogation which may constitute a flagrant abuse of his rights, or he can take his chances and decline to testify, hoping that months or even years later the courts will agree with him that the interrogation was unjustified.

The time has come for a uniform code of procedures for congressional investigations, just as we have the Federal Rules of Civil Procedure and the Federal Rules of Criminal Procedure for judicial trials. At present the committees formulate their own rules, and the rights extended to witnesses range from the very fair to the nonexistent. There have been numerous proposals both from within and without Congress for reform.

These proposed codes differ in detail and in degree, but almost all of them have certain basic points in common. They recognize the danger of one-man control by committee chairmen and one-man subcommittees. They recognize the right to counsel. They recognize the right to notice of the subject under inquiry. They recognize the necessity of protection for third persons who may be irreparably defamed by testimony before a committee. They recognize the problem presented by broadcasting and televising the testimony of a witness against his will.

The last two of these problems are perhaps the most difficult of solution. Insistence by committees investigating subversive activities that a witness must "name names" has focused public attention upon the plight of a person who is defamed and who has no forum in which to clear his name. The problem of defamation, however, is not limited to these committees. Almost any major investigation can result in charges of crime, malfeasance or fraud against some person who has no right to tell his side of the story unless the committee chooses to hear it. The requirement of the House rules that defamatory testimony must be heard initially in executive session and released only by majority vote affords at best illusory protection, because the witness can always be recalled in open session to repeat the defamatory testimony.

If a committee elects to publish testimony which may cost a man not only his good name but even his means of livelihood, it would seem only fair that he should be allowed a reasonable opportunity to cross-examine his accuser and that the committee should call a reasonable number of witnesses on his behalf. When the committee feels that this procedure would constitute an undue burden on its operations, its course is simple: the defamatory testimony should be taken in secret and kept in secret.

Of course the American people have a right to be informed about the operations of their government, including congressional committees. They do not, however, have a right to know that X called Y a Communist or a labor racketeer unless and until Y is given a fair opportunity to reply —which includes the right to testify on his own behalf, to cross-examine X and to present the testimony of Z, a responsible citizen who may be able to establish the complete falsity of X's charge.

A somewhat allied problem involves the recall of witnesses who have testified in executive session to repeat their testimony in open session. It is impossible to see any legitimate legislative objective which can be served by this practice. Of course, it is perfectly proper to recall a witness for the purpose of obtaining additional information from him. But when the committee intends to ask precisely the same questions and expects to obtain precisely the same answers in open session as in a previous executive session, the only possible purpose is sensationalism. It does not even rise to the dignity of exposure, since that objective could be more easily attained by releasing the executive-session transcript. This abusive practice is frequently employed when a witness in executive session has invoked the privilege against self-incrimination. He is then recalled in open session and the incriminating question is framed in as many embarrassing ways as possible. Often the witness is lectured for the benefit of radio and television audiences. It is then reported that this particular witness has invoked the Fifth Amendment forty times or one hundred and forty times, and the public is left with the inference that he is guilty of forty crimes or one hundred and forty crimes, as the case may be.

Another problem deserving further discussion is raised

by the broadcasting and televising of committee hearings, especially when the witness objects. Senate committees at present are free to permit television, broadcasting and newsreels. The Kefauver crime probe, the Army-McCarthy hearings and the McClellan investigation have been among the most popular "shows" in the history of television.

In the House, on the other hand, television has charted a rocky course. In 1952 Speaker Rayburn held that the silence of the House rules on this subject meant that the House had no authority to permit broadcasting or television. In the Eighty-third Congress, Speaker Martin informally indicated a contrary interpretation of the rules, and some House hearings were televised. When Rayburn again became Speaker in the Eighty-fourth Congress, he formally reiterated his ruling that both broadcasting and television were prohibited.

The second Rayburn ruling was precipitated by the suicide of a San Francisco biochemist who was scheduled to testify during televised hearings conducted by the House Committee on Un-American Activities. He left a note stating that he had "fierce resentment" against being televised. His widow thereupon filed a wrongful-death action against the committee, demanding damages of $500,000. Since this incident many bills to permit the broadcasting and televising of House hearings have been introduced, but none has so far reached the floor.

There are, in my opinion, weighty reasons supporting an outright ban against broadcasting or televising any congressional hearing. The chief danger posed by microphones and cameras is that both committee members and witnesses often become more conscious of their audience than of their legislative responsibility. When a witness objects to having his testimony broadcast or telecast, I think his wish should be respected. The average person is extremely nervous when he appears as a witness before any court or committee. It is unfair to ask him to appear before the entire country as well. In the first place, if he has strenuous objection to broadcasting or television, his answers may very well be affected by nervousness or by fear of public opinion. In the second place, it is a serious and unnecessary invasion of his privacy to project his face and voice into millions of homes without his consent. Consequently, the best course seems to be a rule that no testimony will be broadcast or televised without the consent of the witness.

It is difficult to distill the best points from all of the bills, resolutions and bar-association proposals in this field. I would like, however, to see both houses of Congress adopt a code of procedure which embodies substantially the following points. Most of them are not new; they are drawn from one or more prior proposals. Some of them, on the other hand, are based solely upon my own experience. I might add that these proposals are not, and were not intended to be, couched in the formal language of legislative draftsmanship.

1. All subpoenas or requests to testify shall be in writing, shall state the question under inquiry and the subject matter of the interrogation to be directed toward the witness, and shall be served at least forty-eight hours in advance of his appearance. No witness may be held subject to the same subpoena for a period longer than ten days from the date on which he first testifies in response thereto.

2. No subpoena shall be issued without the approval of a majority of the committee, unless a majority of the committee has delegated the power to issue subpoenas to the chairman and a member of the minority political party. If a subpoena requiring the production of documents is issued without the specific prior approval of a majority of the com-

mittee, the witness shall have the right to demand that its legality be passed upon by the full committee.

3. Every witness shall have the right to be accompanied by counsel, who shall be entitled to interpose proper objections to the jurisdiction of the committee, the questions propounded and any failure to follow procedural requirements; to submit legal memoranda in support of such objections; to advise the witness of his legal and constitutional rights before the committee; and to ask clarifying questions of the witness, subject to control of the length of such interrogation by a majority of the members present.

4. Every witness shall have the right to read a prepared statement of reasonable length into the record, provided that it is pertinent to the subject under inquiry and that it was submitted to the committee in advance of the hearing.

5. No witness shall be compelled to testify at any hearing unless at least two members of the committee are present.

6. No witness shall be compelled to have his testimony broadcast, televised or filmed for newsreels.

7. No witness who has testified in executive session shall be required over his objection to repeat his testimony on the same subject matter in open session.

8. All testimony which is likely to defame another person shall be heard in executive session. No testimony given in executive session or any summary thereof shall be released without approval by a majority of the committee. If defamatory testimony is to be released, the person defamed shall be notified in advance and shall be entitled to testify on his own behalf at the same hearing, to cross-examine the witnesses against him in person or by counsel, to have the committee subpoena a reasonable number of witnesses to testify in executive session on his behalf and to examine such witnesses in person or by counsel. All rebuttal testi-

mony shall be released simultaneously with the defamatory testimony. The extent of the examination and cross-examination on behalf of a person defamed shall be subject to reasonable limitations by the committee to prevent abuse.

9. No committee report containing defamatory statements shall be made public unless the person defamed has been given an opportunity to testify before the committee and such testimony is published or summarized as part of the report.

10. Every witness shall be afforded a reasonable opportunity to inspect the transcript of his testimony in person and by counsel and to make proper corrections therein. If a witness testifies in public or if his testimony in executive session is released, he shall be entitled to a copy of the transcript at reasonable expense.

There is one important area which is not covered by the foregoing points, and that is the area of enforcement. It has been suggested that a committee be set up in each house to ensure compliance with any procedural code. Most of these suggestions rely upon public opinion and possible censure of offending committee members as their sole sanctions. Because of the well-known reluctance of both Senators and Representatives to indulge in personal criticism of their fellow members, however, some additional sanction is clearly necessary. The best proposal, in my view, is that no witness should be punished for contempt unless and until the committee has extended to him all of the rights guaranteed by the code. This should go a long way toward assuring that procedural rights will not become empty phrases.

When President Truman resigned as chairman of the Senate special committee investigating the national defense program in 1944, he delivered a speech stressing the vital role of congressional investigations. He said: "In my opinion, the power of investigation is one of the most important powers of the Congress. The manner in which that power is exercised will largely determine the position and prestige of the Congress in the future. An informed Congress is a wise Congress; an uninformed Congress surely will forfeit a large portion of the respect and confidence of the people." He might well have added that a Congress which seeks to inform itself by violating the rights of its citizens will forfeit all the respect and confidence of the people.

This respect and this confidence can be safeguarded only by fair procedural rules that will prevent an irresponsible minority of investigators from continuing to overshadow the responsible majority. That the majority should be thus overshadowed is particularly tragic in view of the fact that most congressional investigations are conducted for preeminently proper purposes and with due regard for the rights of all witnesses.

It is always difficult to single out one or two committees as examples of proper investigative procedure. Most of my personal experience has, unfortunately, been with the minority of committees which abuse their powers, because it is these committees which give rise to litigation. I did, however, have the privilege of testifying several times before the Subcommittee on Constitutional Rights of the Senate Judiciary Committee, and I have watched its work with interest. All of the hearings conducted by this subcommittee have been designed to produce information which will help Congress in legislating, not to produce headlines or convictions. When it was investigating the subject of confessions obtained during police detention, it heard from law-school professors, prosecuting attorneys, police officials, defense counsel and representatives of bar associations and other interested groups. It did not call prospective defendants or convicted felons to suggest how our criminal procedure in this field might be improved. Obviously, none of the witnesses had any occasion to evade the subcommittee's questions or to rely upon the privilege against self-incrimination. The subcommittee was consequently able to compile over 700 pages of pertinent testimony and exhibits in two days of hearings.

William S. White, a distinguished observer of Congress in action, has described in *Citadel* the work of other committees which discharge their investigative function with distinction. Of particular interest is his discussion of the investigation following General Douglas MacArthur's recall by President Truman, when an explosive topic was investigated with restraint and respect for the rights of witnesses as well as for the national security. Mr. White's examples prove that the power of investigation can be properly and perceptively exercised even in controversial fields.

CHAPTER VI

THE LISTENERS AT THE WALL

EQUALLY as important as the purpose, scope and legal basis of investigations in our society are the means and methods by which the investigations are conducted. We all have a vital stake in the preservation of the right to privacy—the privacy of the home, the privacy of our thoughts and words, the privacy of our conversations, both face to face and telephonic. We also have an interest in the right to silence, the right not to communicate.

The rapid development of electronic listening devices in the past few years has greatly multiplied the number of clandestine invasions of these rights. Conversations within the home or the office are invaded by eavesdropping equipment and those over telephones by wiretapping devices. A mechanism which can accomplish both is now in existence, and it can be manufactured at a cost below $25.

Justice William O. Douglas has described the threat of eavesdropping this way: "With modern electronic devices, conversations within the home and the office can be recorded without tapping any wires. The intimacies of private life can be made public without a key being turned or a window being raised. And those who listen may be private detectives and blackmailers, as well as law enforcement officials."

Eavesdropping is a threat that few people really understand, because it is surrounded by a conspiracy of silence. Only occasionally is there an incident which demonstrates to the public that no conversation, however confidential, is beyond the reach of a hidden microphone. This unhappy situation was well illustrated in two cases in which I participated in 1959. One involved Bernard Goldfine, the New England textile manufacturer who was a close confidant and benefactor of Presidential Assistant Sherman Adams. The other was a gambling indictment brought against Julius Silverman of Washington.

Goldfine was the victim of one of the oldest tricks of the private investigator. He had come to Washington in 1958 to testify before a committee which was investigating improper pressure on the federal regulatory agencies. Some of the testimony which the committee heard indicated that Goldfine had used his contacts with high-ranking officials, such as Sherman Adams, to obtain special favors for his business enterprises.

By the time Goldfine arrived to testify, the hearing had taken on all the atmosphere of a Hollywood production. The newspapers were full every day of charges and countercharges made by committee members and staff or by Goldfine's collection of lawyers and public-relations men. Halfway through the hearings, however, a midnight event at the Sheraton-Carlton Hotel in downtown Washington temporarily took the spotlight away from the show on Capitol Hill. Roger Robb, then chief counsel for Goldfine, came to the hotel on a night late in June to talk to his client. While he was there, Robb went to the eighth floor, where Jack Lotto, a New York public-relations man, was trying to offset some of the bad publicity which Goldfine had been getting. Robb later told in court this story of what happened that evening:

Well, Mr. Lotto and I were discussing getting out some sort of press statement to make the morning newspapers and Mr. Lotto finally suggested some statement about some letters that Mr. Goldfine had received from governors acknowledging receipt of certain vicuna coats. I didn't have the letters and I sent for them. Mr. Lotto, meanwhile, called up some newspaper people and told them that we would have something for them. While we were waiting, I was sort of walking up and down the room and I noticed there was a door leading from the Lotto suite into the adjoining room. There was an aperture, perhaps an eighth of an inch, between the bottom of that door and the sill and I noticed that there was light coming from under that door. Being curious, I thought I would see if I could look under there and see if anybody was next door who might be listening to what we were saying. I leaned down and finally got flat on my belly on the floor and looked under the door.

When I did so, I saw within two or three inches of the door on the other side the toes of a man's shoes. They were pointing toward the door and my first thought was that somebody had put his shoes down. Then they moved and I knew there was a man in the shoes. He was obviously standing facing the door and in close proximity to it, in a position that one would occupy if he were eavesdropping.

I immediately got up and asked another man who was present, Mr. Phil Brennan, who was also one of Mr. Goldfine's press representatives, to take a look. He did and he jumped back up and said, "I saw a man's hand on the floor down there. He is apparently on the floor."

So I went downstairs to the pay telephone in the

lobby and called Mr. Lloyd Furr [a private detective]. I asked him if he could come down right away, because I thought we were being spied on by the people next door. Mr. Furr came down and brought with him some electronic equipment that he had. He reported, after a little while, that there was a microphone next door.

About this time, the newspaper people had come in to get our letters and I called them aside and told them what we had just discovered. We looked at the door and Mr. Furr looked under the door. Then he turned to me and said, "I can see the microphone under there. Do you want me to get it?" I said, "Sure."

So he took a coathanger out of the closet and bent a hook in the end of it and inserted the hook under the door. With a very quick movement he snaked out the microphone and about eight or ten feet of wire.

The microphone, it turned out, had been installed by Baron Shacklette, chief investigator for the Special Subcommittee on Legislative Oversight, and Jack Anderson, a Washington newsman. They wanted to listen in while Goldfine conferred with his staff, and they had spent several days in rooms adjoining those of various members of the Goldfine party.

Robb vigorously protested this invasion of Goldfine's privacy. Shacklette promptly resigned from the committee staff, and the committee members denied that they had authorized him to engage in eavesdropping. But there were no regrets over what Shacklette had done. The regrets were for the fact that he had been caught doing it.

As the hearings proceeded, Goldfine refused to answer some of the questions asked him by the committee, and for this he was indicted for contempt of Congress. He asked me to defend him. When the case went to court, a long hearing was held to ascertain what the eavesdroppers had overheard. We brought out that Goldfine had conferred with his lawyers in the very rooms in question and that there had been an invasion of the confidential and private communications between lawyer and client. Shacklette denied he could hear Goldfine talking to his lawyers. He claimed he had heard only conversations of a purely personal nature between Goldfine and his wife and other members of his family.

On the strength of this testimony from an admitted eavesdropper the government contended that there had been no invasion of the lawyer-client relationship. The force of this argument, of course, was that it was all right for Shacklette to eavesdrop as long as he didn't hear the things he was trying to hear.

The government also argued that Goldfine's rights were not violated, because there had been no physical trespass into his room when the microphone was installed. The microphone had been placed on the floor next to Goldfine's door and was attached to an amplifier and recorder which sat several feet away in another room.

Judge James W. Morris, who presided over the hearing, felt that the law obliged him to uphold the government's position. But he said: "It is certainly understandable that the defendant should complain of and be indignant at the intrusion on his conversations . . . and it may well be such should be considered in mitigation of any punishment which would be visited upon him if convicted of the charges in the indictment." Later the judge permitted Goldfine to enter a plea of *nolo contendere* despite the prosecutor's objection, and he gave him a suspended sentence.

A few months after this incident in the Sheraton-Carlton Hotel, Julius Silverman asked me to represent him in what appeared to be a routine gambling case. I had not appeared for a client in a gambling case in ten years and I was not interested in this one until he showed me a copy of the affidavit which supported the issuance of the warrant authorizing the search of the house he occupied. In the affidavit a District of Columbia policeman and two Internal Revenue agents said they had overheard conversations which indicated that Silverman and two other men were conducting a gambling operation inside this house. I quickly realized that all of the conversations these officers swore they had overheard were telephone conversations. There were many direct quotes from one end of such conversations. No other colloquy was quoted.

I immediately suspected that the federal agents had illegally used wiretaps and had exposed their hand. But it puzzled me that the agents were so inept in concealing the source of their information.

I went to the Silverman house to see if it was possible for someone who lived next door to overhear conversations through the wall. The houses on either side of Silverman had common walls with his house. These party walls were twelve inches thick. An acoustical engineer whom I asked to run sound tests quickly demonstrated that it was impossible to hear sounds through the walls with the naked ear. I was then sure that the prosecution had obtained its evidence through some form of electronic invasion.

A few days later we filed motions in court to suppress all of the evidence which the police had seized when they raided the house. Under the law evidence which is illegally seized cannot be used in a criminal trial and a motion to suppress is the normal way to block the use of it. Such a motion is granted if the search warrant under which the evidence was seized was illegally issued. A search warrant based on evidence obtained through wiretapping is by my lights clearly illegal. We said in our motion that the government's evidence for the search warrant in this case had come either from wiretapping or from some kind of electronic eavesdropping. When this motion came on for a hearing in court the prosecutor conceded that the police had overheard conversations inside the house occupied by Silverman through the use of a spike microphone.

A spike microphone is a long, thin piece of steel with an attachment. It looks like a long nail. The one used in this case was almost twelve inches in length and about a quarter of an inch in diameter. It had an amplifier and a set of earphones attached to one end. When the point of the spike was placed in contact with a sounding board, the instrument was capable of amplifying sound waves through a wall.

The sounding board for a spike microphone can be almost any flat surface—a plasterboard wall in a room, a pane of glass in a window, or even a door. The principle of its operation is that the sound waves which emanate from a human voice set up mechanical vibrations in almost everything they touch. When a person talks inside a room, the windows vibrate ever so slightly. If the spike microphone is in contact with the glass, it takes those vibrations and converts them back into electrical energy, which is amplified and reconverted back into sound energy—the sound of the spoken words. The best sounding boards are thin sheets of metal which vibrate easily and freely.

When we learned that such a microphone had been used in the Silverman case, we bought one and took it to the Silverman house to see how it worked. We carefully inspected the party wall of the house next door and we found a small hole under the molding in an upstairs bedroom. The spike fitted this hole perfectly. We looked at the blueprints of the building and discovered that while the wall was twelve inches thick at that point, it was not the solid wall it appeared to be. Inside the wall was a heating duct which supplied hot air to Silverman's house. By pushing the spike microphone up against that heating duct, the police had obtained a perfect sounding board. They could hear everything that was said in Silverman's house—not only everything that was said in the room immediately adjacent to the duct, but everything that was said in any room in the house. The heating duct had been converted into a giant transmitter of sound and the heating registers of each room had become microphones.

Eventually all of these facts emerged at trial. But the prosecutor insisted there was nothing wrong or illegal in what the federal officers had done. He conceded that if a wire had been tapped and conversations overheard, the agents would have been acting illegally. He also conceded that if agents had entered Silverman's house to install the microphone the law would have been broken. But, he argued, because the marvels of modern science make it possible for police officers to eavesdrop on conversations without tapping a wire or entering a room, the search warrant was valid. No law prohibited such eavesdropping and no constitutional rights were violated.

We lost the motion to suppress the evidence and we lost the case at the trial level. Silverman and his co-defendants were sentenced to prison terms. When we took the case to the Supreme Court, however, that court reversed the conviction by a vote of 9 to 0. The court clearly indicated that it would not tolerate the kind of electronic eavesdropping employed in this case. But it based its decision on the fact that the spike had actually penetrated into Silverman's premises. It had been pressed up against his heating duct. Therefore, the court reasoned, there had been a physical trespass and this made the eavesdropping unlawful. The court refused to pass upon whether the eavesdropping would have been unlawful if it had been accomplished by a device having no physical contact with Silverman's house.

The character of the government's "defenses" in these two cases and the reaction of the Supreme Court in the Silverman case demonstrate that the time has arrived for the law to be clarified. Something is radically wrong when the federal government can defend electronic eavesdropping on the citizenry with the argument that everything overheard was purely personal and that the eavesdropping device was all right because it was located outside of the victim's house.

There have been proposals to adopt a federal statute authorizing warrants for eavesdropping. Under our Constitution, however, no warrant can authorize so sweeping an invasion of individual privacy. Indeed, one of the reasons for the American Revolution was to abolish the use of dragnet warrants from which no man's privacy was safe. John Adams tells us that the American Revolution was born in a Massachusetts courtroom when the Paxton case was decided in 1761.

Paxton, a collector of customs in colonial Massachusetts, asked the court for a "writ of assistance." This writ would enable him to enter any house at any time and search every part of it as he pleased if he suspected the presence of goods upon which the custom duty had not been paid. The prior experience of the American people with writs of assistance had been so bitter that the case aroused tremendous interest. Paxton won and the writ was granted. John Adams later wrote: "American independence was then and there born. . . . Every man of a crowded audience appeared to me to go away, as I did, ready to take arms against writs of assistance. Then and there was the first scene of the first act of opposition to the arbitrary claims of

Great Britain. Then and there the child Independence was born."

Ultimately the English courts came to agree with Adams that such unbridled invasion of the individual's privacy was inconsistent with a free society. In 1765 Lord Camden wrote a famous opinion holding that no writ or warrant could authorize government officials to ransack a man's papers in the hope of finding evidence to convict him of crime.

This decision did not stem the tide of revolution in the colonies but its fruits found enduring expression in the Fourth Amendment. That amendment says:

> The right of the people to be secure in their persons, houses, papers, and effects, against unreasonable searches and seizures, shall not be violated, and no Warrants shall issue, but upon probable cause, supported by Oath or affirmation, and particularly describing the place to be searched, and the persons or things to be seized.

This was the effort of this nation's founding fathers to protect the individual's right to privacy. It was an effort to ensure that a man's papers and his thoughts would be his alone unless he chose to make them public. The Supreme Court explained much of what this means and endorsed much of what Lord Camden had written when, in 1886, it decided the case of *Boyd* v. *United States.*

In a decision which Justice Brandeis has described as one that "will be remembered as long as civil liberty lives in the United States," the court verbalized the basic right of privacy that every American citizen enjoys under the Bill of Rights. He is secure not only against the "breaking of his doors and the rummaging of his drawers" by the federal police, but against the invasion of his "indefeasible right of personal security, personal liberty, and private property, where that right has never been forfeited by his conviction of some public offense." The court denied to the government the right to search for and seize the private papers of a citizen in the hope of securing some evidence to convict him of a crime or bring a forfeiture of his goods. No valid warrant may issue out of a court of law for this purpose. The right of the federal police to search and seize under a warrant is limited to specifically described articles which fall into one of three categories—stolen property, contraband and actual instruments of crime. The court struck down as unlawful any extortion of a man's private papers in a hunt for evidence to convict him of a crime.

It is this right of personal security and personal liberty upon which eavesdropping impinges. If the words a man writes to his wife or to his lawyer or to himself are protected by the Constitution from seizure by the police, surely the words he speaks to them or even to himself should be protected.

But as recently as 1928 the Supreme Court was unwilling to extend the protection of the Fourth Amendment to the spoken word. In *Olmstead* v. *United States* the majority of the court ruled that the protection against unreasonable searches and seizures applied only to physical, tangible objects. A conversation, since it is not physical, cannot be "searched" or "seized," the court said. A second rationale underlying the decision was that the listening in by the police in the Olmstead case did not involve a trespass on Olmstead's premises.

Four of the nine justices disagreed and, in a brilliant and often quoted dissent, Justice Brandeis said that listening in on conversations accomplishes exactly what the Fourth Amendment was designed to prevent—invasion of the citizen's privacy. He pointed out that when the Constitution was adopted force and violence were the only known methods of compelling incriminatory testimony or the production of private papers. But, he added,

> Subtler and more far-reaching means for invading privacy have become available to the government. Discovery and invention have made it possible for the government, by means far more effective than stretching upon the rack, to obtain disclosure in court of what is whispered in the closet. . . . The progress of science in furnishing the government with means of espionage is not likely to stop with wiretapping. Ways may some day be developed by which the government, without removing papers from secret drawers, can reproduce them in court, and by which it will be enabled to expose to a jury the most intimate occurrences of the home. . . . Can it be that the Constitution affords no protection against such invasions of individual security?

He urged that the Fourth Amendment be interpreted to keep pace with the advances in modern science so that it would continue to do what the authors of the Constitution intended it to do when it was written. His opinion says: "The makers of our Constitution . . . sought to protect Americans in their beliefs, their thoughts, their emotions and their sensations. They conferred, as against the government, the right to be let alone—the most comprehensive of rights and the right most valued by civilized men."

Justice Brandeis' prophetic fears have now become a reality. Today it is possible to expose to a jury and to the public the most intimate occurrences of the home. Recent advances in electronic eavesdropping devices would be incredible if they were not so authoritatively documented. In a few minutes' time any telephone can be transformed into a microphone which transmits every sound in the room, even when the receiver is on the hook, to the ear of a surreptitious listener in another building. Tiny microphones can be secreted behind a picture or dropped into a vase of flowers. If wires cannot be concealed, a strip of special paint will act as a wire.

Even more sinister are devices which can, without physical contact, pick up from the outside every sound made inside a room. Many of these make the spike microphone of the Silverman case look amateurish. There are devices which can pick up conversations hundreds of feet away. For instance, a parabolic microphone can pick up a conversation through an open window from across the street or from across a park. The possibility of beaming ultrasonic or electromagnetic waves into a room through the window and thereby overhearing everything said in that room has in recent months been made into a reality. A detailed study of eavesdropping in the United States was completed in 1959 by Samuel Dash, a former district attorney in Philadelphia. Dash and his associates published their conclusions under the title *The Eavesdroppers.* The study was carried on under the sponsorship of the Pennsylvania Bar Association Endowment, with a grant from the Fund for the Republic. It sounds the warning that "to be certain of defense against any eavesdropping of this kind [and, incidentally, against wireless microphones as well], one should shield his room completely with a continuous covering of aluminum foil and substitute for his window glass a special conducting glass made by several of the large glass companies."

This study also revealed widespread use of concealed microphones by police and private detectives. Private eavesdroppers use these microphones in an endless variety of situations, from wives' checking on their husbands' fidelity to business firms' checking on their employees' attitudes and efficiency.

Several widely publicized incidents have underscored the frightening potentialities of these practices. One involved a concealed microphone in a prison room assigned to an attorney for conferences with his client. Public indignation ran high when it was discovered that in this same room priests heard the confessions of Catholic prisoners. There was a similar reaction to the revelation that the New York Transit Authority was using hidden microphones to spy on a transit workers' union during a strike.

All of these incidents are outgrowths of the refusal of the Supreme Court in 1928 to protect private conversations from scientific invasion by the police.

In the Goldfine and Silverman cases the government prosecutors did not and could not seriously contend that conversations are not now regarded as within the protection of the Fourth Amendment. But one of the arguments they advanced was certainly justified under existing law. This argument was based upon the holding in the Olmstead case that a physical entry onto the victim's premises was necessary before he could complain that his rights were violated. Thirteen years later this principle was reaffirmed in *Goldman* v. *United States*. In that case federal agents had placed a highly sensitive microphone called a detectaphone *against* the wall of an office. They were able to hear conversations of Goldman in the office on the other side of the wall. In affirming Goldman's conviction the court pointed out that there had been no physical entry into Goldman's premises for purposes of installing the detectaphone.

But, when the court was asked in the Silverman case to approve use by the police of a microphone inserted *into* a wall, it refused. Justice Potter Stewart wrote, "We find no occasion to re-examine *Goldman* here, but we decline to go beyond it by even a fraction of an inch." From his opinion in that case and from what other Justices have said in other cases, I am convinced that the court will overturn completely its decision in the Olmstead case. It will not only continue to protect private conversations as being within the purview of the Fourth Amendment, but will also rule that a physical entry by the eavesdropper for the purpose of installing his equipment, or a physical penetration of the equipment onto the premises, is not necessary before the victim can invoke his Fourth Amendment rights.

Such a ruling would restore the right to privacy to the high place which the Constitution gave it. It would give all Americans a new assurance that this deeply cherished right is being protected by the courts against the advances of modern science.

Our law has always held that a man's house is his castle. This principle was eloquently expressed by William Pitt, Earl of Chatham, many years ago when he said: "The poorest man may in his cottage bid defiance to all the forces of the crown. It may be frail; its roof may shake; the wind may blow through it; the storm may enter; the rain may enter; but the King of England cannot enter—all his force dares not cross the threshold of the ruined tenement."

The concept of a man's house as his castle is completely inconsistent with surreptitious police surveillance of every conversation in that house. If the police may not enter physically, they may not enter scientifically. An entry by electronic eavesdropping equipment is the most effective, clandestine and sinister kind of entry.

Electronic eavesdropping must be considered as a search and seizure. It must be brought under the Fourth Amendment. In my view, this would end the practice by federal officers. No law purporting to authorize the issuance of warrants for eavesdropping would be constitutional, because the Fourth Amendment prohibits any attempt to authorize a hunt for incriminating admissions.

The Boyd case made it an axiom of American constitutional law that no court can issue a search warrant authorizing a policeman to look for mere evidence of crime. A search warrant must specify the things for which the police are to search, and these must be instruments of crime, fruits of crime or contraband. By "instruments of crime" the courts mean things like burglar tools, gambling tables and weapons; by "fruits of crime," ransom money from a kidnaping or the stolen money or merchandise from a theft; and by "contraband," those things the very possession of which is unlawful, such as narcotics and untaxed whisky.

A search for objects which are only evidence of the commission of a crime is unconstitutional. For example, no search warrant can be issued to seize a person's letters or his diary because there are references to a crime in them. But eavesdropping is almost by definition a search for evidence alone. It is a search for incriminating statements.

As the late Jerome Frank once wrote:

> A dictaphone, by its very nature, conducts an exploratory search for evidence of a house-owner's guilt. Such exploratory searches for evidence are forbidden with or without warrants by the Fourth Amendment. . . . A search warrant must describe the things to be seized and those things can only be (a) instrumentalities of the crime, or (b) contraband. Speech can be neither. A listening to all talk inside a house serves only one purpose—evidence gathering. No valid warrant for such listening or for the installation of a dictaphone can be issued. Such conduct is lawless, and an unconstitutional violation of the owner's privacy.

A distinction, however, must be drawn where a conversation is recorded or transmitted with the consent of one party. Law-enforcement officers, for example, may wear a concealed recording device when interviewing suspects or witnesses. An informer may agree to have a microphone concealed in his clothing and engage the suspect in an incriminating conversation, so that police officers can overhear the conversation and testify about it in court. Such conduct may be unethical, but it does not seem to me to be the kind of conduct which the Fourth Amendment should bar.

Every time we have a conversation we run the risk that the other party may play us false. He may reveal what we said to our personal enemies, business competitors or the police. He may try to blackmail us. These are risks inherent in human relationships. They are in essence no different from the risk that the person in whom we confide has arranged to record or broadcast what we say by means of some concealed device. The only real distinction is that a simultaneous record or broadcast is fuller and more exact than any subsequent report. This is a distinction in degree but not in essence.

But when a conversation is recorded or transmitted without the consent of any participant, an entirely new set of concepts must apply. This is a real invasion of privacy. Physical searches, even wiretapping, pale by comparison.

Independently of the Fourth Amendment, moreover, I think that electronic eavesdropping ought to be outlawed. Its dangerous potentialities far outweigh its aid to law enforcement. Judge Frank once warned us:

> The practice of broadcasting private inside-the-house conversations through concealed radios is singularly terrifying when one considers how this snide device has already been used in totalitarian lands. Under Hitler, it became known that the secret police planted dictaphones in houses. Members of families often gathered in bathrooms to conduct whispered discussions

of intimate affairs, hoping thus to escape the reach of the sending apparatus. Orwell, depicting the horrors of a completely regimented society, could think of no more frightening instrument thus to be employed than the "telescreen" compulsorily installed in every house.

To permit electronic eavesdropping by law-enforcement officers would, in my opinion, require a constitutional amendment permitting search warrants to be issued for *evidence of crime.* But before such an amendment should even be considered, a strong demonstration must be made by federal law-enforcement agencies that our collective security is so imperiled by treason, espionage and sabotage that drastic measures are needed. A demonstration must further be made that eavesdropping is a useful and necessary weapon for combating these crimes. I have grave doubts whether such a showing could ever be made. And, as Judge Frank pointed out, we defeat our own ends if we adopt the techniques of totalitarianism in security cases. Like the heroes of Shakespeare's tragedies, we should be our own undoing. If we really believe in democracy, we must have faith enough to fight for its preservation with the tools of freedom.

CHAPTER VII

THE PARTY LINE

UNLIKE eavesdropping, wiretapping is a federal crime. Congress in 1934 made it a criminal act to tap a telephone wire, listen to a conversation and divulge or make use of what is overheard. Despite this fact, wiretapping is rampant in the nation today. It is perpetrated by private investigators in all kinds of cases. It is clandestinely and illegally used to find evidence for divorce cases and to learn trade or personal secrets. It is perpetrated by public law-enforcement officers both surreptitiously and under a self-serving declaration that what they are doing is necessary for adequate law enforcement. Necessity has been the argument used for every infringement of human rights since the birth of this country. William Pitt called it the argument of tyrants and the creed of slaves.

Justice Douglas has remarked that "wiretapping today is a plague on the nation. It is a far more serious intrusion on privacy than the general writs of assistance used in colonial days. Now all the intimacies of one's private life can be recorded. This is far worse than ransacking one's desk and closets. This is a practice that strikes as deep as an invasion of the confessional."

While preparing to write *The Eavesdroppers* Samuel Dash and his associates interviewed law-enforcement officers all over the country. To determine how widespread wiretapping actually is, they spent many weeks in New York City interviewing police officers, telephone-company employees, private investigators and other persons knowledgeable on the subject. They concluded that the reports of the New York City police, who say they tap 300 or 400 lines a year, show only a trace of how much wiretapping actually occurs. They estimated that the police in New York City alone make 16,000 to 29,000 wiretaps a year. Hundreds, perhaps thousands, more are made by private investigators.

In one reported case a convict released from prison suspected his wife of squandering large sums of his money on a secret lover. He hired a wiretapper to tap his home telephone and to record any conversations his wife had with her suspected lover. The wiretapper was friendly with another wiretapper who had been hired by the lover to tap the same telephone for different reasons. The two wiretappers got together, pooled their efforts and tapped the phone only once. Then they made duplicate copies of the conversations and sold them to both sides.

I received a full exposure to the problems and evils of wiretapping in 1956 when I agreed to represent Frank Costello in his denaturalization case. As we prepared for trial, it became evident that much of the government's case was built on wiretapped evidence. Costello at the time was serving a prison term on a conviction of income-tax evasion. When I examined the record of that trial, I concluded that some of the evidence used against him in that case had been obtained through wiretaps. As we delved more deeply into the matter, we discovered that there had been a tap on Costello's home telephone at intermittent intervals over many years.

During the period of the taps, six policemen sat in eight-hour shifts, working in teams of two. They listened to and transcribed every conversation over Costello's telephone, whether he was a participant or not. Through an order of the federal court in New York I obtained the transcripts of those conversations. It was necessary for my associates and me to read literally hundreds of them. Then, for the first time, I think I understood what Justice Oliver Wendell Holmes meant when he characterized wiretapping as "dirty business."

The transcripts included conversations between Costello and his wife, his doctor and his lawyer; conversations between Mrs. Costello and members of her family, her doctor and her friends; conversations between one of the Costellos' maids and her husband, baring the most confidential and intimate family secrets.

Literally scores of persons who were suspected of no crime and who had committed no crime were subjected to this kind of surveillance. What they believed to be private conversations were invaded by the ears of the police. The most intimate details of the lives of these people became a matter of record in the files of the New York City police department as a result of this one wiretap.

But the persons victimized by these wiretaps were not just persons who used Costello's telephone. Taps were placed on public telephones in restaurants frequented by him. Everyone who used those pay-station telephones had a hidden third party listening to every word he said. Confidential business matters between wholly honest and unsuspecting businessmen were invaded. Husband-and-wife calls were monitored. The tender words of sweethearts were heard by a third ear. In short, hundreds of wholly innocent, law-abiding and unsuspecting citizens were deprived of their right to communicate privately by the efforts of the law-enforcement agencies to listen in on Costello.

When we talk about wiretapping, it is important to remember that we are not talking about a wiretap on a particular telephone to pick up the conversations of a particular man. The Costello taps picked up a hundred conversations of other people for every one to which Costello was a party. There is just no way to circumscribe the number of innocent victims of any tap. It's like an atom bomb. You can't pick your victims. As many people can be killed by the fallout as by the hit.

The federal government's attitude toward wiretapping has served only to augment the problem, because it has been riddled with inconsistencies. During World War I, Congress prohibited all wiretapping because of widespread fear that government communications were being intercepted. When this prohibition expired at the end of the war, the government began to use wiretapping as one of the chief weapons against prohibition violators. This was discontinued under Attorney General Harlan F. Stone in 1925, but was resumed under Attorney General Mitchell in 1931.

Wiretapping by federal officers was again stopped by Attorney General Robert H. Jackson in 1941, but was resumed the next year at the direction of President Franklin D. Roosevelt. On May 11, 1961, the Justice Department announced through an official spokesman that the Federal Bureau of Investigation was operating eighty-seven wiretaps across the country as of that day. All of these were purportedly connected with national-security cases. Admittedly, the FBI also uses wiretaps in kidnaping cases. The Justice Department defends these wiretaps as being both necessary and legal. To understand how this argument of legality is made and why it is unsound, it is necessary to trace the law as it has developed.

There was great dissatisfaction with the Olmstead case when the Supreme Court ruled by a bare 5-to-4 majority that wiretapping did not violate the Fourth Amendment.

It meant that policemen and private citizens alike could tap telephone lines with impunity. There was much sympathy with the dissenting position taken by Justice Brandeis—and by Justices Holmes, Stone and Butler—that the citizen's privacy should be protected against this kind of intrusion.

This right to telephone privacy was recognized by Congress six years later when it enacted the Communications Act of 1934. Section 605 of this law provides that "no person not being authorized by the sender shall intercept any communication and divulge or publish the existence, contents, substance, purport, effect, or meaning of such intercepted communication to any person." It goes on to provide that no person having received or becoming acquainted with an intercepted communication shall "use the same or any information therein contained for his own benefit or for the benefit of another not entitled thereto." Violation of this law is a criminal offense punishable by a term of imprisonment up to one year.

The Supreme Court gave effect to the sweeping terms of this statute in the Nardone case in 1937. This decision held that evidence obtained through wiretapping by federal officers cannot be used against the victim in a federal court. The court was then, as now, unwilling to allow law-enforcement officers to break the law to ferret out crime. It was applying the philosophical principle, basic to our system of justice, that a good objective does not justify an illicit means.

Despite this clear holding that wiretapping by federal officers is illegal, Section 605 has been consistently violated. The federal government has continuously engaged in wiretapping ever since 1931, except for that brief period when it was forbidden by Attorney General Jackson. The Department of Justice seeks to defend this defiance of the law on the theory that Section 605 does not prohibit interception of telephone and telegraph messages, but only *interception and divulgence.*

On May 18, 1958, J. Edgar Hoover, the director of the FBI, told a television audience that his bureau had ninety wiretaps installed as of that day. On the same day a prosecutor from the same Department of Justice was asking a New York jury to convict James Hoffa of the Teamsters Union for allegedly installing one wiretap. This seemed to me to be a classic illustration of the dangers and evils of lawless law enforcement. One division of the Justice Department was prosecuting a man for breaking a law which another division of the department was itself breaking at that very moment.

I took occasion to say this to a large audience at Georgetown University in Washington at one of its traditional Gaston lectures. A few days later I received a letter from one of the assistant directors of the FBI, who took me to task for criticizing his agency for wiretapping. He set out the rationale of the Department of Justice in employing wiretapping this way:

> . . . I am unaware of any court decision which has ruled that wire taps are illegal per se. What the courts have done is to ban evidence secured from wire taps and this whole matter was explored rather fully in the attached statement of the late Mr. Justice Robert H. Jackson when he was Attorney General. In the FBI, telephone taps are utilized only with the written approval of the Attorney General in cases involving internal security or those involving kidnapping.

He annexed to his letter an opinion the late Justice Jackson wrote when he was Attorney General in 1941. It says:

> There is no Federal statute which prohibits or punishes wire tapping alone. The only offense under the present law is to "intercept any communication and divulge or publish" the same. Any person, with no risk of penalty, may tap telephone wires and eavesdrop on his competitor, employer, workman or others and act upon what he hears or make any use of it that does not involve divulging or publication.

I am convinced that if Justice Jackson had faced this same question after he went on the bench, he would have concluded that his 1941 opinion was incorrect. Jackson faced the problem of changing his position at least once while he served on the Supreme Court. I like to think that he would have said of his wiretapping opinion what he said in changing his view in a naturalization case. Then he quoted Lord West, who once said, "I can only say that I am amazed that a man of my intelligence should have been guilty of giving such an opinion." Jackson added, "If there are other ways of gracefully and good-naturedly surrendering former views to a better considered position, I invoke them all."

I say this because even a quick look at the wiretapping statute shows that Attorney General Jackson was wrong. The statute outlaws not only tapping and divulging but also *tapping and making use of the information* obtained through the wiretap. The last part of Section 605 says it is a crime for the wiretapper to "*use the same or any information therein contained for his own benefit or for the benefit of another not entitled thereto.*"

I think that if wiretapping is regarded by the responsible heads of the FBI as necessary to successful law enforcement, they should press Congress vigorously for a change in the law. But their argument for a change would be far more cogent if they went before Congress with a record of obedience to the existing law rather than with a long history of cavalier defiance of it.

The record compels the conclusion that the Department of Justice is not confident of its own position. Despite widespread private wiretapping, which everyone agrees is illegal, there was for many years only one reported prosecution for wiretapping. In 1940 the Department of Justice told the United States Attorney for Rhode Island to stop investigating wiretapping because federal officers were tapping wires there themselves. In 1950 a grand-jury investigation of wiretapping in the District of Columbia did not result in a single indictment. A congressional committee subsequently learned that the government's technical construction of the word "divulgence" had made indictments impossible. With few exceptions, the Department of Justice has been forced to take the position that it cannot tap wires with one hand and prosecute wiretappers with the other.

While public pressure has compelled several prosecutions of private tappers during the past few years, there has never been a prosecution of a state policeman for wiretapping. Local police have taken extensive advantage of this immunity to prosecution. The study conducted under the auspices of the Pennsylvania Bar Association Endowment revealed widespread police wiretapping in every state surveyed.

Some states have laws specifically permitting what the federal law prohibits. The best known of these state laws is that of New York, which authorizes the state courts to issue orders which permit the tapping of wires for a specified length of time. The order tells the policeman he can tap the wire. The courts in that state then let him testify about what he overheard. The Supreme Court of the United States held in 1957 that every New York policeman who taps a wire under one of these orders and subsequently repeats what he has heard is guilty of a federal crime. But, despite the Supreme Court's clear statement that this is a federal crime, New York courts continue to issue wiretap orders, New York police continue to tap wires and to testify in court and the Department of Justice continues to look the other way.

In these circumstances it is not surprising that there have been repeated proposals to amend the Communications Act. Former Attorney General William P. Rogers published an article in 1954 which summarizes the case for wiretapping. He argued that wiretapping is an essential weapon which federal law-enforcement officers must have if they are to protect the nation against spies, saboteurs and other subversives. He further argued that wiretapping is not worse than the use of informants, decoys, detectaphones, peeping through windows and the like, all of which have been accepted practices for policemen for many years.

In one form or another, the two arguments advanced by Rogers have been the only ones relied upon by the advocates of legislation to legalize wiretapping. Neither argument, however, really disposes of the issue. Responsible sources have questioned the utility of wiretaps in any criminal case. There is certainly grave doubt about the value of taps in national-security cases. For example, in the celebrated case of Judith Coplon, who was charged with attempting to deliver defense information to the Soviet Union, the government convinced the court that none of its evidence came from wiretapping, although Miss Coplon's telephone was almost continuously tapped. Her conviction was reversed only because these wiretaps interfered with her right to hold private conferences with her attorney. There has never been a prosecution of an alleged spy, traitor or saboteur in which the government gained its evidence from wiretapping.

Interestingly enough, the view that wiretaps do not substantially aid in law enforcement was once held by J. Edgar Hoover. Mr. Hoover's public attacks on wiretapping were numerous in the six years following the passage of the Communications Act in 1934. During that time he called wiretapping an "archaic and inefficient practice" which "has proved a definite handicap or barrier in the development of ethical, scientific, and sound investigative technique." He let it be represented that he was "the first federal official to oppose wiretapping . . . and he has never in court used evidence so gathered."

In a news interview he declared that he had "consistently opposed the practice." He said in a formal press release: "Statements have . . . appeared to the effect that wiretapping has been used by representatives of the Federal Bureau of Investigation in violation of existing laws. At no time has there been a single instance of any action of this kind on the part of any representative of the Federal Bureau of Investigation since I have been the Director of the Bureau."

He advised the Department of Justice itself: "While I concede that the telephone tap is from time to time of limited value in the criminal investigative field, I frankly and sincerely believe that if a statute of this kind were enacted the abuses arising therefrom would far outweigh the value which might accrue to law enforcement as a whole." In a Department of Justice press release it was represented that Mr. Hoover believed that "the discredit and suspicion of the law enforcing branch which arises from the occasional use of wiretapping more than offsets the good which is likely to come of it."

Perhaps it is easier to catch spies—or even gamblers—by wiretapping than by other methods. I suppose it would also be easier if the police could use torture, general search warrants, mass arrests and indefinite police detention for purposes of questioning. It would also be easier to convict spies if one could suspend the Fifth and Sixth Amendments in such cases so that the spy would have no privilege against self-incrimination and no right to counsel. The difficulty with all these methods is that if we used them we would have lost what we are seeking to preserve. We would be trying to protect democracy with the tools of totalitarianism.

There is reason to fear, moreover, that a law authorizing federal agents to wiretap in national-security cases would be an opening wedge to authorize them to wiretap in all cases. During the Eighty-third Congress a bill was introduced to permit wiretapping in cases involving national security. During the Eighty-fourth Congress the sponsor of this bill introduced a new bill which would authorize wiretapping in all felony cases. During the Eighty-sixth Congress the same Congressman introduced a bill to permit wiretapping in all cases. He explained his shift in position on the ground that the telephone and telegraph are now dangerous channels through which criminal conspiracies can operate with impunity.

The record in New York City bears out the conclusion that wiretapping is most useful when it is used against organized vice. The overwhelming majority of the wiretaps authorized by the New York courts have been in cases involving gambling and prostitution. There have been very few wiretapping orders in cases involving the most serious crimes, such as rape, robbery and murder. The number of such orders in any case remotely affecting national security directly or indirectly has been negligible. The evils inherent in wiretapping assume very different proportions when they are balanced, not against the evils of subversion, but against the evils of gambling and prostitution.

There are even more serious objections to the argument that wiretapping is essentially no different from many accepted law-enforcement practices. A crucial difference lies in the extent to which wiretapping invades the privacy of wholly innocent people. None of the proposals to authorize wiretapping would restrict tapping to the wires of people suspected of crime. It appears to be standard practice in New York for the police to tap public telephones which may be used by suspects. These taps, like those in the Costello case, record one conversation involving a gambler or a prostitute among a hundred involving wholly innocent and unsuspecting persons whose most personal affairs are thus laid bare.

No search warrant could ever involve so sweeping an intrusion into private affairs. A search warrant must specify the things for which the police are to search, and these, as already shown, must be instruments of crime, fruits of crime or contraband. This principle of constitutional law is as old as our country. Wiretapping is always a search for evidence; it is a search for incriminatory statements. Since no one can predict when these statements will be made, the hunt may go on for months. A search warrant, on the other hand, must be specific, and it always has a time limitation.

Another significant difference between wiretapping and ordinary physical searches is that the victim seldom learns that his telephone wire is tapped. If government agents search a man's property and seize either his papers or his property, he knows it almost immediately. If it has been done without a valid warrant, he can go to court to get back his belongings. But if government agents listen to a man's conversations for weeks or months or even years, he may never learn about it. Abuses cannot be corrected either in a court of law or in the court of public opinion. Only when something incriminating is disclosed do the courts enter the picture. It is the innocent person who is left completely without remedy for this violation of his right to privacy.

The only solution to these problems is to bring wiretapping under the Fourth Amendment. This was the course advocated thirty years ago by the dissenters in the Olmstead case. It is the course advocated today by Justice Douglas and many other serious students of the law. The intervening years have yielded no acceptable alternative. This course would forever lay to rest the arguments that wiretapping is lawful so long as there is no divulgence outside the Department of Justice. It would also bring an end to attempted legislative encroachment upon present prohibitions. Congress can amend or repeal the Communications Act, but it cannot by its action alone amend or repeal the Fourth Amendment.

But if the courts bring wiretapping under the Fourth Amendment, as I believe they soon will, the problem will not be so easily solved as some lawyers and Congressmen think. Their solution is to pass a law under which the federal courts would issue warrants to wiretap much as they now issue search warrants. On the surface this appears to be a plausible solution. It would allow the courts to strike a balance between the rights of the individual and the rights of society. But it has, I think, a fatal flaw.

The Fourth Amendment authorizes searches and seizures which are reasonable. A warrant to wiretap can be only a search for evidence, and under the Constitution, as it has been interpreted since its advent, such a warrant would be invalid.

The only solution I can see is for Congress to approve for submission to the states a revision of the Fourth

Amendment, if the FBI can show that it desperately needs the right to tap wires in national-security cases. Such a revision would allow the courts to abandon our traditional policy against searches for evidence, and would authorize searches of that kind, but only in cases where the national security is at stake.

Even the most dedicated civil-libertarian must agree that individual liberties must be subordinated to our security as a nation. If we lose this, we lose the whole foundation of our individual freedom. So if it can be demonstrated that wiretapping is a necessary tool for the federal agencies charged with the responsibility to protect that security in ferreting out treason, espionage and sabotage, I would be for such a constitutional amendment. The necessity may be difficult to demonstrate, because traitors, spies and saboteurs traditionally avoid the telephone like the plague. Wiretapping might well be a useless weapon against such crimes. But if it can be shown that wiretapping is necessary for such purposes, I am confident there would be no difficulty in providing a constitutional base for it by means of an amendment.

This would authorize the invasion of privacy only in the protection of the most vital interests of society. It would also bring wiretapping under judicial supervision. The judiciary is the traditional bulwark between citizen and prosecutor. Law-enforcement officers, like defense attorneys, are sometimes carried away by the justice of their own causes. It is unfair to ask the Department of Justice to pass upon the propriety of its own requests for wiretapping authorization. Yet that is precisely what many of the proponents of wiretapping legislation wish to do. They wish to give the Attorney General the authority to authorize wiretaps when they are requested by members of his staff.

Finally, this change in the law would make it possible to

end wiretapping by private individuals and eliminate tapping by state officers. If the FBI taps wires only when the requirements of the Fourth Amendment are satisfied, the Department of Justice can in good faith prosecute wiretapping by others. For the first time Congress will be able to pass an effective wiretapping law which would make it a crime to intercept any communication regardless of whether or not it is "divulged." Once we have ended the sorry spectacle of federal officers tapping in defiance of federal law, we can enforce wiretapping laws just as stringently as we enforce other criminal statutes.

The dangerous consequences of continuing to countenance lawless law enforcement were recognized years ago by Justice Brandeis, who said:

> Crime is contagious. If the government becomes a lawbreaker, it breeds contempt for law; it invites every man to become a law unto himself; it invites anarchy. To declare that in the administration of the criminal law the end justifies the means—to declare that the government may commit crimes in order to secure the conviction of a private criminal—would bring terrible retribution. Against that pernicious doctrine this court should resolutely set its face.

By the suggested changes I am convinced we would be striking the time-honored balance between the right to privacy and the necessity for law enforcement. Perhaps even more important, we would be adopting the only alternative to the pernicious doctrine so forcefully condemned by Justice Brandeis. When we bring wiretapping under the Constitution and wiretappers under the law, we will be taking a long step toward restoration of popular respect for both the Constitution and the law.

The odious writs of assistance and the general warrants against which James Otis thundered in the Boston State House in February, 1761, were puny instruments of tyranny compared to the 1961 induction coil and contactless wiretap.

CHAPTER VIII

THE RIGHT TO SILENCE

It was All Saints Day in 1586. The prisoner lay on his bed of straw in a windowless cell in the Tower of London, too weak to move, too ill to speak. He had been stretched on the rack earlier that day in the hope that he would finally confess to complicity in plots against Queen Elizabeth. Three weeks later he could not lift his hand at his trial to take the oath. His fingers had been torn out in an effort to extract the "truth." He stood silent, invoking his right not to give evidence against himself. History knows him as Blessed Edmund Campion.

Two decades later an old man stood before the judges of the High Commission Court of James I. They were interrogating him in the hope of finding some charge to lay against him in connection with certain barrels of gunpowder which had been found in the basement of Parliament. The old man invoked his privilege against self-incrimination, saying, "When one is asked a question before a magistrate, he is not bound to answer before some witnesses be produced against him." He was not protecting himself because of the gunpowder plot. Instead, he was protecting himself against a law which said that anyone suspected of being a Jesuit priest could be imprisoned if under interrogation he did not give completely "direct and true" answers to questions about his membership in the Society of Jesus.

The old man was Father Henry Garnett, revered Provincial of the Jesuit Order in England.

A few years later, in 1637, John Lilburn, an opponent of the ruling Stuarts, was charged with printing seditious books. Under questioning by the Attorney General of England about many things, he denied the basic charge and then said, "I am not willing to answer you to any more of these questions, because I see you go about by this examination to ensnare me; for, seeing the things for which I am imprisoned cannot be proved against me, you will get other matter out of my examination." For this he was whipped and pilloried.

A dozen years later, when he was on trial for treason, Lilburn again refused to answer questions, saying, "I am upon Christ's terms, when Pilate asked him whether he was the Son of God, and adjured him to tell him whether he was or no; he replied, 'Thou sayest it.' So say I: Thou, Mr. Prideaux, sayest it, they are my books. But prove it."

The principle of immunity from self-incrimination is expressed and accepted in the Jewish Talmud. The Code of Canon Law of the Catholic Church includes the principle in Canon 1743. In the earliest days of the common law, *nemo tenetur seipsum accusare* (no one is obliged to testify against himself) was a recognized principle of law. It was against this background that the men who wrote the Constitution and the Bill of Rights realized the need for expression of the privilege against self-incrimination. Thus was born what is now commonly referred to simply as the Fifth Amendment, the amendment which has become the most maligned part of the Constitution.

But the right not to incriminate oneself is only a part of that amendment. Too many persons have forgotten that the Fifth Amendment is a citadel of liberty, guaranteeing far more than immunity from compulsory self-incrimination. It is the amendment which requires indictment by a grand jury, prohibits double prosecution for a single crime, requires just compensation when private property is taken for public use and, most important of all, provides that no person shall be deprived of life, liberty or property without due process of law. This one amendment is the greatest protection to individual rights ever written.

Nevertheless, the Fifth Amendment is widely regarded today as an obsolete obstacle to law and order. It has become almost indissolubly linked with the image of a guilty man parroting words he does not understand in order to avoid punishment he surely deserves: "I refuse to answer that question on the ground that the answer might tend to incriminate me."

The particularly precarious position of the privilege today was recognized by Judge Harold R. Medina when he wrote:

> Whether we like it or not, indeed, whether some of us realize it or not, the fact is that today we live in critical times; and there is grave danger that some or all of our freedoms, such as free speech, freedom of religion, the equality of all men before the law, freedom from unreasonable searches and seizures, the guarantee that our property will not be taken except by due process of law, and others may be diluted, whittled away, diminished, or even torn out of the Constitution by amendment, as with the right of a person to refuse to incriminate himself, which has been under open attack.

If our primary goal were the punishment of the guilty at all costs, it would be difficult to find contemporary justification for this privilege. Without doubt it hinders the conviction of the guilty far more frequently than it protects the rights of the innocent. Attempts at pragmatic justification of the privilege are often made on the ground that it prevents the third degree and encourages more scientific methods of crime detection. These arguments are far from conclusive.

Where the third degree exists, it is practiced by law-enforcement officers who have no right to compel testimony at all and who would have no right to compel testimony even if the privilege against self-incrimination were abolished altogether. There are safeguards against police brutality, to be sure, but the privilege against self-incrimination is not one of them.

The effect of the privilege upon scientific methods of crime detection is equally dubious. Of course the third degree hinders scientific methods. It is easier to beat a man until he confesses than it is to seek evidence which will result in a conviction without a confession. Sir James Fitzjames Stephen, in his *History of the Criminal Law of England,* observes:

> During the discussions which took place on the Indian Code of Criminal Procedure in 1872 some observations were made on the reasons which occasionally lead native police officers to apply torture to prisoners. An experienced civil officer observed, "There is a great deal of laziness in it. It is far pleasanter to sit comfortably in the shade rubbing red pepper into a poor devil's eyes than to go about in the sun hunting up evidence." This was a new view to me, but I have no doubt of its truth.

There is a difference, however, between torturing the accused and compelling him to answer questions in an orderly judicial inquiry. While the origin of the privilege against self-incrimination is closely linked with the abolition of torture, the restriction of the privilege would not necessarily result in a restoration of torture. If the accused could be compelled to testify before the grand jury or the committing magistrate, for example, it might actually further scientific methods of crime detection. Especially would this be true if the testimony itself could not be introduced at the trial. Law-enforcement officers would have the benefit of the accused's testimony in locating other witnesses and documentary evidence, but they could not use a false confession of guilt to secure a conviction.

The real justification for the privilege must rest upon higher grounds. It seems basically unfair and unfree to confront a suspect with conviction if he confesses guilt, perjury if he denies guilt, and contempt if he stands mute. Essentially, it is like telling a child that you suspect him of taking your loose change and that you intend to thrash him for stealing if he admits it, for lying if he denies it, and for disobedience if he refuses to tell you whether he took it or not. This is not the way to discipline children, and it is not the way to discipline a free society.

Dean Erwin Griswold of Harvard gave one of the clearest expressions of the justification for the privilege when he wrote:

> I would like to venture the suggestion that the privilege against self-incrimination is one of the great landmarks in man's struggle to make himself civilized. As I have already pointed out, the establishment of the privilege is closely linked historically with the abolition of torture. Now we look upon torture with abhorrence. But torture was once used by honest and conscientious public servants as a means of obtaining information about crimes which could not otherwise be disclosed. We want none of that today, I am sure.

> For a very similar reason, we do not make even the most hardened criminal sign his own death warrant, or dig his own grave, or pull the lever that springs the trap on which he stands. We have through the course of history developed a considerable feeling of the dignity and intrinsic importance of the individual man. Even the evil man is a human being.

The same view was adopted by Abe Fortas of the District of Columbia bar, who stated:

> The fundamental value that the privilege reflects is intangible, it is true; but so is liberty, and so is man's immortal soul. A man may be punished, even put to death, by the state; but if he is an American or an Englishman or a free man anywhere, he should not be made to prostrate himself before its majesty. *Mea culpa* belongs to a man and his God. It is a plea that cannot be exacted from free men by human authority. To require it is to insist that the state is the superior of the individuals who compose it, instead of their instrument.

This justification of the privilege has been challenged on the ground that it consists of a conclusion without explanation or proof. The problem is that explanation and proof require reference to more basic principles. The privilege against self-incrimination is a most basic principle. It is a fundamental attitude rather than a conclusion of law. As such it can be accepted or rejected, but it cannot easily be proved.

Perhaps much of the current hostility to the privilege stems from the fact that its invocation is so widely regarded as an admission of guilt or a conclusive presumption of perjury. The Supreme Court has repeatedly taken occasion to condemn this view. In 1956 Justice Felix Frankfurter wrote:

> This constitutional protection must not be interpreted in a hostile or niggardly spirit. Too many, even those who should be better advised, view this privilege as a shelter for wrongdoers. They too readily assume that those who invoke it are either guilty of crime or commit perjury in claiming the privilege. Such a view does scant honor to the patriots who sponsored the Bill of Rights as a condition to acceptance of the Constitution by the ratifying States.

Justice Tom C. Clark, a former Attorney General who is no sentimentalist on the subject of criminal law, has expressed the same view:

> In *Ullmann* v. *United States* . . . we scored the assumption that those who claim this privilege are either criminals or perjurers. The privilege against self-incrimination would be reduced to a hollow mockery if its exercise could be taken as equivalent either to a confession of guilt or a conclusive presumption of perjury. As we pointed out in *Ullmann,* a witness may have a reasonable fear of prosecution and yet be innocent of any wrongdoing. The privilege serves to protect the innocent who otherwise might be ensnared by ambiguous circumstances.

Justice John M. Harlan recently wrote an opinion to the same effect, stating:

> We need not tarry long to reiterate our view that, as the two courts below held, no implication of guilt could be drawn from Halperin's invocation of his Fifth Amendment privilege before the grand jury. Recent

re-examination of the history and meaning of the Fifth Amendment has emphasized anew that one of the basic functions of the privilege is to protect *innocent* men.

Situations may easily be envisioned in which the protection of the Fifth Amendment might be vital to an innocent man. For example, a man who has killed another in self-defense might be well advised to plead the privilege. Similarly, a man who has attended meetings of the Communist Party might be well advised to plead the privilege even if he had no understanding at the time of the Party's illegal objectives and hence was not guilty of any crime. A man who has close ties with a narcotics offender or a dealer in illegal alcohol might be well advised to plead the privilege even if he had no part in the illegal enterprise.

Despite the fact that invocation of the privilege is not tantamount to proof of guilt, very serious consequences may flow from it. Loss of employment, exclusion from union office and exclusion from the bar are only a few of the possible penalties. The problems posed by these collateral consequences are very complex. In essence, the Supreme Court has held that no such penalties can be based solely upon invocation of the privilege, but they can be based upon the refusal to supply information lawfully demanded, even though the reason for refusal is fear of self-incrimination.

This distinction is excellent in theory but difficult to apply. If a government employee is fired after claiming his privilege in response to questions about Communism, what is the real reason for his discharge? Is he being fired because the government thinks that he must be a Communist? Or is he being fired because he is under a duty to answer questions on this subject, and when he refuses for any reason he shows himself unsuitable for continued employment? Sometimes it is really impossible to resolve this problem, but no better solution has been proposed.

Another significant factor in current hostility to the privilege lies in its repeated invocation when the questions are apparently harmless. Many people felt that the privilege had reached its nadir when one of my clients declined to tell the McClellan Committee whether he knew his own son. The exchange went like this:

> THE CHAIRMAN [Senator John McClellan]: I see a name here we have been trying to locate—a Mr. Dave Beck, Jr. Would you know him?
>
> MR. BECK: I must decline to answer the question.
>
> SENATOR MUNDT: I would like to know on what grounds Mr. Dave Beck, Sr., declines to answer whether he knows who Dave Beck, Jr., is. I would like to have a full recital of the grounds for refusing to answer; that is, from Mr. Beck.
>
> MR. WILLIAMS: I will be glad to help you on that.
>
> SENATOR MUNDT: By Mr. Beck, please.
>
> MR. BECK: I decline to answer on the advice of my counsel.
>
> SENATOR MUNDT: That is scarcely adequate for the purposes of our hearing. You may tell us on what grounds your counsel advised you.
>
> MR. WILLIAMS: I will be glad to give you the advice.
>
> SENATOR MUNDT: From Mr. Beck; I am sorry. You may tell him and he may tell us.
>
> MR. BECK: The only answer that I have is that I decline to answer on the advice of my counsel.
>
> SENATOR MUNDT: Mr. Chairman, I suggest that you instruct the witness to answer, if that is the only

grounds he has. I am perfectly confident Mr. Dave Beck, Sr., would never take the fifth amendment with regard to Dave Beck, Jr., and so I wondered what ground it would be.

THE CHAIRMAN: I will ask the witness these questions and then order him to answer.

Do you know Dave Beck, Jr.?

(The witness conferred with his counsel.)

MR. BECK: I decline to answer the question.

THE CHAIRMAN: You are ordered and directed to answer the question.

MR. BECK: I decline to answer this question on the grounds it might open up avenues of questions that would tend to incriminate me.

THE CHAIRMAN: With the permission of the committee and approval of the committee, the Chair orders and directs you to answer the question. You understand that order is being given?

(The witness conferred with his counsel.)

MR. BECK: My answer is the same, Mr. Chairman.

THE CHAIRMAN: Do you honestly and truthfully believe that if you answered the question as to whether you know Dave Beck, Jr., a truthful answer might tend to incriminate you?

(The witness conferred with his counsel.)

MR. BECK: It might, yes, sir.

Under the authorities, however, this claim of privilege was clearly correct. In the first place, Beck was under federal indictment for income-tax evasion. This was the first time in the history of congressional investigations when a committee had called a witness to testify on a matter for which he was under federal indictment. The hazards to the witness were myriad and obvious. Everything to which he testified would be screened by the prosecutor for use against him at his trial. Everything to which he had testified during his prior appearance before the McClellan Committee had been used against him at the grand-jury stage of his tax prosecution. The primary thrust of the committee's investigation turned on his financial transactions, all of which were the very subject matter of his coming income-tax trial. The committee was in effect attempting to make him disclose all the evidence of his defense at a time when it could not help him, before a tribunal which could not acquit him, and in an atmosphere filled with hostility and predilection. I felt then and still feel that the basic dictates of fair play required that his appearance should have been deferred until after his trial.

But, you may ask, how could an admission that he knew his own son tend to incriminate him under the income-tax laws? For a member of the United States Senate to ask Beck if he knew his own son, a son whom he had raised from infancy and who lived with him at the time, afforded a basis for one of two inferences. Either it was a fatuous and captious question asked for no legislative purpose and designed only as a means to taunt the witness, or it was asked as the opening question in a line of inquiry regarding financial transactions between father and son. If it was the former, Beck was justified in not dignifying it with response. If it was the latter, he was justified in saying "it might open up avenues of questions that would tend to incriminate me." In the circumstances he had the right to engage in what may have been a gratuitous presumption that his interrogators were not being fatuous and captious.

The courts have held time and again that once a witness begins to testify about a given subject, he may not then invoke the privilege against self-incrimination in response to a question on the same subject. Once the interrogator gets the witness to open the door a crack, he has full right of ingress. The only safe and prudent course for the witness in a danger area is to keep the door closed tight. The committee was anxious to probe into Beck's financial dealings with his son and turn over all the testimony to the prosecution in the tax case. Thus the prosecutor would have the benefit of the defense testimony before trial, while Beck would remain in the dark with respect to what evidence would be offered against him. It was a one-way street down which I would not let Beck go.

The open-door doctrine was crystallized in the case of Jane Rogers, who admitted that she had served as treasurer of the Communist Party in Colorado but claimed her privilege against self-incrimination when asked to name her successor in office. The Supreme Court ruled that she had waived her privilege by testifying freely about her own occupancy of the office. This result seems fair enough, because obviously the witness was not fearful that her testimony would tend to incriminate her. Her real motive for belatedly claiming the privilege was to protect someone else, and concededly the protection of the privilege is personal.

Unfortunately, however, the doctrine of waiver has now become a legal monstrosity. No one is sure just how far it extends. The decision to answer or not to answer must be made almost instantaneously. A wrong decision is fraught with danger. The only safe course is to invoke the privilege at the very beginning of the line of inquiry and constantly thereafter until the questioning moves to an entirely different field. Beck, for example, testified fully when questioned about union shops, secondary boycotts and locals under trusteeships, but he refused to answer any questions, however apparently innocuous, while the questioning remained in the field of financial transactions.

Much valuable testimony is obviously lost to both courts and Congress because of this doctrine. One possible solution is to empower the court or the committee, as the case may be, to rule upon whether the witness will waive his privilege by answering certain questions. As matters now stand, he must take his chances and wait for a ruling until he is prosecuted for contempt.

In May, 1952, the distinguished playwright Lillian Hellman was summoned before the House Un-American Activities Committee. She wrote to the chairman just prior to her appearance:

> I am not willing, now or in the future, to bring bad trouble to people who, in my past association with them, were completely innocent of any talk or any action that was disloyal or subversive. I do not like subversion or disloyalty in any form, and if I had ever seen any I would have considered it my duty to have reported it to the proper authorities. But to hurt innocent people whom I knew many years ago in order to save myself is, to me, inhuman and indecent and dishonorable. . . .
>
> I am prepared to waive the privilege against self-incrimination and to tell you anything you wish to know about my views or actions, if your committee will agree to refrain from asking me to name other people. If the committee is unwilling to give me this assurance, I will be forced to plead the privilege of the Fifth Amendment at the hearing.

The committee chairman declined to give Miss Hellman the requested assurance. She availed herself of the privilege against self-incrimination and refused to testify at all. This result benefited nobody.

These two cases highlight another significant problem in this field. Admittedly, the privilege is often invoked for the purpose of protecting others. It is clear, however, that the privilege is personal and that it may be invoked only where the testimony sought would tend to incriminate the witness himself. Often a witness is willing to confess his own past errors but unwilling to inform on others. This problem is especially acute with former Communists or Communist sympathizers.

On September 20, 1951, a Hollywood writer startled the entertainment world by admitting that he had been a member of the Communist Party and by naming almost 100 other Hollywood personalities who, he said, had also been Party members. The writer, Martin Berkeley, had joined the Party in 1936 in New York and had met Communists in Hollywood after he went there to work on movie scripts. I was his counsel when he decided to tell all he knew to the House Un-American Activities Committee when it met in Los Angeles.

During the next few days many of those Berkeley had named also took the witness stand. Some declined to answer any questions about the Communist Party, claiming their privilege against self-incrimination. But one of them, Sidney Buchman, chose to proceed differently. Buchman, then forty-nine, had been highly successful in Hollywood as a writer-producer. He had written and produced some of the finest and most successful motion pictures in the previous decade. None of them had any political significance. Buchman was questioned by Committee Counsel Frank S. Tavenner, Jr.:

MR. TAVENNER: Mr. Buchman, during the course of the testimony during this hearing you have been identified by Mr. Martin Berkeley as having been a member of the Communist Party. Were you at any time a member of the Communist Party?

MR. BUCHMAN: Yes, Mr. Tavenner, I was. I was a member of the Communist Party from the years—it is difficult for me to fix, but I assume they are from the year 1938 to approximately 1942 or 1943 . . .

MR. TAVENNER: I want to know what inducement the Communist Party gave to you to become a member of it and how it recruited you into the Communist Party. Those are the things I am chiefly concerned with.

MR. BUCHMAN: May I say honestly, Mr. Tavenner, as a basis of perhaps many questions of this sort, that I am not a political theorist or political scientist. I don't believe that I ever cracked a work of a fundamental character on the subject. My entering the Communist Party was of an emotional character.

I joined the party when the world was troubled by fascism, the rising tide of fascism abroad. We in America were worried about many problems dealing with economic inequality and political inequality. The Communist Party seemed to be the only political force both concerned and willing to take action to stop the threat of fascism abroad and to work for economic and political reform in this country.

Another reason was ideological. I placed this ideological matter in a certain emotional context, what I could call perhaps an instinctive context. Communism seemed to be an ideal experiment in trying to achieve a state where all persons had greater democracy. I might add, like other persons here and elsewhere, I found myself concerned with the problem of increasing need for greater economic and political democracy for greater numbers of people. Dislocations of the First

World War were evident all over and I was worried about the future for my co-citizens and myself. I was attracted to the philosophy, such as I knew of it, and idealism of Communism, which at the time seemed to make a better way of life. I hope that answers your question.

MR. TAVENNER: I noticed that you used the words, "which at the time seemed better." Did your study and understanding of principles of the Communist Party lead you to come to any other conclusion at a later time?

MR. BUCHMAN: . . . I obviously came to a different conclusion. With the Duclos letter and resulting deposition of Browder, there came a sudden reversal of position of the American Communist Party. The Party line completely switched and we were expected to go blindly along. The pact between the Soviet Union and Hitler shattered the illusions of many who had believed in the idealism of Communism, and I had found it difficult to accept. With the Duclos letter I felt that I could no longer understand or live with the Party. Finding I had no freedom of thought within the Party was wholly unacceptable to me. I got out.

Tavenner went on to question Buchman about what he did while he was a Party member, how much money he contributed to it and what his Party meetings were like. Buchman answered all these questions as fully as he could. Then the questioning took a sudden turn.

MR. TAVENNER: In whose homes did you meet?

MR. BUCHMAN: . . . Mr. Tavenner, I would like to answer and explain this and some other questions. Most respectfully, I must decline to answer the question. There are several grounds. First, as to the persons involved. These persons, like others you may ask me about, never, to my knowledge, planned or committed or suggested an illegal act. Secondly, the names of such a person or persons already have been made public by you, and I, therefore, do not see how it will aid you if I repeat them. If this person or any person who may not have been mentioned by this committee is ever accused of subversion or any ever comes to my attention linking this person to such an act, and if I have any knowledge which may be of interest to the authorities I will bring it to their attention. Thirdly, it is repugnant to an American to inform on his fellow citizens. I refer you on that score to what Congressman Doyle said only yesterday in the interrogating of a witness when he explained that he wanted information only about the witness and did not want him to be a tattletale or snitcher. I realize my position may doom a career which has taken twenty years to build, but I have to take that risk. If I may, I want to suggest, however, that it seems to me that the important thing in this investigation of subversion is that I, myself, love America; that I will defend it with my life against any foe, Russia or otherwise, if my country is ever at war, and that never for a second have I felt otherwise.

* * *

MR. TAVENNER: But you will not, I understand, cooperate with this committee in giving it possession of information within your knowledge relating to the extent of Communist infiltration into the moving-picture industry? Is that the position you are taking?

MR. BUCHMAN: May I have a moment, please? . . . Well, Mr. Tavenner, as to this question, I . . . do make such a statement. . . . I have searched my memory, my best feelings on this subject. I have considered, and without desiring or intending in any way to be contumacious or disrespectful, I decline to answer. . . .

MR. TAVENNER: That ground is not that to do so might tend to incriminate you? You are not taking that position, are you?

MR. BUCHMAN: No, sir.

Three days later, Buchman left Hollywood and the movie industry. As he had predicted, his career was ruined. Because he had refused to "cooperate" with the committee by "naming names," he was no longer employable. But, worse than that, he faced certain conviction for contempt. No conviction would have been possible had he declined, on the basis of the privilege, to give the committee any information at all. But Buchman took a position dictated by his conscience. He understood the problem. He could not in conscience inform on others. He could not in conscience refuse to answer questions about his own membership in the Communist Party, because he had done nothing incriminating and he did not fear criminal prosecution. Furthermore, he wanted to help the committee to the fullest extent conscientiously possible for him. His case dramatizes the "all or nothing at all" aspect of the privilege as presently construed by the courts.

A witness who claims the privilege when asked about his own Communist activities does not have to face the problem of contempt. He can continue to claim the privilege when asked to "name names." There is no problem of waiver, and the cases are clear that he is entitled to refuse to answer any question whatsoever. This course is less courageous than the course followed by Buchman, but it has the virtue of being also less dangerous.

Several members of Congress have suggested that abuse

of the Fifth Amendment is often related to abuse of witnesses by congressional committees. Four members of the House opposed enactment of a recent immunity statute on the following grounds:

> It is admitted that there are those who testifying before congressional committees abuse the privilege against self-incrimination accorded by the Constitution. Yet we know many do not now answer who would do so if they were assured of fair treatment by the committee. These witnesses refuse to subject themselves to abuse. A committee conscious of the rights of witnesses and operating under rules to protect those rights would elicit much information now denied them. We could then see how unnecessary the proposal now before us would be. There are those few who always will abuse this privilege but this is the price we must pay for the maintenance of our liberties.

Many people, on the other hand, feel that immunity statutes offer the answer to much abuse of the privilege against self-incrimination. If a witness is invoking the privilege to protect others, he can be promised immunity from prosecution and then compelled to tell what he knows. Since he is not guilty himself, law-enforcement authorities have everything to gain and nothing to lose.

In 1857 Congress enacted a broad immunity statute covering witnesses before congressional committees and in the federal courts. It was soon repealed, however, because so many prospective defendants were rushing forward to confess their misdeeds and thereby avoid prosecution. Congress instead provided that no testimony given by a witness before a congressional committee or a federal court could later be introduced into evidence against the witness. The Supreme Court held that this statute did not preclude reliance upon the privilege against self-incrimination, because the protection of the statute was not as broad as the protection of the privilege. The government was still free to use the testimony for leads in building a case against the witness, even though his exact words could not be introduced before the jury. Nothing less than complete immunity from prosecution for any offense to which the incriminating testimony relates will compel the witness to forgo his privilege.

In recent years Congress has enacted many statutes granting complete immunity. Most of them relate to witnesses before the federal regulatory agencies. In 1954 Congress adopted an immunity statute covering witnesses before congressional committees and federal courts in national-security matters, and in 1956 Congress adopted a similar statute covering narcotics cases. It has been generally agreed that these statutes offer protection against both federal and state prosecution. Under present decisions, however, a federal statute offering protection only against federal prosecution might well be held valid.

The states have also enacted many immunity statutes. These statutes are powerless to confer immunity from federal prosecution. The resulting dilemma for the witness is illustrated by a case involving Frank Costello. On the night of May 2, 1957, after Costello was shot in the lobby of his apartment house, he was taken to Roosevelt Hospital for treatment. As he was leaving the hospital he discovered that certain articles of personal property had been removed from his vest pocket by the police while he was being treated. Among them was a piece of paper with the notations:

Gross Casino Wins as of 4/26/57 $651,284
Casino Wins Less Markers, $434,695
Slot Wins, $62,844, Markers, $153,745
Mike, $150 per week

Jake, $100 per week
L, $30,000
H, $9,000

The police returned this paper, but only after photostating it. A few days later Costello was called before a New York grand jury and asked to explain the notations. He was promised immunity from prosecution under a New York statute. He insisted, however, that his testimony might tend to incriminate him under federal income-tax statutes. This was a very reasonable position, because he was then seeking to set aside a conviction for income-tax evasion and he had reason to believe that the government was contemplating another prosecution for income-tax evasion. Concededly, the New York statute could afford no protection against federal prosecution.

When Costello persisted in his refusal to answer, he was sentenced to thirty days in the workhouse. This sentence was ultimately sustained despite several strong dissenting opinions. The majority of the New York court relied upon a recent Supreme Court case holding that the state can compel a witness to confess the commission of federal crimes merely by promising him protection against state prosecution. Under another Supreme Court decision, the federal courts are free to base a conviction upon admissions so secured.

Justice William Brennan has called for a re-examination of this latter holding. I hope that his views will be shared by a majority of the court. The privilege against self-incrimination becomes little more than a formality if state officers can compel a man to confess himself into the federal penitentiary. As Justice Black has pointed out, ". . . a person can be whipsawed into incriminating himself under both state and federal law even though there is a privilege against self-incrimination in the Constitution of both." This is truly to keep the words of promise to the ear but break them to the hope.

The solution to this dilemma is to forbid federal prosecutions based, directly or indirectly, upon evidence secured from the defendant pursuant to a state immunity statute. Neither the incriminating answers nor any evidence developed through leads from the incriminating answers should be used in a federal court. Moreover, by analogy to wiretapping cases, once the defendant has shown that he has given testimony pursuant to a state immunity statute which is relevant to the federal charge against him, the government should have the burden of showing that none of its evidence is the fruit of his compelled testimony. Only in this way can we reconcile the interest of the state in local law enforcement with the privilege against compulsory self-incrimination.

In resolving all of these problems, we must remember that we are dealing with a privilege which was hard earned by our forefathers. When the protection afforded by the privilege seems to thwart the prevention of crime and the punishment of the guilty, we must remember that these objectives are not absolutes. Efficiency is not the sole criterion of law enforcement in a free society.

As Dean Griswold expressed it:

> If a man has done wrong, he should be punished. But the evidence against him should be produced and evaluated by a proper court in a fair trial. Neither torture nor an oath nor the threat of punishment, such as imprisonment for contempt, should be used to compel him to provide the evidence to accuse or to convict himself. If his crime is a serious one, careful and often laborious police work may be required to prove it by

other evidence. Sometimes no other evidence can be found. But for about three centuries in the Anglo-American legal system we have accepted the standard that even then we do not compel the accused to provide that evidence.

The right to silence is more than the mere right to refuse to answer incriminating questions. It is the respect which society pays to the inviolability of each man's soul in an era when hypnotism, narco-analysis, truth serums, lie detectors and other scientific devices are being used to force the revelation of truths by persons who desire to keep them secret. The right should not be cast aside as a device exploited by hoodlums, for it is a last bastion against an ever more omnipotent government. It is the final shield against invasion of the soul. Protection from this kind of assault is the *sine qua non* of the essential dignity of man.

The freedom of the individual as we have known it since the birth of this nation will be at an end if the time ever comes when the state can confront the suspected person with conviction if he confesses guilt, perjury if he denies it and contempt if he stands silent.

CHAPTER IX

ARREST AT LARGE, INTERROGATE AT LEISURE

IT HAS often been said that the history of liberty is largely a history of procedural safeguards. These safeguards are not "technicalities." Rather they are the rules which our experience has shown are necessary in the interplay between the rights of society and the rights of the individual. This is why we have placed a judicial officer between the policeman and the citizen to determine the validity of an arrest. It is why an accused has the right to know specifically the nature of the charge against him and to confront his accuser face to face. It is why he has the right to have questions affecting his liberty determined in a dispassionate forum free from extrinsic influences. These are some of the principles which govern the administration of criminal justice in our American courtrooms. When these principles break down through violation or erosion, injustices follow. In the next few chapters I shall try to demonstrate this by example where possible.

About five P.M. on January 20, 1958, three teen-age boys walked into the Chips Grill on 11th Street Northwest in Washington, D.C., and ordered Edith Barkley, the waitress on duty, to hand over the receipts of the day. When she was slow in responding to the order, one of the trio struck her a savage blow in the face. They scooped $48 out of the cash register and fled into the street.

Within thirty minutes squads of plain-clothes men and uniformed officers fanned out in a dragnet throughout the whole Second Precinct, an area inhabited almost exclusively by Negroes. The dragnet was spurred by indignation over a continuing wave of yoke robberies and assaults in the city. Mrs. Barkley was able to describe the boys only as "colored," "stocky," and "between seventeen and nineteen."

By eleven P.M. the police had arrested ninety suspects. They ranged from fifteen to twenty-three years in age. The juveniles were released to their parents pending questioning the next day. Sixty-three of the others were locked up in the central cell block at headquarters, where they were questioned throughout the night. In the morning they were placed in the line-up in groups. Those who complained that they might lose their jobs if they failed to appear on time were told: "That's too bad."

When Mrs. Barkley was unable to identify a single suspect after carefully examining all of them throughout the morning, they were released. Ultimately the police apprehended the culprits, but not one of the youths arrested in the round-up was involved in the crime directly or indirectly.

Such an incident would never happen in an affluent white neighborhood in any city. If it did, it would create a thunder that would reverberate through the corridors of city hall for weeks and would certainly result in disciplinary action and perhaps dismissal for those involved. But this incident merely elicited an observation from a District of Columbia commissioner that the police had gone "too far." And the observation was made several weeks later in response to a newsman's question in a television interview. The episode is one more illustration of the fact that whenever and wherever there have been invasions of civil liberties and infringements of human rights by those who hold authority, the first victims have been the poor and the downtrodden, the weak and the helpless, or the unpopular and the scorned.

Some weeks after the arrests, and shortly after the commissioner had said that the police had gone "too far," one of the boys who had been picked up and locked up that night came to see me. He was a student who had his heart set on going to law school one day, and he was deeply troubled because this arrest for robbery might rise in the future to haunt him. He told me of his horror at being arrested by two plain-clothes men upon coming out of a colored motion-picture theater. After being questioned for several hours he had been held overnight in the cell block for the morning line-up. His parents had worried through the night, wondering as to his whereabouts. As he told me the story of his night in jail it was clear that he had undergone a horrible emotional experience, and that he felt embarrassment and humiliation over his innocent involvement in the matter.

But his embarrassment and humiliation were secondary. He came to me because he was deeply worried and wanted help. He had heard that he would have to undergo a morals examination in addition to his bar examination if he was ever to become a lawyer. Any arrest would have to be revealed, and he feared that an arrest for robbery might well create a complete impediment to his pursuing his chosen career.

It was clear that he had been the victim of a wholly unlawful arrest. It was equally clear that his detention through the night had been unlawful. He had a case for money damages against the arresting officers. But he wasn't looking for money. He had a right to prefer criminal charges against those responsible for the outrageous violation of his personal security and liberty. But he wasn't seeking vengeance. He simply wanted to undo any permanent injury to his record and reputation. But the fact of his arrest can never be erased. It can only be explained, and he will have the burden of explaining it fully every time he seeks a position of trust where his past is regarded as relevant. His predicament is a dramatic demonstration of the need for the rules that apply to the police in making arrests and the need for community alertness in getting compliance with these rules.

Perhaps one of the most heated legal controversies in recent years was touched off in 1957 when the Supreme Court reversed Andrew Mallory's rape conviction. The principle of law reasserted by the court has come to be known as the Mallory rule. Most people did not consider whether the Mallory rule was a good or bad legal principle. They had been told repeatedly that Mallory was a bad man and they were violently opposed to any rule which blocked his conviction.

Mallory was a nineteen-year-old Negro of limited intelligence who, with two others, was arrested about two o'clock in the afternoon of April 8, 1954. All three youths were questioned intermittently by District of Columbia police through the afternoon and early evening about a brutal and unwitnessed rape. About eight o'clock that evening all three were given lie-detector tests at police headquarters. After the tests Mallory confessed to the crime. He was then put into a cell and the other two youths were released.

The next morning Mallory was taken before a United States commissioner and advised of his constitutional rights. Subsequently he was convicted and sentenced to death, but the Supreme Court reversed the conviction. The court said that Mallory's confession could not be used against him because it was obtained during an unlawful delay between his arrest and his appearance before the commissioner.

The Mallory case was a unanimous decision by what I believe to be one of our greatest Supreme Courts. It is significant that four of the justices who joined in this opinion were former prosecutors.

Under present law no other decision was rationally possible. Rule 5 of the Federal Rules of Criminal Procedure provides that the police shall take an arrested person "without unnecessary delay before the nearest available commissioner" or other committing magistrate, who must inform him of the complaint against him, of his right to retain counsel and of his right to a preliminary examination. The commissioner must also inform him that he is not required to make a statement and that anything he says may be used against him. The commissioner must admit the accused to bail in all non-capital cases and in capital cases where the circumstances warrant it. Unless the accused waives a preliminary examination, the commissioner must hear the evidence against him within a reasonable time and discharge him unless it appears that there is probable cause to believe he has committed an offense.

Rule 5 is the law of the land in federal cases. If a law enforcement officer flouts its requirements, he is flouting the law of the land. It has long been settled that federal officers cannot use the fruits of their own wrongdoing to secure convictions. Evidence secured through physical coercion, unlawful search and seizure, and wiretapping is for this reason inadmissible in the federal courts. Similar considerations apply to confessions secured through violation of Rule 5.

Many times it is asked whether there is not some other effective way to secure police compliance with the law.

Some students of the law are offended by the concept of the culprit going free because the policeman blunders. Chief Justice Vinson, when he sat as a federal appeals-court judge, pondered other remedies for obtaining police compliance with the requirements of the Fourth Amendment:

> The casuist answers—a civil action against the officers. That remedy has been found wanting. Such remedy scarcely satisfies the non-belligerent, non-legal mind of a person whose security has already been violated and who stands convicted. To follow that procedure means delay, expense, unwanted publicity; it asks the individual to stake too much, and to take too great a chance, in the hope of compensating the interference to his privacy. A criminal remedy is also possible, but it is likely to be too strict or too lax. If criminal actions are brought consistently against the enforcing officers, before long their diligence will be enervated. If no prosecutions are brought, which appears to be the case, it cannot be said that statutory criminal provisions afford any deterrent to the infringement of the Fourth Amendment. . . . A simple, effective way to assist in the realization of the security guaranteed by the Fourth Amendment, in this type of case, is to dissolve the evidence that the officers obtained after entering and remaining illegally in the defendant's home.

Actually, the Mallory rule is nothing more than the application of an old principle to a new set of facts. In the celebrated McNabb case, decided fourteen years before the Mallory ruling, the Supreme Court reversed three convictions for murder because they were based upon confessions secured as a result of violation of the same principle, at that time expressed in statutory form. The McNabb brothers were Tennessee mountaineers who had never gone beyond the fourth grade. They were arrested on a charge of murdering a federal officer attached to the Alcohol Tax Unit. Instead of being taken before a commissioner and advised of their rights, two of them were questioned by federal officers for more than forty-eight hours and the third for five or six hours.

The Supreme Court held that this was precisely what the law prohibited. It pointed out that almost all of the states have similar statutes, exhibiting a common consciousness of the dangers inherent in unlimited police detention. As Justice Frankfurter put it:

> For this procedural requirement checks resort to those reprehensible practices known as the "third degree" which, though universally rejected as indefensible, still find their way into use. It aims to avoid all the evil implications of secret interrogation of persons accused of crime. It reflects not a sentimental but a sturdy view of law enforcement. It outlaws easy but self-defeating ways in which brutality is substituted for brains as an instrument of crime detection.

The principal arguments advanced against the McNabb-Mallory rule are actually the most cogent evidence of the necessity for it. Police and prosecutors point out that the commissioner must release an arrested person unless there is "probable cause" to believe that he has committed a crime. They say that they are often unable to show "probable cause" until they have secured a confession. Hence they urge that they should be allowed to detain an arrested person for the purpose of securing a confession before they take him to the commissioner.

This logic has one fatal flaw. Under the Fourth Amendment to the Constitution, a warrant cannot be issued for an arrest unless there is "probable cause" to believe that the person to be arrested has committed a crime. Rule 4 of the Federal Rules of Criminal Procedure puts this constitutional requirement into the rules under which federal courts operate. The same requirement of "probable cause" has always applied to arrests without a warrant.

If an arrest is lawful under the Fourth Amendment and Rule 4, therefore, there is already "probable cause" and no confession is necessary in order to hold the accused for prosecution. If, on the other hand, there is no "probable cause" at the time of the arrest, the accused has been arrested illegally and unconstitutionally. In that case, he should be promptly taken before a commissioner and released, as the law requires.

When the police insist upon an opportunity to question arrested persons in order to develop "probable cause," they are really asking for the right to arrest upon suspicion. They are asking for the right to arrest at large and interrogate at leisure. This is a practice which has been universally adopted by totalitarian states. If our police want the right to make dragnet arrests, they should ask for a constitutional amendment. As long as Rule 4 and the Fourth Amendment remain on the books, however, we should demand that our law-enforcement officers obey them.

The second argument commonly advanced against the McNabb-Mallory rule is even more cogent evidence of the necessity for it. Police and prosecutors point out that they need proof beyond a reasonable doubt in order to convict. Even where there is "probable cause" and hence a perfectly proper arrest, the government may not be able to prove guilt beyond a reasonable doubt without a confession. The police say that they cannot secure a confession unless they are allowed to question the accused before he is advised of his rights by the commissioner.

This position was stated very candidly by a Cincinnati prosecutor who said: "Police would never get anything out of anyone but a crazy man if they told him first he doesn't have to talk." An Assistant United States Attorney for the District of Columbia was equally candid when he tried to justify intermittent police questioning of a young Negro for nineteen or twenty hours before he was taken to the commissioner. This prosecutor stated: "They say why didn't we put him downstairs [in a cell block] and call him back the next morning. Why? We would find the place crawling with attorneys telling him 'You don't have to talk to the police.' "

Major Edward Kelly, formerly superintendent of the District of Columbia police, took the same position when he testified before Congress some years ago. Major Kelly pointed out that as soon as the accused is taken before a commissioner he is committed to jail and "when he arrives at the jail or place that he is committed, receives all kinds of advice and information from other persons held in jail; namely, those that are referred to as tier lawyers, and then it is absolutely impossible to proceed further in a proper manner with the investigation."

In other words, the police want a chance to question suspects before they have been advised of their right to counsel, their right to bail or their privilege against self-incrimination. They want a chance to extract a confession before either the commissioner or even fellow prisoners can tell the accused about these things.

This practice works a terrible discrimination against the youthful and uneducated suspect. The hardened criminal does not need a commissioner or anyone else to advise him of his rights—he knows them. It is no accident that the McNabb case involved three boys from the backwoods with fourth-grade educations. It is no accident that the Mallory case involved a nineteen-year-old of limited intelligence. Only a handful of convictions have been reversed in the District of Columbia on the basis of the Mallory case. It is no accident that one of these involved another nineteen-year-old defendant of questionable mental capacity and that another involved an eighteen-year-old defendant with an IQ of 74.

These are the people whom Rule 5 was promulgated to protect. They do not understand about the privilege against self-incrimination. They do not know that the court will appoint a lawyer to defend them if they are without means. They do not know about bail and preliminary examinations. It is a sham to advise such people of their constitutional rights after the police have questioned them for hours or even days to extract admissions which virtually ensure convictions.

Perhaps an even more important reason for the McNabb-Mallory rule is to prevent those practices collectively known as the third degree. In 1929 President Hoover appointed a group of distinguished lawyers, headed by George Wickersham, to survey law enforcement in the United States. Its report on police lawlessness and the prevalence of third-degree methods shocked the nation. For example, the report stated that the methods employed in Chicago "include the application of rubber hose to the back or the pit of the stomach, kicks in the shins, beating the shins with a club, blows struck with a telephone book on the side of the victim's head. The Chicago telephone book is a heavy one and a swinging blow with it may stun a man without leaving a mark."

Today it is generally agreed that cases of physical coercion are rare. But psychological coercion is equally effective and far more difficult to prove. As Judge Jerome Frank put it: "Policemen have discovered that they need neither intricate devices nor violence. The easiest way to persuade a man to confess to whatever you want is to deprive him of sleep beyond the point of normal exhaustion, questioning him endlessly."

A police reporter in the District of Columbia wrote that several years ago he entered a police station early one morning and saw a man leaning against a wall in the detectives' office. When he came back the next day, the man was still standing there. On the third day the man was gone. When the reporter asked about it, a detective told him that the man had gotten tired of standing and had decided to confess.

Protracted police detention is obviously an indispensable condition of such coercion. Conversely, the McNabb-Mallory rule is the most efficacious safeguard against both physical and psychological coercion. Coercion of any kind is hard to prove because it takes place in secret. The police are understandably reluctant to inform on themselves or on one another, and the courts are understandably reluctant to accept the word of a self-confessed criminal with strong motives for fabrication. Prolonged detention, on the other hand, is an objective fact which courts can easily ascertain and penalize. The best penalty is exclusion of evidence obtained by such detention. If the police realize that evidence obtained in this way is useless, there is every reason to hope that they will fully comply with the law.

Undoubtedly, most of the hostility to the McNabb-Mallory rule stems from the fact that so far it has been invoked principally in cases of heinous murders and rapes where guilt seemed clear. Before trial, however, we cannot have one rule for innocent prisoners and another for guilty prisoners, because we do not know which are which until the verdict is returned. Under our law making this judgment is the function of the jury. It must not be usurped by the police, no matter how able and sincere they may be.

Moreover, there is no reason to suppose that illegal detention will be confined principally to murder and rape cases. As pointed out in a memorandum prepared by the American Bar Association Committee on the Bill of Rights:

> And nobody can guarantee that the people who will disappear for days or weeks will all be guilty of some desperate crime. Of course, nobody sheds tears over the plight of kidnapers and bank robbers held incommunicado. But now federal offenses are being rapidly created, so that the potential area of prolonged detentions is constantly widening. For example, certain expressions of opinion are now federal crimes even in peacetime. Protracted questioning is just as appropriate for the investigation of what the enforcing officers consider to be sedition as for crimes of violence. The suspect need not be actually guilty to be unlawfully detained; it is enough if the officers think he might be guilty.

This type of law enforcement violates the most basic principles of our criminal law. As the Supreme Court pointed out more than a decade ago:

> Ours is the accusatorial as opposed to the inquisitorial system. Such has been the characteristic of Anglo-American criminal justice since it freed itself from practices borrowed by the Star Chamber from the Continent whereby an accused is interrogated in secret for hours on end. . . . Under our system society carries the burden of proving its charge against the accused not out of his own mouth. It must establish its case, not by interrogation of the accused even under

judicial safeguards, but by evidence independently secured through skilled investigation.

This simple fact—that ours is an accusatorial system—is one that some law-enforcement agencies are reluctant to learn. This fact is the underlying basis for the Fifth Amendment's guarantee against self-incrimination and the Fourth Amendment's guarantee against arrests without probable cause. When the police ask to arrest and to question at will for the purpose of obtaining a confession, they are asking for a change in the basic criminal system which we have developed throughout our history. And they never ask directly for such a change, because the public outcry against it would be too great.

There is much reason to believe that abolition of the McNabb-Mallory rule would not really increase police efficiency at all. Many experts have said that an efficient police force relies on scientific methods of investigation rather than upon admissions elicited from the accused by protracted questioning. This view has been expressed by J. Edgar Hoover, who has said:

> Civil rights violations are all the more regrettable because they are so unnecessary. . . . Technical crime-detection methods have greatly reduced arbitrary intrusions on civil liberties. The apprehended suspect "won't talk": Third degree methods, the ill-trained officer might think, perhaps a severe beating will force a confession. But the trained officer, schooled in the latest techniques of crime detection, will think otherwise—he will go to work, locating a latent fingerprint, a heel-print in the mud, or a tool print on the safe.

Where no such evidence is available, a confession during unlawful detention is a slender reed to support conviction.

One of the decisions in this field most widely condemned as defeating justice involved Clarence E. Watson, a Negro youth accused of murdering a white woman while attempting to rape her. The only fingerprints the police could find were bloody fingerprints on a book beneath the body of the victim. They were not Watson's fingerprints, and they were never identified. There was no substantial evidence connecting Watson with the crime except his confession, which was secured after he had been detained and questioned almost all night by the police. In these circumstances we are forced to wonder whether the reversal of his conviction was in fact a "miscarriage of justice."

It has been suggested that detention for interrogation protects innocent people from arrest records, because the police will release anyone who appears innocent after interrogation. This is one kind of protection which I would willingly forgo. The fact is that a record must be kept of all arrests. Once a man is arrested and taken to police headquarters, he has an arrest record. His reputation will not be further damaged by taking him before a commissioner who will advise him of his rights and perhaps release him on the ground that there was no "probable cause" to justify his arrest.

In recent hearings before the Senate Subcommittee on Constitutional Rights it was noted that the standard application for federal employment inquires whether the applicant has ever been arrested, not whether he has ever been bound over by the commissioner for prosecution. This is true also of applications for naturalization and for many other things. As a matter of fact, I have never seen any form which asks about appearances before a commissioner. The questions always relate to arrests, charges and convictions.

There have been several recent proposals to change the McNabb-Mallory rule by act of Congress. One proposal would provide that no confession shall be inadmissible solely because of a delay in taking the accused before a commissioner. This proposal is a license for lawless law enforcement. It leaves unchanged the plain commandment of Rule 5, but it invites the police to ignore this commandment whenever they need a confession to validate an invalid arrest.

A second proposal is almost equally dangerous. It would provide that the police must take the accused before a commissioner within a set period after his arrest, such as twelve hours. If no commissioner were then available, the police would continue to hold him until one became available. This proposal invites the police to wait literally until the eleventh hour before making any effort to find a commissioner. It puts a premium, moreover, upon intensive interrogation to extract a confession before the deadline. The police could hold any suspect incommunicado for twelve hours of continuous questioning before he was advised of his right to counsel, his privilege against self-incrimination, his right to bail.

A third proposal would require the police to warn the accused that he is not required to make any statement and that any statement he makes may be used against him. If this warning were given, illegal detention would not invalidate a confession. Such warnings are required by FBI regulations, by the Uniform Code of Military Justice, and by the Judges' Rules followed in England.

If the required warning were broadened to include advice about the right to counsel, the right to bail and the nature of the charge, it would appear superficially sufficient. So long as the accused receives from the police the same advice he would receive from a commissioner, what difference does it make whether he is taken before the commissioner without unnecessary delay?

There are several answers to this question. An important reason for the McNabb-Mallory rule is the prevention of an opportunity for coercion. Obviously, this objective is not attained by requiring the police to warn the accused of his rights and then permitting them to detain him indefinitely for questioning. Moreover, there would be a tremendous temptation to delay the warning until after the accused had made enough incriminating admissions to ensure a subsequent signed confession. Some English police have admitted to employing this strategy. Finally, there may be a vast difference between advice given in a police station and advice given in a commissioner's office. Most suspects feel that they are in hostile territory so long as they are held by the police. They may be advised of their rights in such a way that they conclude it would be unwise to insist upon them. This is an intangible factor, difficult to prove but very dangerous.

The McNabb case provoked the same sort of crisis in 1943 that the Mallory case provoked in 1957. Bills were introduced in Congress to nullify its effects, just as bills have been introduced to nullify the effects of the Mallory decision. For more than fifteen years we have lived under the McNabb decision, and it has released few, if any, dangerous criminals to prey upon society. The latest statistics from the Department of Justice show that approximately 90 per cent of the criminal prosecutions initiated by the federal government end in convictions. It is a safe prediction that the Mallory case will have no discernible effect upon these statistics.

My objection to the Mallory rule is that it does not go far

enough. There are two tremendously broad fields where it cannot afford any protection. When a citizen is unlawfully arrested, illegally detained and then released with no charge preferred against him, for all practical purposes he has no recourse against those who perpetrated the wrong. I think that we need protection for the ninety boys rounded up in the District of Columbia dragnet arrest of January 20, 1958.

Unfortunately, experience has shown that civil suits against the offending police officers are not a practical remedy. The only alternative is increased public awareness of the problem. No community gets a better police force than it demands. Popular indignation at lawless law enforcement is sometimes the best available weapon against it.

A second inadequacy in the Mallory rule is that it does not apply to state police. This is because the Federal Rules of Criminal Procedure apply only to the federal government. The American Civil Liberties Union recently published a study of illegal detention by the Chicago police which is truly shocking. Although Illinois statutes require that all arrested persons shall be taken before a magistrate "without unnecessary delay" or "immediately," Chicago court records show that one out of every four persons arrested was held for more than seventeen hours before he saw a magistrate. Of those detained more than seventeen hours, moreover, almost 60 per cent were held for more than twenty-four hours and 10 per cent of these were held for more than forty-eight hours.

There is no reason to believe that the Chicago police are different in this respect from the police in other large cities. The staggering statistics from that city indicate that hundreds of thousands of Americans are unlawfully held incommunicado by state police every year. The state courts generally allow a jury to convict on the basis of a confession secured during unlawful detention as long as it is "voluntary."

Popular awareness and indignation are the first step toward reform. So long as we tolerate lawless law enforcement by state police, we shall have it. We must understand that the occasional release of a guilty man is a small price to pay for a society where the police are under the law. We must understand also that the good intentions of police officers make their violations of procedural rules all the more dangerous.

Justice Brandeis once said that the real threat to our liberties does not come from men of bad faith. We have always been alert to their designs. The great danger has lurked in insidious encroachments by men of zeal who have forgotten that a good end does not justify an illicit means. The Mallory decision is a great decision because it reasserts this elementary principle. Instead of trying to abolish its effects by legislation, we should concentrate our efforts to extend its application.

CHAPTER X

COMBAT BY SURPRISE

THE large Washington law firm with which I was associated when I was first admitted to the bar had a great volume of civil litigation, and I spent my days trying negligence cases. Sometimes we represented the injured plaintiff, but more often we represented the local streetcar company, the railroad or the store which had been sued by a pedestrian, a passenger or a customer.

The Federal Rules of Civil Procedure were then only a few years old. Under these rules, I found that I need never enter the courtroom ignorant of the case against my client. I was entitled to the names and addresses of my opponent's witnesses before the trial began. Even more important, I could take sworn testimony from these witnesses before trial. When I entered the courtroom I knew all the witnesses who would be called to testify on behalf of my opponent. I knew what they would say. More than that, I knew their backgrounds. I had checked their reputations for truthfulness and veracity, and the credibility of their testimony in the particular case to be tried. I was like a quarterback trotting onto the field for the kickoff with a set of the opposition's plays and signals. I had all this information because, in the defense of property rights, the rules permitted me to get it.

These rules had been widely hailed as ending the old idea

that a trial is "a game of combat by surprise." Of course, there is an inevitable element of surprise in any trial. But too many surprises too often produce an unjust result. False or misleading testimony can win a case for the wrong party simply because his opponent did not know about it soon enough to refute it. The purpose of liberal discovery procedures is to prevent such results while still preserving the adversary character of litigation.

In 1947 I was assigned as court-appointed counsel to defend a forty-year-old musician named Paul Collins. As the result of a problem with alcohol he had lost a series of jobs with various orchestras and had finally taken a job as a driver-salesman with a large milk company. He had been assigned to a route in the Washington area. Collins was distraught when I first talked to him. He had been indicted by a grand jury and charged with the felony of embezzlement, a crime punishable by imprisonment. He had never before been arrested and, except for his alcohol problem, his record was unblemished.

The indictment was simply drawn. It alleged that Collins had been in the employ of the milk company for a period of about three months and that during the last four weeks of his employment he had "converted fraudulently and feloniously to his own use" approximately $700 of the dairy's money. In other words, he was charged with spending money which belonged to his employer.

Two weeks earlier he had been told he was short in his accounts and discharged. His employer asked for no explanation, and no hearing was given him. The next Collins heard of the matter was when he was arrested by a federal marshal. As he unfolded his story, it seemed fantastic to me, but it was true. I later learned that the company had been plagued by a series of shortages in drivers' accounts and had determined to make an example of the next offender.

Collins was without funds or friends. Before I was assigned to the case he had languished in jail for twenty-three days because he couldn't afford a bail bond and no one had made any effort on his behalf. I was able to secure his release before trial by getting his bail sharply reduced.

As I began preparation for trial of the case, my mind automatically turned toward the conventional weapons that I had so often employed for the firm's corporate clients when they were sued for money damages. But none of those weapons was now available to me. I could not get the names of the prosecution witnesses. I could not take their testimony before trial, even if I knew who they were. It was only when I began to formulate plans for defending the liberty of Paul Collins that the great contrast between civil and criminal procedures came home to me graphically.

If the dairy had filed a civil suit against Collins for $700 alleging that he owed them this as a result of a shortage in his accounts, he would have had available to him all of the procedural safeguards that any civil litigant can employ. He could have ascertained the names of all the witnesses against him and taken their depositions before trial to find out what their testimony at trial would be. In other words, in the defense of $700 he could have availed himself of what we lawyers call pre-trial discovery procedures.

But this was a criminal case. His liberty was at stake. He faced a possible sentence of five years in the penitentiary, the loss of his civil rights and the destruction of his reputation. Under the criminal rules, the procedural safeguards available to the parties in a civil case were not available to him. We were flying blind as we prepared for trial. And from my many talks with Collins and my study of the available records I became convinced that, while he might have been a bad bookkeeper, he was not a thief.

When we went to trial in the spring of 1947, for the first

time in the two years I had been trying cases I had the feeling of going into court unprepared. It was not for lack of work. I had never before worked so hard on a case. It was just that under the criminal rules I couldn't prepare to defend Collins' liberty the way I had become accustomed to prepare for the defense of corporate bankrolls.

Collins was ultimately acquitted by the jury. Somehow the truth emerged at trial. When a small shortage had first manifested itself, the company had sent investigators to interview each of his customers to find if the books reflected the true state of their accounts. Some of the customers took advantage of the company's uncertainty and claimed payments they had never made, not dreaming they would be called upon to testify in a courtroom under oath on the subject. The company accepted their versions and ultimately pressed for indictment. Under painstaking cross-examination by an uncertain interrogator this testimony collapsed, and the case against Collins collapsed with it. But he could never be repaid for the anguish of facing criminal charges, of his twenty-three days in jail and of the mark on his reputation left by the arrest and the indictment.

The Collins case excited my interest in bringing to the rules of criminal procedure the same advances and improvements that had been introduced on the civil side of the court. Some of the realities of life in the administration of criminal justice had been forcefully impressed upon me. I now realized that the government had the most superb engine for discovery ever invented by the legal mind—namely, the grand jury. Before trial the prosecutor could call every witness with any knowledge of the facts in front of the grand jury and interrogate him with virtually no holds barred. Neither the accused nor his lawyer had any right to be present, to propose questions or to object to procedures. The defendant could not even find out the names of the witnesses who testified against him, much less the substance of their testimony. Even unsworn statements given to government agents were generally shrouded in secrecy. It was perfectly possible for defense counsel to begin a serious criminal trial without knowing the name of any government witness and without knowing what any government witness would tell the jury about the defendant.

There were a few exceptions to these harsh rules. In capital cases the government was obliged to give the defendant a list of witnesses three days before trial. If the defendant could show that the trial testimony of a government witness was inconsistent with his grand-jury testimony or with a statement the witness had previously given to government agents, the court would order production of the grand-jury testimony or the prior statement so that the witness could be cross-examined about such inconsistencies. But it was rare indeed for a witness to admit any inconsistencies before he was physically confronted with his previous written statement or testimony. Normally, defense counsel had no way of knowing whether a witness told the same story before the grand jury and the trial jury, and so he could not make the necessary showing of inconsistency. Sometimes the trial judge would undertake the task of comparing the grand-jury and trial testimony of a witness, but this was satisfactory only when the testimony was brief and the inconsistencies were glaring.

It was obvious to me that the innocent defendant suffered most from this procedure. The guilty defendant may not need liberal discovery procedures. He usually knows the identity of the witnesses against him. He usually knows what they have told the grand jury and what they will tell the trial jury. Presumably he has been indicted because they have told the truth, and he knows what the truth is because he committed the crime.

An innocent defendant, on the other hand, may well be unaware of the identity of the witnesses against him. He has no way of knowing what false or misleading testimony has produced the unfounded charge against him. Let us take, for example, the simplest case of an innocent defendant—namely, a case of mistaken identity. Let us suppose that Jones is accused of a robbery which took place at 10:00 P.M. on Tuesday, September 8, 1959. Several people identify him as the culprit, although the crime was actually committed by another man having somewhat similar physical characteristics.

If Jones can establish an alibi, all will be well. Most of us, however, would experience some difficulty in producing sworn testimony of our whereabouts at 10:00 P.M. on Tuesday, September 8, 1959. Alibi evidence, moreover, is usually regarded with suspicion, as it comes most often from the defendant's friends and family. Even if Jones has a wife who is prepared to swear that he was home in bed when the robbery occurred, the jury may not believe her.

There is really very little that any lawyer can do to protect Jones unless he knows who testified before the grand jury and what they said. If counsel had this information, he might be able to show uncertainties and inconsistencies in the identification evidence at trial. But, you may ask, why can't this be done through cross-examination? The answer is that perhaps it can. Every lawyer knows, however, that skillful cross-examination is much easier when the questions are based on facts rather than on intuition. Moreover, it often takes days or weeks to secure a witness or scientific proof which can destroy a fabricated story. If the fabricated story is not revealed until trial, it may be too late. For example, a witness sometimes claims that he saw or heard something which it was physically impossible for him to have seen or heard from the position which he says he was occupying at the time. Unfortunately, such testimony often sounds plausible until there is an opportunity for measurements and tests. Other examples can be readily imagined.

I do not believe that the founding fathers intended to surround property rights with greater procedural safeguards than those which protect liberty. Actually, liberal discovery is more important in criminal cases than in civil cases, because personal liberty is more important than personal property. Our present procedural rules are archaic because they express the converse of this proposition. They date back to medieval days when land was more valuable than the serfs who tilled it.

Civilized societies are remarkably similar in the substance of their criminal law. Murder, rape, robbery, larceny and treason are crimes the world over. The difference between a free and an unfree society lies in the way these crimes are prosecuted—namely, in criminal procedure. Even in the Soviet Union the prosecution's evidence is revealed to the defendant before trial, to assist him in preparing his defense. I think that this is a sorry commentary upon our own practice.

Supposedly, under our system of law an accused is presumed innocent until proven guilty. Opposition to liberal discovery procedure, however, rests upon the assumption that the accused is guilty until proven innocent. The essence of such opposition rests in the fear that the accused, being a depraved criminal, may suborn perjury and intimidate adverse witnesses if he knows anything about the government's case before trial. This position was candidly stated by Judge Alexander Holtzoff, one of the authors of the Federal Rules of Criminal Procedure, who said:

> As a matter of public policy and in the interest of the protection of the community, defendants should not be permitted as a matter of right to inspect statements of witnesses contained in government files, unless in exceptional and unusual situations. To permit such unbridled and unlimited inspection in every case may result in a defeat of justice. It may lead to fabrication of countervailing testimony, to intimidation of witnesses, to bribery of witnesses, and other similar consequences. This remark is not intended as a reflection on members of the Bar. It is a well-known fact, however, that in criminal cases particularly, counsel frequently cannot control their clients, and that defendants themselves at times resort to unscrupulous methods to thwart the ends of justice. These considerations do not exist in civil cases.

The only provision of the present rules which permits real discovery is, unhappily, honored in the breach. Rule 5 provides that the commissioner shall inform the accused of his right to a preliminary examination. Unless the accused waives this right, the commissioner must hear the evidence against him "within a reasonable time." The accused may cross-examine the witnesses against him and may introduce evidence in his own behalf. If it appears that there is probable cause to believe that an offense has been committed and that the accused has committed it, the commissioner will hold him for prosecution. Otherwise the accused must be discharged.

Admittedly, the purpose of a preliminary examination is to prevent the government from holding an arrested person indefinitely when there is no probable cause to believe him guilty of anything. But it has a collateral and sometimes more important effect. It gives the defendant a chance before trial to find out who is accusing him and exactly what the accusation is.

When the government does not want to give the defendant this chance, it resorts to a simple stratagem. It tells the commissioner that it is not yet prepared to present its evidence and it asks for a continuance of the preliminary examination. It then proceeds to present the case to the grand jury and secures an indictment before the date fixed for the preliminary examination. Since the purpose of this examination is to determine whether the defendant should be held for action by the grand jury, it is apparent that no examination will be conducted after indictment. The accused is thus deprived of his rights under Rule 5.

I had firsthand experience with this strategy when I defended James Hoffa. The FBI arrested Hoffa on the night of March 13, 1957. At approximately 1:00 A.M. on March 14, 1957, he was taken before the commissioner. An Assistant United States Attorney asked to have the preliminary examination postponed for two weeks, on the ground that it would take the government two weeks to prepare its evidence. I objected violently, because I felt sure that this postponement would deprive my client of any preliminary examination at all. I was convinced that the FBI would not have arrested Hoffa until the government had all the evidence it could possibly find against him.

The commissioner, however, accepted the government's representation that it was unprepared to present its evidence and granted the postponement. Nine hours later the prosecutor began to present his evidence before the grand jury. Five days later the grand jury returned an indictment. The preliminary examination never took place.

In essence, the indictment charged Hoffa with bribing

an employee of the McClellan Committee named John Cye Cheasty to give him confidential information from the committee files relating to the Teamsters Union. I cross-examined Cheasty for several days. Apparently the jury did not believe his testimony, because they acquitted Hoffa. I have often wondered how much of this exhaustive and exhausting cross-examination would have been unnecessary if I had been given a chance to question Cheasty at a preliminary examination when the facts were fresh and he had had no chance for extensive preparation before testifying. Cheasty had spent days with the prosecutor preparing his testimony before he actually went on the witness stand. Under cross-examination at the trial, which began on June 19, 1957, he testified on this as follows:

> Q. In addition to your testimony in this case before the Grand Jury, and your testimony before the McClellan Committee, you answered questions for the prosecutor, did you not, over a period of days?
>
> A. Yes, sure. You mean trial preparation?
>
> Q. Yes.
>
> * * *
>
> A. Yes; there was trial preparation, sir.
>
> Q. In other words, questions were put to you and you gave answers, is that right?
>
> A. That is correct, sir.
>
> * * *
>
> Q. Over how many days did that go, Mr. Cheasty?
>
> A. Well, there were parts of each day from June 3rd until the opening gun in this case.
>
> Q. Beginning on June 3rd—
>
> A. (Interposing) With the exception of Saturdays and Sundays.
>
> Q. Beginning on June 3rd you met with [the prose-

cutor] and he put questions to you and you would give him answers, is that right?

A. Yes, sir.

* * *

Q. And over how many hours a day, sir, did you go over it on the average?

A. About two in the morning and maybe two in the afternoon.

Q. Just about the same amount of time as we have here in court, is that right?

A. No, not so much, not that I recall.

Q. In other words, four hours a day is what your best guess is; is that right?

A. I am not guessing; I am not guessing.

Q. So you have been testifying about these events for four hours a day since June 3rd of this year, is that right?

A. That is incorrect, sir. That is incorrect.

Q. Except for Saturdays and Sundays.

THE COURT: Just a minute. Will you finish your answer, Mr. Cheasty?

THE WITNESS: I have not been testifying about it, Mr. Williams.

BY MR. WILLIAMS:

Q. You have been responding to questions for four hours a day except for Saturdays and Sundays since June 3rd, is that right?

A. That "responding to questions" isn't an accurate description of what went on there, Mr. Williams. It is a very inaccurate description.

Q. Well, you have been preparing—

THE PROSECUTOR: May the witness answer the question in his own way?

MR. WILLIAMS: Have you finished, Mr. Cheasty?

THE WITNESS: I say it is a very inaccurate description of what transpired in that room.

BY MR. WILLIAMS:

Q. Well, you have been preparing your testimony. Is that an accurate description?

A. I have been refreshing my recollection, would be more accurate.

Q. And you have been preparing your testimony?

A. Yes, sir.

The only way for the court to cope with an obviously unfair situation is to dismiss the indictment if the government begins immediately to present its evidence to the grand jury after it has represented to the commissioner that it is not prepared to present this evidence to him. In other words, the government should not be permitted to profit from its own wrongdoing. Such an amendment to the rules would protect the defendant, but it would not result in the release of people who should be prosecuted. If it still appeared after the preliminary examination that there was probable cause to believe the accused guilty, the matter could be presented to another grand jury and another indictment could be returned.

This change would not solve the entire problem for two reasons. In some cases the accused is not arrested until after an indictment or an information has been filed against him. In these circumstances there is no occasion for a preliminary hearing. Moreover, many witnesses may testify before the grand jury and at trial who do not testify during the course of the preliminary examination. As to their identity and testimony the defendant remains as much in the dark as ever, even if his right to a preliminary examination is scrupulously regarded by the prosecution.

The Supreme Court took a long step toward remedying

these inequities in 1957, when it decided the Jencks case. Jencks was a union officer charged with filing a false non-Communist affidavit. The principal witnesses against him, Harvey Matusow and J. W. Ford, were FBI informers. The trial judge refused to let Jencks's lawyer see the reports which Matusow and Ford had made to the FBI concerning Jencks, because Jencks's lawyer was not able to show any inconsistency between their trial testimony and their reports. Jencks's conviction was reversed by the Supreme Court.

In a celebrated and highly controversial opinion the Supreme Court held that a defendant is entitled to inspect prior statements by government witnesses. It pointed out the absurdity of requiring the defendant to show an inconsistency between their testimony and their statements before he has seen the statements. It also pointed out that inspection by the trial judge to determine whether there is any inconsistency cannot be satisfactory. In support of its position, the court quoted no less venerable an authority than Chief Justice Marshall, who in 1807 ordered a letter in the possession of President Thomas Jefferson turned over to defendant Aaron Burr, notwithstanding that the prosecutor contended that parts of the letter were confidential. To the prosecutor's argument that Burr had not designated which passages of the letter were relevant to his defense, Chief Justice Marshall said, "It is objected that the particular passages of the letter which are required are not pointed out. But how can this be done while the letter itself is withheld? Or how can the applicability be shown without requiring the accused prematurely to disclose his defense?"

The Jencks decision raised a storm of conflict. It was wildly predicted that every FBI file would be opened to the forces of subversion and that law enforcement would become impossible. Congress proceeded to enact a statute confirming the essential holding of the case, but providing that no statement should be turned over to the defense until after the witness had testified. This statute also made it clear that only prior statements by the witness, and not the FBI's evaluation of such statements, need be disclosed.

While the court will recess briefly to permit defense counsel to study statements obtained under this statute, I think that it would be preferable to furnish the statements several days or a week before trial. This would ensure an opportunity for careful study without the pressure of trial, and it would also give an opportunity to run down leads suggested by the statements. Of course, defense counsel would thereby learn the identity of the government's witnesses before trial. This is already the rule in capital cases. If fairness requires it in capital cases, I think fairness requires it in non-capital cases. Likewise, the defendant, through counsel, should be required under the rules to submit a list of the witnesses he expects to call if he wants the government to give him the same information before trial. This would keep the scales fairly balanced between prosecution and accused. The important thing, however, is that no defendant should ever enter the courtroom ignorant of both the identity of his accusers and the nature of their accusation.

A classic example of the need for fair discovery procedures can be found in a trial that was held in Oklahoma City in 1933. The consequences of the inequity that took place then were being felt a quarter of a century later.

George "Machine-Gun" Kelly and his wife, Kathryn, were tried in federal court for kidnaping the multimillionaire oil tycoon Charles F. Urschel. The facts surrounding the case were highly dramatic and showed the investigative techniques of the FBI at their best. Urschel and his wife were playing bridge at their home in Oklahoma City on July 22, 1933, when two men armed with a machine gun and a pistol made entrance. They seized Urschel, blindfolded him and drove for twenty-four hours to a farmhouse, where he was held prisoner. Eight days later he was released when $200,000 in ransom was paid.

After his release Urschel gave the FBI a remarkably detailed account of his ordeal. He had noted that an airplane flew over the farmhouse where he was held prisoner every day at 9:45 A.M. and at 5:45 P.M. except on July 30, when there was a heavy storm in the morning. The FBI quickly found an airline route on which a storm had forced a detour on July 30 and discovered that a plane on that route passed near Paradise, Texas, at 9:45 A.M. and 5:45 P.M. daily. Near Paradise the agents found the farm that Urschel described. It belonged to Mr. and Mrs. R. G. Shannon, the parents of Kathryn Kelly.

The Shannons and a dozen others were soon arrested. George Kelly and Albert Bates were identified as the kidnapers. Bates, too, was quickly apprehended. The entire group was placed on trial in Oklahoma City in September, 1933, while the FBI continued to search for Kelly.

Newspapers across the country carried large headlines about the search, often coupling the story with another—the search for John Dillinger in the Wisconsin woods. It was a time of big kidnapings in this country. The tragic case of the Lindbergh baby was still fresh in people's minds.

On September 20, two days after Bates, the Shannons and their co-defendants went on trial, Urschel and a local newspaper, the *Daily Oklahoman,* received letters postmarked from Chicago threatening dire reprisals if the Urschels testified and averring that the defendants were innocent. Six days later George and Kathryn Kelly were arrested in Memphis, Tennessee.

Kelly made no denial of his role in the crime. But Mrs.

Kelly vigorously protested that she was innocent. She told police that her husband had forced her to accompany him and that she had wanted to leave him but could not escape.

Sixteen days later the Kellys were put on trial, charged with violation of the federal kidnaping statute. The defense lawyers put in no real defense for Kelly. Instead they concentrated on trying to convince the jury that Mrs. Kelly was an unwilling and coerced wife who had resisted participation in the crime. But the prosecutor offered a damaging piece of evidence against her. The two letters from Chicago were introduced and one D. C. Patterson, a local handwriting expert, swore they had been signed by Kathryn Kelly.

Mrs. Kelly took the stand and testified that she had begged Kelly to release Urschel when she found out about the kidnaping. She testified that Kelly had told her it was "none of [her] business," and that he intended to kill Urschel if no ransom were paid.

When asked if she had signed the letters postmarked from Chicago, she cried out, "I did not!" She said the signatures were her husband's. Her lawyer asked for a recess so that he could secure the testimony of another handwriting expert. The request was denied.

The jury did not believe Kathryn Kelly. She and her husband were both convicted and given life sentences. He died in prison a few years ago. She remained in prison for twenty-five years until her case was reopened in 1958. At that time a new attorney argued that her 1933 trial had been unfair. He claimed that Mrs. Kelly should have had time to get another handwriting expert, and also that she had received an inadequate defense because her lawyer was intimidated by knowledge that the FBI was conducting an investigation of him.

The federal judge who heard these claims ordered the

prosecution to produce all of its records on the case, by now twenty-five years old, so that he could inspect them to ascertain if there were any substance to the claims. The Department of Justice refused to produce the files. Thereupon the judge set aside Mrs. Kelly's conviction and freed her on bond pending a new trial. His ruling was later reversed by the United States Court of Appeals for the Tenth Circuit. The case was sent back to the lower court for a continuation of the hearing.

At this writing there has been no hearing. Perhaps the reason is that the FBI had in its possession in 1933, at the time of Kathryn Kelly's trial, evidence of the most persuasive character that she had not signed the letters in question. After the letters had been examined by the local expert, they were sent to the FBI laboratory in Washington. There they were intensively examined by the bureau's top handwriting analyst, Charles A. Appel, who concluded that the signatures had not been written by Mrs. Kelly. He pointed out that a casual examination might lead one to think they were in her writing, but that a thorough analysis proved they were not. Appel concluded that the writing might be that of George Kelly.

This evidence was kept from the jury that tried Kathryn Kelly. If the jury had known that the local expert who testified was wrong, according to the bureau's own expert, and that Mrs. Kelly was undoubtedly telling the truth about the letters, the result might have been different. This, of course, can be small consolation for twenty-five years in prison. But the most disturbing facet of the case is that this evidence was not even disclosed in the 1958 hearing. Instead the government chose to keep the file closed and forget the case.

This story, perhaps as well as any I know, demonstrates why a major change is needed in pre-trial discovery procedures. If Mrs. Kelly had known in advance that a handwriting expert would testify, she might have obtained another expert to challenge his testimony. If she had known that the FBI's own expert had concluded after intensive analysis that she had not signed the letters, she could have called him as a witness. But the game of combat by surprise and disguise had dealt a lethal blow to her chance to defend herself.

The whole problem of the availability of grand-jury testimony to the defense was left unanswered at the time the Supreme Court handed down the Jencks decision, and not until two years later did the court discuss this problem. It then ruled that neither the Jencks case nor the so-called "Jencks Statute" applies to grand-jury testimony. It held that a defendant must show some "particularized need" before he can have the grand-jury testimony of a government witness. The definition of "particularized need" was left to future cases. As the reason for this result the court relied upon the traditional secrecy of grand-jury proceedings.

The reasons for this secrecy have been stated and restated by the authorities. Probably the most often quoted statement is as follows:

> (1) To prevent the escape of those whose indictment may be contemplated; (2) to insure the utmost freedom to the grand jury in its deliberations, and to prevent persons subject to indictment or their friends from importuning the grand jurors; (3) to prevent subornation of perjury or tampering with the witnesses who may testify before the grand jury and later appear at the trial of those indicted by it; (4) to encourage free and untrammeled disclosures by persons

who have information with respect to the commission of crimes; (5) to protect the innocent accused who is exonerated from disclosure of the fact that he has been under investigation, and from the expense of standing trial where there was no probability of guilt.

After an indictment has been returned, reasons 1, 2, and 5 are obviously no longer applicable. The same may be said about reason 4, because presumably the witnesses whose testimony results in an indictment will be called by the government to repeat their testimony at trial. While the possibility of having to testify in open court may discourage some people from disclosing information about crimes, the possibility that their grand-jury testimony may be turned over to defense counsel scarcely discourages them further. The only reason for secrecy which can apply after indictment is reason 3.

This reason always fills me with a sense of outrage. It assumes that defendants are criminals because they are defendants. It assumes, moreover, that counsel for the defense in criminal cases are willing to use suborned testimony and to acquiesce in the intimidation of witnesses. I do not mean to suggest that subornation and intimidation never take place at present or that they might not take place somewhat more often if defendants knew the witnesses against them and the testimony against them at the grand-jury level. Such cases, however, are only a small fraction of the total. I think it is wrong that the overwhelming majority of defendants whose counsel defend them with honesty and integrity should be penalized merely because there are some few who would resort to other weapons. The possibility of subornation and intimidation could be further reduced if the right to bail were abolished, so that all defendants would be held in jail pending trial. Everyone agrees, however, that this would be barbarous. In my view, it is almost equally barbarous to deny all defendants discovery for the sole purpose of reducing the possibility of subornation and intimidation by a few unscrupulous counsel and their clients.

California and several other states give the defendant access to the grand-jury testimony. I have never heard that these states have any more difficulty with improper pressure than do other jurisdictions. A similar procedure is followed in England. There the function of the grand jury has been taken over by the committing magistrate, and these proceedings are open to the accused, who is given full knowledge of the witnesses against him and the nature of their testimony before his trial. This system has proved eminently satisfactory.

The practice followed by some courts of having the trial judge inspect the grand-jury testimony for inconsistencies is far from satisfactory. In the first place, it gives the defendant no access to the testimony of any witness who does not testify at trial. Presumably the government will produce at trial only the witnesses favorable to its position. It will not normally call a witness whose testimony before the grand jury was favorable to the accused. If the defendant is unaware of the identity of such a witness, or if the witness has refused to give the defendant's lawyer a statement because he does not want to become involved in the case, a grave miscarriage of justice may be avoided only by giving the defendant all the grand-jury testimony.

Moreover, if the trial judge gives defense counsel only such parts of the grand-jury testimony as may be inconsistent with the testimony at trial, the defendant may be deprived of an opportunity to investigate leads suggested by the grand-jury testimony. A witness, for example, may mention a name or a document before the grand jury which he is not asked about at trial. This name or this document might lead to vital evidence for the defense.

Finally, the function of the trial judge does not qualify him to search the grand-jury testimony for impeaching evidence. This problem was recognized in the Jencks case, where the Supreme Court held that inspection of prior statements by the judge was insufficient. There the court said:

> Flat contradiction between the witness' testimony and the version of the events given in his report is not the only test of inconsistency. The omission from the reports of facts related at the trial, or a contrast in emphasis upon the same facts, even a different order of treatment, are also relevant to the cross-examining process of testing the credibility of a witness' trial testimony. . . . Because only the defense is adequately equipped to determine the effective use for purpose of discrediting the Government's witness and thereby furthering the accused's defense, the defense must initially be entitled to see them to determine what use may be made of them. Justice requires no less.

All that the trial judge normally knows about a case is what he has heard during the days or perhaps hours since it began. Defense counsel, if he is doing his job, has been living with the facts and the law for an extended period. Moreover, unlike the judge, he knows about the aspects of the case which have not been unfolded in the courtroom. It is obvious that he is in a far better position to determine whether grand-jury testimony casts any cloud over the credibility of testimony given at trial.

The major argument against the application of the civil rules of discovery to criminal procedure is that the prosecution, under constitutional prohibitions, cannot compel the defendant to testify. He may always invoke the privilege against self-incrimination. I do not believe this is a valid reason for denying the discovery procedures on the civil side of the court to the accused defendant. The 90-per-cent record of convictions in criminal cases obtained by the government each year is ample testimony to the fact that the scales are weighted heavily for the prosecutor once the case gets into court. And, under the proposal I make, the prosecutor would have all the same discovery procedures available to him with the one exception that he could not get a pre-trial deposition from the defendant himself, if the defendant invoked the privilege against self-incrimination.

But if this argument (which is traditionally made by the Department of Justice when the liberalization of the rules is suggested) is to be accepted by the rule-makers, then certainly the rationale of the argument fails completely in the case of a defendant who is willing to waive his rights safeguarding against self-incrimination. In our time we should make at least this much advance in the administration of criminal justice: we should at least have an "open skies" policy for defendants who are willing that such rules be reciprocally applicable in the pre-trial stage.

Instead of attacking the Jencks decision, we should concentrate our efforts toward applying its philosophy more broadly. There will be plenty of opposition, just as there was plenty of opposition when the federal courts abandoned the complexities of common-law pleading and instituted liberal discovery procedures in civil cases. The same considerations of justice and fair play which compelled those reforms today compel radical reform of our criminal discovery procedures. The objective is the same as it was in the civil-procedural reforms—namely, to end the concept of a trial as "a game of combat by surprise" and to make it a search for truth.

CHAPTER XI

SUSANNA AND THE ELDERS

ONE of the oldest and most important rights which Americans have is the right to confront one's accusers and to question them. This is a right which is built upon common sense and which has been recognized since biblical times. Many incidents throughout history have shown why this right is vital, but perhaps none has shown it more movingly than the story of Susanna as told in Chapter 13 of the Book of Daniel.

There was a man living in Babylon whose name was Joakim. And he took a wife named Susanna, the daughter of Hilkiah, a very beautiful woman and one who feared the Lord. Her parents were righteous and had taught their daughter according to the law of Moses. Joakim was very rich, and had a spacious garden adjoining his house; and the Jews used to come to him because he was the most honored of them all.

In that year two elders from the people were appointed as judges. Concerning them the Lord had said: "Iniquity came forth from Babylon, from elders who were judges, who were supposed to govern the people." These men were frequently at Joakim's house, and all who had suits at law came to them.

When the people departed at noon, Susanna would go into her husband's garden to walk. The two elders used to see her every day, going in and walking about, and they began to desire her. And they perverted their minds and turned away their eyes from looking to Heaven or rendering righteous judgments. Both were overwhelmed with passion for her, but they did not tell each other of their distress, for they were ashamed to disclose their lustful desire to possess her. And they watched eagerly, day after day, to see her.

One day they said to each other, "Let us go home, for it is mealtime." And when they went out, they parted from each other. But turning back, they met again; and when each pressed the other for the reason, they confessed their lust. And then together they arranged for a time when they could find her alone.

Once, while they were watching for an opportune day, she went in as before with only two maids, and wished to bathe in the garden, for it was very hot. And no one was there except the two elders, who had hid themselves and were watching her. She said to her maids, "Bring me oil and ointments, and shut the garden doors so that I may bathe." They did as she said, shut the garden doors, and went out by the side doors to bring what they had been commanded; and they did not see the elders, because they were hidden.

When the maids had gone out, the two elders rose and ran to her, and said: "Look, the garden doors are shut, no one sees us, and we are in love with you; so give your consent and lie with us. If you refuse, we will testify against you that a young man was with you, and this was why you sent your maids away."

Susanna sighed deeply, and said, "I am hemmed in on every side. For if I do this thing, it is death for me; and if I do not, I shall not escape your hands. I choose not to do it and to fall into your hands, rather than to sin in the sight of the Lord."

Then Susanna cried out with a loud voice, and the two elders shouted against her. And one of them ran and opened the garden doors. When the household servants heard the shouting in the garden, they rushed in at the side door to see what had happened to her. And when the elders told their tale, the servants were greatly ashamed, for nothing like this had ever been said about Susanna.

The next day, when the people gathered at the house of her husband Joakim, the two elders came, full of their wicked plot to have Susanna put to death. They said before the people, "Send for Susanna, the daughter of Hilkiah, who is the wife of Joakim." So they sent for her. And she came, with her parents, her children, and all her kindred.

Now Susanna was a woman of great refinement, and beautiful in appearance. As she was veiled, the wicked men ordered her to be unveiled, that they might feast upon her beauty. But her family and friends and all who saw her wept.

Then the two elders stood up in the midst of the people, and laid their hands upon her head. And she, weeping, looked up toward Heaven, for her heart trusted in the Lord. The elders said, "As we were walking in the garden alone, this woman came in with two maids, shut the garden doors, and dismissed the maids. Then a young man, who had been hidden, came to her and lay with her. We were in a corner of the garden, and when we saw this wickedness we ran to them. We saw them embracing, but we could not hold the man, for he was too strong for us, and he opened the doors and dashed out. So we seized this woman and asked her who the young man was, but she would not tell us. These things we testify."

The assembly believed them, because they were elders of the people and judges; and they condemned her to death.

Then Susanna cried out with a loud voice, and said, "O eternal God, who dost discern what is secret, who art aware of all things before they come to be, thou knowest that these men have borne false witness against me. And now I am to die! Yet I have done none of the things that they have wickedly invented against me!"

The Lord heard her cry. And as she was being led away to be put to death, God aroused the holy spirit of a young lad named Daniel; and he cried with a loud voice, "I am innocent of the blood of this woman."

All the people turned to him and said, "What is this that you have said?" Taking his stand in the midst of them, he said, "Are you such fools, you sons of Israel? Have you condemned a daughter of Israel without examination and without learning the facts? Return to the place of judgment. For these men have borne false witness against her."

Then all the people returned in haste. And the elders said to him, "Come, sit among us and inform us, for God has given you that right." And Daniel said to them, "Separate them far from each other, and I will examine them."

When they were separated from each other, he summoned one of them and said to him, "You old relic of wicked days, your sins have now come home, which you have committed in the past, pronouncing unjust judgments, condemning the innocent and letting the guilty go free, though the Lord said, 'Do not put to death an innocent and righteous person.' Now then, if you really saw her, tell me this: Under what tree did you see them being intimate with each other?"

He answered, "Under a mastic tree."

And Daniel said, "Very well. You have lied against your own head, for the angel of God has received the sentence from God and will immediately cut you in two."

Then he put him aside and commanded them to bring the other. And he said to him, "You offspring of Canaan and not of Judah, beauty has deceived you and lust has perverted your heart. This is how you both have been dealing with the daughters of Israel, and they were intimate with you through fear; but a daughter of Judah would not endure your wickedness. Now then, tell me: Under what tree did you catch them being intimate with each other?"

He answered, "Under an evergreen oak."

And Daniel said to him, "Very well! You also have lied against your own head, for the angel of God is waiting with his sword to saw you in two, that he may destroy you both."

Then all the assembly shouted loudly and blessed God, who saves those who hope in him. And they rose against the two elders, for out of their own mouths Daniel had convicted them of bearing false witness; and they did to them as they had wickedly planned to do to their neighbor; acting in accordance with the law of Moses, they put them to death. Thus innocent blood was saved that day.

And Hilkiah and his wife praised God for their daughter, Susanna, and so did Joakim her husband and all her kindred, because nothing shameful was found in her. And from that day onward Daniel had a great reputation among the people.

This was probably the first transcript made of a cross-examination in all history. But no record made since dramatizes more effectively that the right to confront and cross-examine one's accusers is an indispensable safeguard in any system of justice. Yet many Americans identify cross-examination with trickery or with unsavory efforts to confuse or berate honest witnesses. Hundreds of motion pictures and television shows have created the image of the crafty lawyer who conceals truth or who deliberately confuses truth with falsehood through cross-examination. Since the days of Socrates cross-examination has been thought a sophist's trick designed to make the guilty appear innocent. No doubt the truth is sometimes concealed or confused through skillful use of cross-examination. Even so, the opportunity to face and to question one's accusers is the most effective instrument ever devised for exposing error and falsehood. Confrontation forces the witness to face the accused in open court and to state all he knows of the crime under fear of punishment if he lies. Cross-examination allows the accused or his counsel to scrutinize the testimony, to find its weaknesses or its errors and to expose the prejudice or character of the witness.

Sir Matthew Hale wrote in the seventeenth century that cross-examination "beats and boults out the truth" far more effectively than a naked statement by a witness who cannot be questioned. With it a lawyer can expose a witness who is a habitual criminal or a perjurer or whose relation to the parties in the case ought to be known. He can, like Daniel, expose and denounce those who have borne false witness. But he can do more than that. Most witnesses are honest and truthful when they testify in court, but they, like the rest of us, observe and remember events far less accurately and completely than they think. In recalling events gone by, all of us, without knowing it, make small errors about the details and the sequence of happenings. Yet it is those details which often become the substance of controversy in the courtroom. The color of a cap, the precise amount of time, the exact words—these may be unimportant facts to which we pay no attention. But they may also be the facts which save or convict an accused man. Cross-examination is vital because it gives the accused an opportunity to draw out the forgotten facts or to make plain the lapses in memory.

Cross-examination also gives an accused man the chance to discover whether a witness is remembering things which he never saw or heard. Most of us are highly susceptible to suggestion. Suppose, for example, that you saw an automobile accident but you did not remember clearly the color of one car. A week or so later when a policeman interviews you, he suggests that the car was blue. A few days later, in another conversation, a lawyer says that it was a blue car. It is quite possible for you to become convinced then that you remembered all along that the car was blue. Cross-examination gives the accused a chance to show this development in memory. A few years ago an exchange between a lawyer and a doctor during a trial in New York City gave a perfect example of how even experienced witnesses and observers can remember things which never happened:

> Q. I suppose, of course, that you must be familiar with Professor Munsterberg's recent book, *On the Witness Stand,* which has created so much comment?
>
> A. Yes, indeed.
>
> Q. Do you remember the stress he laid on the power of suggestion, and the illusions of memory; and can you recall some of the curious examples he gave of these phenomena?
>
> A. Yes; if you will call my attention to them, I am sure I will.
>
> Q. For instance (reading from the book): "In the midst of a scholarly meeting, the doors open, a clown in highly colored costume rushes in in mad excitement, and a Negro with a revolver in hand follows

him. They both shout wild phrases; then one falls to the ground, the other jumps on him; then a shot, and suddenly both are out of the room. The whole affair, which was prearranged, took not more than twenty seconds. The scholars are asked immediately to write down a report of what they saw. Out of forty reports there were only six which did not contain positive wrong statements; only four noticed that the Negro had nothing on his head; the others gave him a derby, or a high hat and so on; different colors and styles of clothing were invented for him; some said he had a coat on, others that he was in his shirt sleeves; and it was determined that a majority of the observers had omitted or falsified about half of the processes which occurred completely in their field of vision." Do you remember that example of the frailty of memory?

A. Yes, sir, I remember it well.

Q. Then do you remember this one: "A picture of a room in a farmhouse was shown to a class of picked students; then each was asked questions as to what he had seen. 'Did you see where the stove was located?' Fifty-nine out of one hundred replied and gave the stove a definite place. 'Did you see the farmer's wife winding the clock?' Thirty of the class described the clock, and so on. There was neither stove nor clock shown in the picture." You remember that, do you not?

A. Yes, that was one of his examples which quite forcibly impressed me.

Q. I am going to burden you with the relation of one more incident from Munsterberg's book, and then I am going to ask you if you can see the relation of these cases to the one [we are now trying]. Do you remember this further example . . . "A Negro was being tried for murder committed on a highway at night. A disinterested witness, who claimed to have seen the whole occurrence, was asked these suggestive questions on cross-examination:

> 'Q. Did you see by the moonlight, the kind of trousers and coat the prisoner was wearing at the time?
>
> 'A. Yes, I am sure they were brown or at least dark.'

As a matter of fact there was no moonlight; and all the other witnesses who had testified earlier said that the prisoner's attire consisted of blue trousers, white shirt and no coat." (To witness) Do you remember this example of the remarkable power of suggestion recorded by Professor Munsterberg?

A. Yes, sir, I do.

Q. Do you appreciate, Dr. Allison, that you are yourself easily subject to the power of suggestion?

A. . . . Do you mean to imply that I am testifying falsely?

Q. Not intentionally, no; but that you are what is known as a suggestible witness.

A. Prove it!

Q. Very well. Would it surprise you to know that of the three instances I apparently read from Munsterberg's book, all of which you said you remembered perfectly, only the first one was actually in the book, the second was only half true, and the third was an entire fabrication of my own? Here, take the book, and see for yourself.

A. Mr. Smyth, I am afraid you are making a fool of me.

Q. Not more so than any one of us is liable to be honestly mistaken. . . .

Cross-examination allows counsel to discover instances like this when a witness's memory has played tricks on him. Without confrontation and cross-examination, a man accused of crime would be at the mercy of all these factors plus the possibility, as illustrated in the story of Susanna, of perjured testimony. Without confrontation and cross-examination, he could not probe into errors or omissions in the testimony, he could not force a witness to search his own memory, he could not expose ignorance or cast doubt on the credibility and reliability of a witness, and he could not be sure that a witness really remembered all the events he described. It is clear that even when men try to testify honestly and fully, cross-examination is an important element of any just hearing.

Sometimes the development through cross-examination of a difference in emphasis or inflection can change the whole meaning of what appears to be damaging testimony. This was illustrated in a famous English murder trial in which Marshall Hall, the great British advocate, appeared for the defense. Annie Dyer was accused of killing her illegitimate child. The nurse who attended her testified for the Crown that the defendant had asked her: "How can anyone get rid of a baby like this?" It was shortly after this question was asked that Miss Dyer took the child into her bed, where it suffocated.

Marshall Hall turned what appeared to be the most damaging testimony in the case into a defense. On cross-examination he asked the nurse: "Did she say how *can* anyone get rid of a baby like this?" When he posed the question he put the emphasis on the word "can." The nurse affirmed that this was the precise way in which Annie

Dyer had made the statement. She conceded that the emphasis had been placed this way. What appeared to be almost an admission of guilt was exploded by an ingenious bit of cross-examination, and the full truth emerged. Only by cross-examination could this all-important nuance have been developed.

Vigorous, hard-hitting cross-examination will often extract the truth when all else fails. Sometimes the witness unwittingly gives it up, and occasionally he is forced into conscious collapse. Lloyd Paul Stryker in his fine book *The Art of Advocacy* illustrated the use of cross-examination as the means of causing an attractive feminine witness to unveil her true character for the appraisal of the court. Stryker was involved in a hotly contested divorce case in which the client had alleged adultery against his wife. The evidence of infidelity was so strong that this issue was not contested. The real contest was for the custody of the couple's two young daughters. The wife's position was that, while she had erred in the past, she was still a fit and proper custodian of her children. This is the way Stryker dealt with her during cross-examination:

> Q. In other words, you, a married woman, supported by your husband, and with growing daughters, thought that you would see how you liked living with this Frenchman who himself had a wife in France and children?
>
> A. Well, that is one way of putting it.
>
> Q. You think what you have done here was perfectly moral and fine?
>
> A. I think it was moral under the circumstances, yes.
>
> * * *

Q. Do you feel at all that the inculcation of decent moral principles is important in the raising of a girl?
A. I certainly do.
Q. Is it one of your principles that the only way to know a man is to live with him?
A. For me, yes.
Q. And that is in your opinion a moral and ethical principle, is it; yes or no?
A. For me, yes.
Q. That, however, would not be a good principle for anyone else in the world but you?
A. I didn't say that.
Q. I am trying to get your standard, as the person who wants to have the custody of children. Is that principle that you expressed a principle applicable, not only to yourself, but to other women as well; yes or no?

(Long hesitation)

A. To full-grown adults, yes, but not when they are young—to full-grown adults who are mature and who know something about life and who understand people. Then I think they are free; otherwise they have no right.
Q. What is your definition of a full-grown adult?
A. I feel a full-grown adult—

(Long hesitation)

I don't think any woman is a full-grown adult until she reaches the age of over twenty-eight.
Q. Then it is your standard and moral principle that a woman over the age of twenty-eight is following proper ethical standards who chooses to sleep and have intercourse with a man other than her husband; is that right?

A. If she wishes it, it is right. I think it is wrong for young girls to go out and have intercourse with men. I do.

Q. But not after twenty-eight?

A. You know, people vary. There are some people of twenty-eight who never grow up and there are some people who are younger that are matured.

Q. Then for some persons it would be all right to go out and do what you did at an age considerably younger than twenty-eight?

A. I wouldn't want my children to do it, no.

Q. At any age?

A. I wouldn't want them to do that until they were absolutely fully grown. As a matter of fact, I wouldn't want my daughters to do that until they reached the age that I gave you, or over.

Stryker had artfully and deftly pushed her into a position which was almost as unavoidable as it was lethal to her hopes for custody. He had caused her to destroy her case from her own lips by articulating her sliding moral code.

In my own courtroom experience I have seen witnesses collapse on the stand during cross-examination, but none so completely and pathetically as Ella Thomas, a somewhat neurotic spinster who filed suit against the Capital Transit Company of Washington, D.C. The trial took place early in my career and left me with an indelible impression of the potential efficacy of cross-examination.

Ella Thomas was a passenger on a Transit Company bus which was involved in a collision with another bus owned by the same company. The impact was slight and none of the many passengers appeared to be injured. Weeks passed and only one claim was filed—that of Ella Thomas. She claimed a back injury. She was examined by several specialists and no organic disorder could be found. There was no objective finding whatever to support her complaints. But the complaints worsened. She went through a series of hospitalizations and a series of doctors, none of whom could find evidence of injury. Her damages mounted from loss of income, hospital bills and doctors' bills. By the time of trial they had risen to several thousand dollars.

In preparation for trial I read what seemed to be reams of hospital records. I recall sitting up most of one night studying them. Bleary-eyed and sleepy after hours of study, I finally discovered what I believed to be a pattern of similar episodes in the records. One of the things that troubled the doctors about her case was that she ran high temperatures sporadically. As I studied the records I noted that in every instance where a high temperature was recorded, an entry in the nurses' notes showed that about a half-hour earlier she had asked for and received a hot-water bottle.

At the trial I asked her during cross-examination about the frequency of fever. She expounded at length on how she would periodically flush and become hot with fever and then it would pass. I took her over the recorded instances of fever, and she eagerly described her pain and discomfort during each episode. Then I took her back to the first of these fifty-odd episodes and asked her if she had requested a hot-water bottle a half-hour before her temperature was taken. Slowly I took her back through the history of these episodes. The pattern became clearer. She squirmed uncomfortably in the witness chair and bit her lips. She nervously eyed the now suspecting jury. Finally she broke into tears:

"You think I put the thermometer on the hot-water bottle, don't you? . . . Well, how else could I make them know how sick I was?"

Professor Wigmore, probably the foremost legal scholar

this country has produced on the rules of evidence, once said that the "difference between getting the same facts from other witnesses and from cross-examination is the difference between slow-burning gunpowder and quick flashing dynamite; each does its appointed work, but the one burns along its marked line only, the other rends in all directions." The rending of Ella Thomas well illustrated what he meant.

Few people today dispute the need for confrontation and cross-examination in the courtroom. The right is too deeply embedded in our constitutional system. But there is often dispute as to whether confrontation and cross-examination are essential in quasi-judicial hearings, where Americans have lost their jobs, their property and their reputations on the basis of testimony given by unknown accusers. This problem became particularly acute during the heyday of the Communist scare in the early 1950's. Men were fired from government jobs and branded "security risks" without a chance to know or to question those who accused them. Men were smeared as Communists or Communist sympathizers and lost their reputations without an opportunity to probe by cross-examination the testimony of those who spoke against them. Those days do not make bright pages in our history. But the worst may have passed, because we have begun to see the justice and wisdom of confrontation and cross-examination. There still remains in the nation, however, a type of thinking which sees confrontation and cross-examination as an unnecessary procedure which delays and confuses without clarifying.

This was brought home to me forcibly when a famous radio and television singer who had been closed out of network television appearances for more than a year came to my office. Several times, she explained, she had been hired for major television shows, but her appearances were always canceled at the last moment with unconvincing excuses. She had no idea why this was happening and she had not been able to get a good reason from the network officials. I traced the cause of her problem to a small-town grocer. As a member of a veterans' patriotic group, this man felt a personal responsibility to fight subversion. His group kept a file—and very likely still keeps it—on prominent people in the entertainment world, listing any evidences they may have shown of Communist sympathy or affiliation. He saw to it that his small chain of grocery stores boycotted the sponsors of television broadcasts on which any suspected person appeared. When he had come across the name of my client a year before, he had withdrawn her sponsor's products from the shelves of his stores and told the sponsor's salesmen that he had done it because they were supporting a subversive. The sponsor's sales office, unwilling to risk even so small a protest, had notified the advertising agency, which had forced the networks to cancel her future performances. Eventually this grocer agreed to show me his file on her subversive activities. The only "evidence" against her was that she had sung at a benefit for Henry Wallace in 1948 when Wallace, a former Vice President of the United States, was running for President on the Progressive Party ticket. The engagement had been arranged through her agent, and she had been paid $500 for her appearance. Because of this incident, this grocer and others like him were willing to drive her out of her profession without ever telling her why and without giving her a chance to defend her reputation. As soon as the accuser was stripped of his anonymity and the basis for the accusation was exposed, she was able to meet and answer it. The shameful boycott was ended by shamefaced men.

I find it terrifying and disheartening to think that there are men in America who would act against a fellow citizen on evidence as thin as that on which the grocer acted. But it is far more terrifying when government acts on this kind of evidence to brand a man as disloyal or as a security risk. When we allow congressional committees or government hearing boards to act on the evidence they have received without confrontation and cross-examination, we take the chance that they, too, will act in the same arbitrary and capricious way. Without confrontation and cross-examination, a man brought before a hearing board is subject to trial by inquisition. His accuser may be a trained FBI informant, or he may be a malicious busybody, or he may be an incompetent with a flair for melodrama. We saw all three kinds during the early 1950's. Without cross-examination and confrontation, the accuser is faceless and nameless. He may be stable or unstable, bright or stupid, right or wrong, but the man who is accused can never challenge him. The charge may be a mistake. It may be a bureaucratic error. But the accused may never know enough of the evidence against him to disprove the charge.

I have seen cases in which a man was accused of disloyalty through the simplest of mistakes. I represented a motion-picture writer who wanted to travel to Europe with his family during a summer vacation. He was flabbergasted when his application for a passport was turned down by the State Department. When I, on his behalf, pressed the department for a reason, I was told there was information suggesting disloyalty in his files. The department had information from an informer whose identity it would not reveal that the writer had at one time belonged to the Communist Party. He categorically denied the charge in a sworn statement. Still no passport was issued. We demanded the identification of the faceless informer. It was not the policy to give such information and we were refused it even after the allegation had been denied. The writer's vacation plans were scrapped and he went through a nightmare for almost five months until we finally ferreted out the fact that he had been confused with another man of the same name—all because there was no right of confrontation.

Of course, it is possible to conjure up situations in which the disclosure of the informant's identity could do serious damage to national security. Where this is true, and where it is further true that the continuation of the accused in a sensitive job would equally damage national security, there is basis for exception to the over-all rule. But the truth of these facts should be certified in writing by the cabinet officer or agency chief of the affected department or agency. He should further certify to his belief in the credibility of the information involved. Only upon such certification should the hearing board in question be empowered to make a ruling depriving the accused of confrontation and cross-examination. And this decision should be subject to full review by a board of appeals and, finally, full judicial review by courts which have available the concealed information that was before the board. Only the most carefully circumscribed application of this exception can be allowed, for secret evidence is abhorrent to a free society. It protects from exposure the malevolent and the prejudiced, the meddlesome and the misinformed, the corrupt and the venal.

Ever since the first communities were formed, men have been concerned with security and loyalty problems. Citizens throughout the centuries have been condemned hastily, and when condemnation was based on uncontested evidence from a faceless, nameless informer, the results have been uniformly evil. Plato tells us that in ancient Greece Socrates was condemned for subversion in exactly this fashion. At his trial Socrates protested:

> And, hardest of all, I do not know and cannot tell the names of my accusers. . . . All who from envy and malice have persuaded you—some of them having first convinced themselves—all this class of men are most difficult to deal with, for I cannot have them up here, and cross-examine them, and therefore I must simply fight with shadows in my own defense, and argue when there is no one who answers.

The problems of loyalty and security are acute in a day when the United States stands face to face with the growing Communist challenge. But the solution to those problems should not be one requiring Americans to give up rights which have been established by our ancestors down through the years of history. Too many Americans, like the grocer, are ready to seize upon the necessities of the moment, to dispense with the protections given to the individual, and to cry for quick justice. Justice which is quick and which dispenses with the protections of freedom is rarely justice. The Bill of Rights and the fundamental rights which all Americans can claim have no clauses excepting those accused of disloyalty from their protection.

The right to confrontation and cross-examination is one of those rights which should be protected not solely because it is a right, but because it is fair. Former President Eisenhower once explained that right this way:

> I was raised in a little town of which most of you have never heard . . . called Abilene, Kansas. Now that town had a code, and I was raised as a boy to prize that code. It was: Meet anyone face to face with whom

> you disagree. . . . In this country, if someone dislikes you, or accuses you, he must come up in front. He cannot hide behind the shadow. He cannot assassinate you or your character from behind.

The real reason for the right of confrontation and cross-examination is precisely that. We cannot allow men to be assassinated, either in person or in reputation, from behind.

CHAPTER XII

FINGERS ON THE SCALES OF JUSTICE

A FEW years ago, when the late Dorothy Thompson was asked to address a section of the American Bar Association, she chose to talk about one of the great dangers which hangs over our legal system—mob influence on the processes of justice. Recalling all the safeguards which we use to make the system fair and impartial, Miss Thompson said, "One might say that the judiciary exists to protect democracy against its own excesses." She explained:

> It has taken centuries of evolution to take the conduct of justice *out* of the hands of the multitude; away from the mob and the market place, where rumor, hearsay, passion, prejudice, malice, and mass emotion so easily hold sway; to take justice out of the hands of those who, for such reasons, "know not what they do," and to take it into the quiet chambers, surround it with rules and restrictions, conduct it with dignity and decorum, and establish the conditions and atmosphere to make it possible, at least, that those who sit in judgment do know what they do. Only thus can the law be the guardian and protector of men's liberty. . . .

Far too often bystanders in the mob and in the market place even today influence the outcome of individual cases.

In many instances the result of this meddling is a miscarriage of justice—the conviction of a man because extensive and defamatory newspaper publicity deprived him of a fair trial, or the indictment of a man because pressure applied to the grand jury deprived him of its carefully weighed judgment.

An example of meddling with the judicial process came forcefully to my attention in the case of Adam Clayton Powell, a Congressman from New York who was indicted in 1958 for evading income taxes.

For twenty years Powell has been one of the most controversial and newsworthy figures in public life in New York City. His political power over his congressional district seems unbreakable. His eloquent articulation of his convictions on racial equality and his personal dynamism have won him hordes of idolaters and hordes of detractors. Small wonder that when a federal grand jury began to look into his income taxes in December, 1956, the press gave the matter full attention. Immediately speculation was rife as to whether he would be indicted. But it was eighteen months before the grand jury acted. Not until May 8, 1958, did they return an indictment. It was on that day that I first met Adam Clayton Powell.

He called me on the telephone and we arranged a meeting in my office, where we spent several hours in discussion of the case. The indictment charged him with understating his wife's income by $5,365.77 for the year 1951. At the time he was married to Hazel Scott, the famous jazz pianist. Another count in the indictment charged him with understating his own income by $3,700 for the year 1952. I was astounded when he told me that at no time had he been interviewed by an Internal Revenue agent regarding these returns. It is routine policy to interview the taxpayer whose return is in question and give him a chance to explain his position. More than that, it is routine for the Internal Revenue Service to attempt civil compromise in such a case. None was attempted here. The least prominent citizen is entitled to these procedures. It would seem that a Congressman and the pastor of the largest Protestant church in New York would be accorded the same courtesy.

I was even more astounded when he told me such facts as he knew about the grand-jury proceedings out of which his indictment came. My astonishment turned to incredulity when he detailed some of the unorthodox and highly irregular things that had happened. I thought his story just a manifestation of the persecution complex that so many people in public life develop when they become the target of a criminal prosecution. But Adam Powell is a persuasive and dynamic man and he convinced me that what he was saying certainly warranted careful investigation. That's what I gave it, and what follows is an account of what I found.

The Powell grand jury had convened in December, 1956, under the direction of Assistant United States Attorney Thomas A. Bolan. It met and heard evidence twenty times during December of 1956 and January and February of 1957. Thirty-nine witnesses appeared before it. Then it went into recess without returning an indictment. The only proper explanation for this was that there was not sufficient evidence on which to indict. At this juncture the Revenue Service had been in possession of all the returns in question for at least four years, and a squad of agents had been investigating them. The grand jury had been sifting evidence about them for three months. In the ordinary case this would seem to be a fair basis for inference that there would not be an indictment. But not so in the case of Adam Powell.

In September, 1957, Mr. Bolan resigned from the United States Attorney's office and went into the private practice of law in New York City. Shortly thereafter he was in communication with William F. Buckley, Jr., editor of *National Review* and author of a book called *God and Man at Yale.*

Following Bolan's conversations with Buckley, *National Review* carried an article in the December 14, 1957, issue called "Death of an Investigation: The Wheels of Justice Stop for Adam Clayton Powell, Jr." The article stated that the tax investigation by the grand jury had been suspended

> in spite of the fact that the agent in charge of the Treasury force detailed to assist the United States Attorney to secure evidence for the grand jury privately stated that in his opinion enough evidence had already been amassed to win an indictment; and . . . in spite of the further fact that the Assistant United States Attorney who had been in direct charge of the investigation from the outset, believed, and so stated to his superiors, that enough evidence had already been marshaled to bring about an indictment, and in spite of the fact that he believed, and so informed his superiors, that two months additional work would even further strengthen the government's case.

The article went on to suggest that the investigation had been suspended either as a result of intimidation of unnamed persons or as a result of a sinister and corrupt election deal of which President Dwight D. Eisenhower had been the beneficiary. The second suggestion implied that Powell, a Democrat, had supported Eisenhower in the 1956 election in return for assurances that the tax investigation would be dropped. Of course, the absurdity of the charge was quickly demonstrable from the fact that the Powell grand jury was not even empaneled until after the election.

Buckley obtained the names and addresses of the grand

jurors sitting on the Powell case and had copies of the December 14, 1957, issue of his magazine mailed to them. Emblazoned across the cover were the words, DEATH OF AN INVESTIGATION, THE WHEELS OF JUSTICE STOP FOR ADAM CLAYTON POWELL JR.

Beginning on February 22, 1958, each issue of *National Review* carried a special box advising the readers exactly how long it would be before the Powell grand jury automatically went out of existence, and how long it had been since it was last convened. The boxes read:

> The grand jury called to investigate the tax returns of Adam Clayton Powell has——weeks to live. ——weeks have gone by since it was last convened to hear evidence.

During the spring of 1958 Bolan actually met by prearrangement with members of the grand jury. On April 2, 1958, Buckley himself met and talked with a member of the jury, who said that he was convinced, as a result of the *National Review* articles and his talks with Bolan, that Washington was arbitrarily interfering in the Powell case. Eight days later Buckley mailed copies of the December, 1957, article to each grand juror with the following covering letter:

> NATIONAL REVIEW, 211 East 37th Street,
> New York 16, N.Y.
> April 10, 1958
>
> Eight weeks ago, *National Review* published the editorial a copy of which I attach. Every week since, we have reminded our readers of the length of life left to the grand jury investigating Mr. Adam Clayton Powell, Jr. As you will remember, last December *National Review* published an article based on affidavits

and other information, establishing the irregularity of the suspension of the investigation, and the abuse of the grand jury by the Department of Justice. It is the purpose of this letter to inform you that not a single fact contained in that article has been challenged, either by Mr. Powell, or by the Department of Justice, or by the Tax Department. I am enclosing, for your information, a copy of the original article, to refresh your memory.

National Review is not interested in persecuting Adam Clayton Powell, Jr., but is interested in the integrity of the judicial process.

Yours sincerely,
WM. F. BUCKLEY, JR.

On May 3, 1958, *National Review* carried an editorial captioned THE JIG IS UP FOR ADAM CLAYTON POWELL, JR. The title bannered on the cover was more revealing about the periodical than it was about the case. The editorial itself said:

> The foreman of the grand jury, having read *National Review's* article . . . addressed U.S. Attorney Paul Williams, and asked him to convene the jury to explain the mysterious inactivity. Mr. Williams, presumably on orders from Washington, stalled.
>
> Two weeks ago *National Review* sent another copy of its expose of last December to every member of the grand jury; and, at last, action resulted. The jury convened on its own motion. . . .
>
> Now the question is, Will the grand jury, having had such direct experience with the politicalization of justice as administered by the Justice Department in the case of Adam Clayton Powell, Jr., take matters into its own hands in the few weeks left to it, and see

to it that, as long as *this jury* has anything to say about it, the laws of this country apply even to big-time politicians?

The pressure on the grand jury produced the desired result. The jurors demanded that they be recalled and that the proceedings be resumed. They felt that their integrity had been challenged. They felt that they were pawns in a game of politics. They talked of renting a room in a midtown hotel and holding their sessions there instead of in the courthouse. They talked of excluding the United States Attorney and his assistants, and of hiring Bolan as an independent counsel. They wanted immediate action.

It was against this background that their first meeting took place. The foreman had been assured by the United States Attorney that the Justice Department had not called off the investigation. The Attorney General had long since written a letter of instruction saying that Powell's case should be investigated fully and that any action warranted by the facts should be taken. But the damage had been done. The charges which impugned the integrity of the Eisenhower Administration, and particularly the Attorney General, had been made and placed in the hands of the grand jurors. The jurors had been told they were being used for a "whitewash." It was a foregone conclusion that there would be an indictment.

It was almost two years before the effect of the external influences upon this grand jury could be fully measured. But what developed during the course of the trial of this case in the spring of 1960 compels the conclusion that the indictment of Congressman Powell was born of hysteria.

The government took five weeks of trial to lay its evidence before the jury. Morton Robson, a skilled and experienced prosecutor, had prepared the case with painstaking care, and he presented it most effectively. He had nothing to do with the presentation of evidence at the grand-jury level and had been assigned to the case by his superiors on the eve of trial. Now at the end of the government's case he was forced into the wholly embarrassing position of admitting that the government had no evidence of a violation of law for the year 1952. The prosecution had been able to produce no evidence to substantiate this count of the indictment and the prosecutor had to consent to its dismissal. The government found itself in this humiliating position despite the fact that an exhaustive investigation designed to buttress the case had continued after the indictment. But the indictment was the result of hasty, improvident action inspired by irresponsible charges, and the chickens came home to roost.

Robson found himself in an even more embarrassing position, not of his own making, with respect to the charge of evasion for the year 1951. The grand jury had indicted Powell for understating his wife's income for that year. In a formal pleading, called a Bill of Particulars, filed in court, the then United States Attorney had stated that the grand-jury indictment was based upon an understatement of Hazel Scott Powell's income. No challenge was made to the deductions taken on that return. But as Robson began to prepare the case for trial, he found that he had no evidence to support this charge either. So he tried feverishly to patch up the case. He changed the whole theory of the prosecution, and at the eleventh hour filed an amended pleading (an Amended Bill of Particulars) alleging that Powell had taken improper deductions on his wife's return.

When the evidence came out in court during weeks of trial it showed clearly that Powell, instead of understating his wife's income for 1951, had actually overstated it. This meant that once again there was absolutely no evidence to support the charge made by the grand jury. Since overstatement of income cancels out excessive deductions dollar for dollar, the government's case once again foundered on the rocks. The formidable New York *Times* was constrained to comment that the indictment had been improvidently and hastily drawn. When this count of the indictment was finally submitted to the jury, ten of them voted for acquittal, but two held out. The government eventually dropped the charge, conceding that it could not prove the case.

It seems clear to me that without the external pressures and without the passion aroused in the grand jurors, Adam Powell would never have been indicted and would never have been forced into a long, expensive and politically damaging trial. If the grand jurors had been left to reach their decision in the calm, careful manner in which grand juries are intended to function, no indictment would have resulted. But because of the meddling with the judicial process which occurred in this case, the grand jury was turned into the "market place" which Miss Thompson spoke of—a market place where "rumor, hearsay, passion, prejudice, malice, and mass emotion so easily hold sway."

Incidents like these do not often happen with regard to grand juries. More frequently the mass emotion and passion of the market place is brought to bear when a case goes to trial. Then these outside influences do even more to contaminate the judicial process, for they can bring about the conviction and perhaps even the execution of an innocent defendant.

There are any number of ways in which extrinsic influences can unbalance the scales of justice. A celebrated case involved five Negro youths who were arrested in Arkansas on September 30, 1913, and charged with killing a white man during a racial disturbance. Only the presence of United

States troops saved them from being lynched while they were being taken to jail after arrest. They were indicted on October 29 and brought to trial five days later. The boys were all convicted, and ultimately the case (*Moore* v. *Dempsey*) reached the Supreme Court of the United States. The record presented to the Supreme Court, as described by Justice Oliver Wendell Holmes, showed they had not been accorded the semblance of due process of law:

> The court and neighborhood were thronged with an adverse crowd that threatened the most dangerous consequences to anyone interfering with the desired result. The counsel did not venture to demand a delay or a change of venue, to challenge a juryman, or to ask for separate trials. He had had no preliminary consultation with the accused, called no witnesses for the defense, although they could have been produced, and did not put the defendants on the stand. The trial lasted about three quarters of an hour, and in less than five minutes the jury brought in a verdict of guilty of murder in the first degree. According to the allegations and affidavits there never was a chance for the [men] to be acquitted; no juryman could have voted for an acquittal and continued to live in Phillips county, and if any prisoner, by any chance, had been acquitted by a jury, he could not have escaped the mob.

A more common way in which juries are influenced, however, is through the publication in the press of highly damaging information which, under the rules of our judicial system, should never reach the minds of jurors. This problem—trial by newspaper—has become of great concern to all judges and to many of our lawyers. It threatens the very basis upon which our judicial system operates, because it brings into the courtroom the rumors and passions of the market place. These must inevitably imperil the constitutional right of every accused to a fair trial. In the early summer of 1961 the Supreme Court had occasion to upset a murder conviction for this very reason. This was a case in which the press had tried and convicted Leslie Irvin of murder long before his courtroom trial began.

Irvin was arrested near Evansville, Indiana, on April 8, 1955. Soon afterward the prosecutor in that county and the Evansville police issued press releases stating that he had confessed to six murders which had occurred in the Evansville area. Newspapers headlined the story and radio and television stations carried extensive newscasts about it. In the following days more news stories were written about Irvin. These revealed the details of his life, including accounts of crimes he had committed when he was a juvenile twenty years before the crime in question was perpetrated. Headlines announced that he had been identified in a police line-up, that he had faced a lie-detector test, that he had been placed at the scene of the crime. Other stories said he had confessed to twenty-four burglaries, and one story related the promise of the sheriff to devote his life to securing Irvin's conviction. He was described as a "confessed slayer of six" and the "mad-dog killer."

The publicity was so intense that when the case finally went to trial, 268 of the 430 prospective jurors on the panel said they had already made up their minds that Irvin was guilty. Eight of the twelve jurors who were finally selected to sit in judgment on Irvin said they thought in advance that he was guilty but they were sure they could give him a fair trial. One of those eight said he "could not . . . give the defendant the benefit of the doubt that he is innocent." One said, "You can't forget what you hear and see."

Is it any wonder that in such an atmosphere Irvin was

convicted and sentenced to death? In telling the state of Indiana that it must try Irvin again if it hoped to convict him, the Supreme Court said, "With his life at stake, it is not requiring too much that [Irvin] be tried in an atmosphere undisturbed by so huge a wave of public passion and by a jury other than one in which two-thirds of the members admit, before hearing any testimony, to possessing a belief in his guilt."

How can incidents like this be avoided in a free society? Some lawyers have urged that a rein be put on newspaper accounts of judicial proceedings and crimes which will be the subject of judicial proceedings. They advocate that editors who permit publication of stories which prejudice the right of a defendant to a fair trial by an impartial jury be punished for contempt of court. This is the system in effect in England, and it does ensure a fair trail for the accused. But this proposal runs squarely into the First Amendment's guarantee of a free press. The delicate balancing of the rights of the press and the rights of the accused has provided for decades a fertile field for debate among legal scholars.

I have long felt that the problem can be solved without tampering in any way with the freedom of the press. Canon 20 of the lawyer's Code of Professional Ethics says:

> Newspaper publications by a lawyer as to pending or anticipated litigation may interfere with a fair trial in the courts and otherwise prejudice the due administration of justice. Generally they are to be condemned. If the extreme circumstances of a particular case justify a statement to the public, it is unprofessional to make it anonymously. An *ex parte* reference to the facts should not go beyond quotation from the records and papers on file in the court; but even in extreme cases it is better to avoid any *ex parte* statement.

If lawyers would meticulously abide by this rule, most of the difficulties would be overcome. Prosecutors would, of course, have to apply a tight rein on the information which the police gave to the press. They would have to see to it that such highly inflammatory materials as confessions, past police records and statements of witnesses were not released to reporters. Defense lawyers would likewise have to refrain from putting out exculpatory materials and previews of the defense. Only the courts and the appropriate disciplinary committees of the bar can enforce compliance with this rule. But if compliance were rigidly enforced, it would go a long way toward the elimination of "trial by newspaper." Enforcement of laws already on the books would eliminate the kind of problem exemplified by the Powell case. Application of existing rules providing for change of venue and postponement of trial date can remove the abuses of which Justice Holmes spoke in *Moore* v. *Dempsey*.

Hazard Gillespie, Jr., former United States Attorney for the Southern District of New York, acted in the highest tradition of the bar when he complained to the New York newspapers that identified a man on trial in a narcotics case being prosecuted by his office as a "convicted narcotics dealer who was present at the gangland meeting three years ago at Apalachin, New York." He said in a letter to the editors:

> On Tuesday, November 22, 1960, your newspaper printed an article concerning the commencement of a narcotics conspiracy prosecution in the Federal Court for the Southern District of New York. In that article you named one of the defendants standing trial, and identified him as "a convicted narcotics dealer who was present at the gangland meeting three years ago at Apalachin, New York."

Despite the Court's admonition not to read about this case in the newspapers, one of the jurors who had been selected to serve the day before inadvertently read a similar article in another New York City newspaper and advised the Court that it so influenced his mental attitude that he did not feel he could serve any longer as an impartial juror. He was thereupon excused.

This incident illustrates the obstructive effect on constitutionally safeguarded judicial processes which the publication of a defendant's prior criminal record can have, irrespective of the Court's admonitions to jurors and the latters' good faith attempts to abide by such instructions.

While this office not only recognizes but supports the right of the press fully to inform the public of judicial proceedings in open court, we would at the same time point out its correlative duty not to publish information in derogation of the rights of individual citizens standing trial until the evidentiary admissibility of such matter has been determined by an appropriate judicial forum. A failure to adhere to this obligation, as exemplified by this case, produces the foreseeable risk of judicial obstruction. I advise you to this effect with the approval of the District Judge before whom this case is being tried.

In view of the incident in this case, and the context in which we have discussed the correlative rights and duties involved, we request that you refrain from publishing such information including particularly any reference to past criminal actions or other prejudicial information regarding defendants on trial until such matter has been accepted in open court as lawfully admissible evidence or until the trial has been completed.

We will very much appreciate your voluntary cooperation in this matter gravely affecting the continued integrity and effectiveness of our trial processes.

The harm which those articles did cost the government and the defendants in the case several hundreds of thousands of dollars. The case went on after the juror in question was excused. An alternate juror was substituted for him. But ultimately, over the course of a five-month trial, all the alternates were used up. At the very end of the trial a juror was hospitalized as the result of an accident and could no longer serve. That left only eleven jurors who had heard the case, and under the rules a jury must consist of twelve unless the parties consent to a lesser number. When the defendants refused to go on with eleven jurors, there was nothing for the judge to do but declare a mistrial. Months of work were wasted. A new trial was ordered and all the evidence had to be presented to a new jury.

So much is said about the defendant's right to a fair trial that sometimes we lose sight of the fact that the same right belongs to the prosecution. A brazen and outrageous attempt was made to put fingers on the scales of justice in the Hoffa bribery trial in Washington in 1957. The trial attracted great national attention in press, television and radio. Several hundred people jammed the courtroom every day and hundreds more were turned away. There were reporters galore, and photographers snapped pictures daily on the courthouse steps as the participants went to and fro.

One afternoon as I returned to court after lunch I was introduced to a woman lawyer from the west coast. She was a Negro. As I stood chatting with her for a moment, a photographer called to us to look his way and snapped our picture. The incident meant absolutely nothing to me at the time. A few days later I was horrified to see the picture in a full-page advertisement in the *Afro-American*, a paper having large circulation among the Negroes of Washington. The advertisement recounted in detail Hoffa's long record of friendship for the Negro people and their causes. The jury trying Hoffa was predominantly Negro. Obviously, the advertisement had been placed in an effort to influence the jury in Hoffa's favor.

This was the darkest day of my professional life. I have never before nor since been so upset about any incident connected with a trial. Neither I nor any lawyer assisting me had an inkling that such an advertisement was to appear. I held a long inquisition of everybody in any way connected with the defense, including the defendant himself. I can honestly say that I satisfied myself that no one directly or indirectly connected with the defense staff knew anything about the appearance of the ad. I can also honestly say that I'm sure Hoffa himself knew nothing of it. It was the work of a well-motivated meddler from Detroit who thought he was helping his friend "Jimmy" and who acted wholly on his own. Judge Matthews immediately locked the jury up for the remainder of the trial, and it was subsequently ascertained that no one of them ever saw the ad. The McClellan Committee probed extensively into the whole episode, and all the evidence showed that it was the work of a self-appointed interloper who understood neither the sanctity of the judicial process nor the dignity of the Negro people.

At this point another episode in the Hoffa case needs recounting. This one I knew about. It was my original intention to put character witnesses on the stand during the defense. I had screened a long list of prospective character witnesses and had selected eight for use at trial. I had tried to get a representative cross-section of people. Among those selected were a labor leader, an owner of a trucking company, a Catholic bishop, a Protestant minister, a college professor, a Congressman—and Joe Louis. All of these people had known Hoffa for years. Joe Louis and he had been close friends for over two decades.

They were asked to testify, and all readily agreed to do so. As the time for putting on defense witnesses approached, they were summoned to Washington. Just as we were about to begin the defense, I came to the decision not to put on any character witnesses. I decided on this course because I believed we would be hurt more than we would be helped by this kind of evidence. One of the rules in a criminal trial is that the defendant may always put in "good character" evidence. But if he does, the prosecutor has the right to cross-examine the witnesses exhaustively about all the derogatory rumors, hearsay and gossip affecting the defendant's reputation. In the case of a controversial figure such as Hoffa, who had many enemies, this could give the prosecutor a field day. He could parade before the jury every derogatory piece of gossip and rumor ever mouthed about the defendant. On balance, it seemed to me the danger of prejudice was too great. So the witnesses were excused.

I met with Joe Louis, who had come all the way from Detroit, and explained to him that we were not going to use him and that he was free to go back to Detroit. This took place at a luncheon recess. That afternoon I was genuinely surprised to see him sitting in the back of the courtroom. He had come to court wholly on his own, insofar as I knew then or have ever found out since. I very much doubt whether any juror ever saw him in that packed courtroom, because the jury never came in until all the spectators were seated, and they always left before any spectator was permitted to leave his seat.

Almost no notice was given the incident at the time.

It was only after Hoffa was acquitted many days later that Louis' appearance took on significance. By now thousands of words have been written about it. But everyone who had any connection with the trial knows his presence had not the remotest effect on the verdict. The prosecutor concedes this. The jury acquitted Hoffa because they did not believe the accusation against him. They acquitted him on the first ballot. They retired to their jury room. They read the indictment aloud and then they read the judge's instructions. One juror suggested that they say a prayer before balloting, and they bowed their heads for a moment. They balloted secretly, and when the ballots were tallied by the foreman, the vote was 12 to 0 for acquittal. Negro and white voted alike.

The Louis story seems to grow each year and more legend and less fact gets into it. Needless to say, I'm sorry he ever came to court. But had I known he was coming to observe the trial that afternoon, I would not have asked him to stay away. I have thought about it a great deal since, and it is almost impossible to project myself back into that hectic frame of reference. But, whether it should have or not, the fact is it never crossed my mind that his presence could have any effect on the jury. And all of the jurors later attested that his appearance at the trial was meaningless insofar as the outcome was concerned.

The Hoffa jury, like every jury, was instructed by the trial judge that it was to arrive at its verdict free from sympathy, prejudice, predilections and all extrinsic influences. The jurors were instructed to decide the case solely upon the evidence presented in court and the law as stated by the judge. If our system is to continue to use trial by jury, the minds of the jurors must be kept free from outside influences. A chemist would not make a test with test tubes contaminated by waste materials. The minds of the jurors are the test tubes of the judicial system. They must be kept clean of extraneous matter if justice is to be done. That's why civilized society removed trials from the market place, surrounded them with safeguards and brought them under the most careful judicial scrutiny. Justice requires that jurors make their decisions solely on the facts properly presented to them. Ways must be found to block those who would put before them material which does not belong there. Only then can we really guarantee the constitutional right to a fair trial.

CHAPTER XIII

NEITHER IN NOR ON CAMERA

In 1934 the *Morro Castle* burned at sea. One of the worst ship disasters of its time, it claimed scores of lives. The United States Board of Steamboat Inspectors held public hearings in New York to ascertain the cause of the disaster and the reason for the tremendous toll of lives. The inquiry was historic in that it marked the first time that hearings of this kind were broadcast over radio. The broadcasts quickly brought a denunciation from the New York County Lawyers' Association. In a strongly worded resolution the association urged that all broadcasts or movies of judicial proceedings be discontinued "in the interests of justice."

The reasons for this kind of resolution were strong and clear. Everyone truly interested in the administration of justice and in the inquiry as a search for truth was revolted at what had happened. The witnesses were more concerned with the microphones than with their oaths. One witness picked up the microphone, put it to his mouth and shouted "Mom—how'm I doin'?" Another said, "I hope the red-headed girl and all the other girls and those I met on shipboard will remember me and the pleasant times we had and send me some postal cards."

It was a travesty, a radio show instead of an inquiry.

This kind of thing was quickly stopped in the 1930's. But with the advent of television came pressure from all over the nation to put trials and hearings on the screen. The industry was, of course, not interested in telecasting all trials or all hearings—only the more sensational ones, and preferably only the most sensational parts of those.

But Canon 35 of the American Bar Association Canons of Judicial Ethics provides:

> The taking of photographs in the courtroom, during sessions of the court or recesses between sessions, and the broadcasting or televising of court proceedings are calculated to detract from the essential dignity of the proceedings, distract the witness in giving his testimony, degrade the court, and create misconception with respect thereto in the mind of the public and should not be permitted.

Rule 53 of the Federal Rules of Criminal Procedure covers the same ground:

> The taking of photographs in the courtroom during the progress of judicial proceedings or radio broadcasts of judicial proceedings from the courtroom shall not be permitted by the court.

The argument advanced by the television industry for the admission of cameras is that the Constitution provides for a "public trial." The matter of a "public trial" now assumes new proportions.

Television spokesmen argue that the advances of modern science should be used to make judicial proceedings more public, that everyone with a television screen should be able to peer into the courtroom and watch his fellow citizen tried for a crime. This is the way to keep the Constitution a viable document adaptable to the advances in knowledge and the changes of the times. "After all," they argue, "the courts don't belong to lawyers. They belong to the public. We have a right to know what goes on in them. We have a right to inspect the judiciary at work. That's why the Constitution provides for 'public trials.' "

There is only one flaw in this logic. But the flaw is fatal. True, the Sixth Amendment guarantees that there shall be a "public trial." But the guarantee is not for the benefit of the press or other news media. It is not to satisfy the curiosity of the mob. It is for the benefit of the accused. "Public trial" in our system of justice does not mean that every member of the public should be able to watch the proceedings. Rather it means a trial that is open, not closed to outsiders. The "public trial" requirement of the Constitution prohibits criminal trials *in camera,* the legal term for trials from which the public is barred. It means that citizens other than court officials and participants may attend. But it is not for educational or entertainment purposes that our courts are open to the public. They are open to prevent secret trials, or Star Chamber proceedings, where outrageous abuses of the judicial process might take place without detection. They are open because of our natural aversion, as a freedom-loving nation, to any proceedings held in secret—especially judicial proceedings.

Another argument is that we discriminate against two of the three media of communication—we let the press in, but not radio and television. The answer is that radio and television correspondents have exactly the same rights as the newspaper writer. Just as the reporter for the press may come to court, observe the proceedings and record his observations in the press that evening, so too may the radio or television reporter come to court, observe the proceedings and record his observations over radio or television the same evening. The newspaper may not send its camera into the federal courtroom or into most state courtrooms any more than the other media.

These restrictions are not archaic rules or legal fetishes. Trial lawyers and trial judges know that the search for truth is tortuous and difficult enough without putting it on stage. Television turns all the participants into actors. If they are unwilling actors, their essential dignity as human beings is offended, and this will affect their conduct. If they are willing actors, there is grave danger that the litigant, whose life, property or liberty is in jeopardy, may be adversely affected by participants who are more concerned with the effectiveness of their histrionics than with the compliance they owe to their oaths. And this goes for all participants—lawyers, judges, witnesses, litigants and jurors.

In almost every trial the evidence comes largely from the mouths of living witnesses. In each case the powers of observation, recollection and expression of the witness must be weighed. A shortcoming in one of these powers may well make an honest witness a purveyor of false information. In addition to those factors, the truthfulness and veracity of the witness come into play. Even if he intends to be honest, his predilection, his bias, his prejudice, his sympathy may shade his testimony. All of these factors must be carefully weighed and evaluated by each of the jurors. The facts must be developed by the lawyers, and the judge must be ever alert to keep the inquiry in proper channels. If the participants are called upon to perform their functions before microphones, klieg lights and cameras, knowing that perhaps millions of people are listening and watching, the temptation to act a little will be overpowering to some. Others will freeze. But the main thing is that the search for truth is not made easier. It is made more difficult, and this alone is sufficient reason for the ban.

I have appeared before many congressional committees, representing witnesses who have been summoned to testify. Some of the hearings have been televised and some have not. The difference has been marked. I dare say that if a grant were made to study the subject, it could be demonstrated convincingly that ten times more useless, irrelevant, repetitive and inane questions are propounded in the televised hearings than in those not televised. Everybody must get on camera. The important thing is to be seen and heard, not to further the legislative purpose of the inquiry.

Television converted the Army-McCarthy hearing into a nightmare. Each member of the committee was allotted ten minutes of questioning of each witness in rotation for so long as the witness remained on the stand. The fine, experienced trial lawyer Joseph Welch operated under the same rule. Any trial lawyer knows that no effective examination can be conducted in ten-minute sessions, each followed by an hour's wait before the thread of questioning can be picked up again. Yet no member of the committee ever yielded to Welch. Each wanted and took as many ten-minute sessions in the sun as he could get. Much of the puerile wrangling and fussing can only be explained by concern for the camera. *Life* magazine, in reporting on the inquiry, was constrained to say: "If the hearings have proved anything to date, it is that courtroom procedure, with its strict rules on conduct and introducing evidence, is a most marvelous human invention."

Witnesses were called before the Kefauver Committee, the McClellan Committee, the McCarthy Committee and the House Un-American Activities Committee when it was known they were going to invoke the Fifth Amendment. Even if it can be argued that the committee had the right to make sure that the privilege was invoked, this still was no justification for continuing the interrogation sometimes for hours while the witness monotonously intoned his refusal to answer. Only the television spectacle benefited.

Other witnesses, such as Frank Costello, testified before the crime investigators for days behind closed doors in executive session. Costello was then called and asked the same questions before television cameras. When he objected to being televised, the carnival spirit reached its apex, for the committee allowed the cameras to focus on his hands nervously fumbling with a cigarette box.

All of this entertained the housewives during the day and the family at night. But it was prostitution of the true function of a legislative committee. And the seduction was accomplished largely by the exploitation of the theatrics of the situation.

Two years ago in Baghdad the government held a televised trial of seventy alleged conspirators charged with plotting the assassination of Premier Karim-el-Kassem. All of the defendants, in chains and handcuffs, were herded into the middle of an arena, where they were tried under floodlights with television cameras working. The trial sessions began at seven o'clock in the evening so that all could watch. A studio audience jammed every available inch of the "courtroom." The spectators hooted, hollered, cheered and booed. The trial lacked the dignity of a prize fight in Madison Square Garden. Each evening the prosecutor, his assistants and the judge all became actors, vying with one another for thespian honors. The tribunal was called "People's Court," but it dispensed mob justice. We had a repetition of this in our own hemisphere in the Castro trials held at the Sports Palace in Cuba. Here, too, television cameras swept the scene and, as in Baghdad, the mob hooted and hollered in derision at those who stood accused.

An inscription over one of the doors of the Department of Justice in Washington says: "The place of justice is a hallowed place." It is also a quiet place. It is a place where the quest for truth is carried on by dedicated men in a dignified manner. It can never be otherwise if we are really to succeed in improving the administration of justice.

CHAPTER XIV

A DEATH FOR A DEATH

EQUALLY as important as the means by which criminal justice is administered are its ends. The whole problem of crime and punishment is ancient. Great progress has been made in this generation, but final solution is still beyond sight. Without question the two points around which the most controversy still turns are the merits of the death penalty and the standards of criminal responsibility. A courtroom episode during a first-degree-murder case poignantly highlighted for me the present posture of society's attitude toward capital punishment.

The prosecutor was interrogating the prospective jurors at the start of the trial. A middle-aged lady, charming and well educated, took her seat in the jury box, and this question was put to her:

"Madam, do you have any conscientious objection to the infliction of the death penalty?"

She hesitated and thought. Finally she answered slowly and deliberately.

"No, not if it isn't too severe."

The courtroom was filled with laughter. This was a spontaneous reaction to an answer she had not intended to be humorous. I have thought often of her response in the past few years. And I have come to wonder if what she said is not a fair reflection of our national thinking on the problem.

Society has moved forward in its concept of punishment. In the Middle Ages there was a grotesque catalogue of tortures, including the Iron Maiden, drawing and quartering, bone crushing, tongue extraction, blinding, nail pulling, burning at the stake, crushing by increasing weights, smearing with honey and spread-eagling over red ants' nests, hanging by the thumbs, flaying and burying alive.

In 1603 Sir Walter Raleigh received this sentence from the court after his conviction for treason:

> That you shall be had from hence to the place whence you came, there to remain until the day of execution. And from thence you shall be drawn upon a hurdle through the open streets to the place of execution, there to be hanged and cut down alive, and your privy members cut off and thrown into the fire before your eyes, and your body shall be opened, your heart and bowels plucked out. Then your head to be stricken off from your body, and your body shall be divided into four quarters, to be disposed of at the King's pleasure. And God have mercy upon your soul.

Less than 150 years ago, over 200 offenses were punishable by death in England, including stealing a lace handkerchief and shooting the king's deer. But in this century we have made many advances in our penological views. Hanging has been all but abolished in the United States. The electric chair and the gas chamber were substituted, because hanging was too "brutal." And now the electric chair is slowly being eliminated—the gas chamber is regarded as more "humane." In short, our sensibilities are not offended by capital punishment "so long as it is not too severe." But the social question concerns the justification for capital punishment itself, not the modernity of the gadget by which it is imposed.

Caryl Chessman's twelve years in "death row" before his execution in 1960 underscored more effectively than any other episode in recent years the inhumanity, the injustice and the inequality of capital punishment. It is inhuman because its deterrent effects are now recognized as a myth. It is unjust because it leaves no remedy for a mistake. It is unequal because it is exacted almost exclusively of the poor and the ignorant. It is, in short, a relic of the barbarous days when our law demanded an eye for an eye.

Criminologists, penologists and sociologists generally agree that there are only two reasons for punishing those who commit crimes: to attempt to rehabilitate them and to deter others from criminal ways. But you can't rehabilitate a dead man, and the record is conclusive that the death penalty does not have greater deterrent effect than life imprisonment.

The District of Columbia for years maintained mandatory capital punishment for first-degree murder. If the jury convicted the defendant of murder in the first degree, the judge was left with no discretion. The sentence was automatically death in the electric chair. In this respect the District has been unique. If, as some law-enforcement officers and criminologists argue, capital punishment acts as a deterrent to atrocious crimes, one might suppose that Washington would have had fewer killings than any other city of comparable size. The record is to the contrary. The criminal-homicide rate in the nation's capital has been as high or higher than in all other American cities of comparable size. In fact, a strong movement to get Congress to change this statute succeeded only this year, and the imposition of the death penalty is now within the discretion of the jury.

Eight states have now abolished capital punishment completely. The latest FBI crime statistics show that most of these states have a lower homicide rate than neighboring states which retain the death penalty. The comparison with neighboring states is significant because similar socio-economic and political factors are presumably at work. Furthermore, homicide rates in the eight states which have abolished the death penalty are lower than the national average. Historians tell us that when England made picking pockets a capital crime, the greatest incidence of pocket picking occurred at the hangings of convicted pickpockets.

All of these statistics may be inconclusive in themselves, but they are in accord with the views of judges, penologists and psychiatrists who have firsthand knowledge in this field. Murder is the offense most often punished by execution. Almost always it is a crime of passion and impulse. If the killer weighs the consequences of his act at all before he kills, he weighs them upon scales distorted by dark and twisted emotions. As Arthur Koestler has put it in his remarkable book *Reflections on Hanging,* "a normal person in a normal state of mind just doesn't commit murder." Penologists have searched in vain for half a century to find a single case of a convicted murderer who weighed and deliberated the consequences of his deed in terms of death or imprisonment for himself before killing.

Moreover, the deterrent effect of any sanction depends in large measure upon its swiftness and sureness rather than upon its severity. Whatever capital punishment may be, it is neither swift nor sure. Caryl Chessman's case is extreme but not unique. On March 12, 1953, Willie Lee Stewart killed an elderly grocer during a hold-up in the District of Columbia. To date, he has been tried four times and three juries have convicted him of first-degree murder. Each time his conviction has been reversed by a higher court. The first two were overturned by the United States Court of Appeals for the District of Columbia Circuit and the last conviction was reversed by the Supreme Court in a 5-to-4 decision.

In announcing his dissenting opinion Mr. Justice Frankfurter gave an extemporaneous summary of it, in the course of which he accused the Supreme Court majority of "plucking out" of the lengthy trial record an isolated episode to justify a reversal of the lower court. He suggested that judges are apt to find "what the mind is looking for," and warned against "turning a criminal appeal into a quest for error." But it is inevitable that where the punishment is death, appeals courts will always scrutinize the record with meticulous care. Delays in the imposition of sentence will be granted with great liberality whenever the ingenuity of defense counsel produces a new point for consideration. The National Prison Statistics put out by the Federal Bureau of Prisons show that the elapsed period of time between sentence of death and execution runs in many cases four years or longer.

Even the Department of Justice finally advocated the abolition of mandatory capital punishment in the District of Columbia because it recognized that in such cases juries were reluctant to convict and the appeals courts reluctant to affirm conviction. From 1953 to 1960, 104 defendants were indicted for first-degree murder in Washington. At the end of 1960 only one had been electrocuted. These statistics were fairly representative of the country as a whole. In 1958 only 49 prisoners were executed under civil authority in the United States, a record low. In 1959 the number was the same. In 1960 there were 57 executions. The record shows that not one in a hundred homicides ends in an execution. Punishment so unswift and unsure can never be an effective deterrent.

Certainly the death penalty is not necessary to protect society. It is almost unheard of for a convicted killer to kill again after release from prison. Parole authorities do not release such prisoners unless convinced that they are no longer dangerous to society. In any event, the risk of recidivism is outweighed by the risk of executing innocent men.

Unfortunately, the execution of the innocent is not a myth. Eyewitnesses make honest mistakes in identification. Circumstantial evidence can point to the wrong man. Perjury can sometimes survive even penetrating cross-examination. Error, fortuity of circumstances and outright perjury have caused the processes of justice to miscarry many times.

The late Alfred E. Smith, when he was governor of New York, played a providential role in preventing the electrocution of an innocent man in Sing Sing Prison. On August 12, 1925, a paymaster in Buffalo, New York, was robbed and killed by a bandit who was wearing dark glasses. Edward Larkman was arrested and charged with the crime. When he was brought to headquarters he was forced to stand alone under a bright light while wearing a pair of dark glasses. It was in this manner that he was identified by the sole eyewitness to the crime. At no time was a line-up used for identification purposes. But the eyewitness, who saw the bandit for a total of five seconds at the scene of the crime, repeated her identification under oath at trial.

Larkman vigorously denied his guilt, but the jury convicted him after deliberating forty-three hours. He was sentenced to die in the electric chair, and his conviction was affirmed by the highest court in New York. Just before he was to be electrocuted, however, Governor Smith commuted his sentence to life imprisonment. In commuting the sentence Governor Smith said that should a later disclosure prove him innocent, "the State would be helpless if [he] were dead."

Two years later a Buffalo gangster named Anthony Kolkiewicz confessed to the crime. Larkman applied for a pardon and Governor Franklin D. Roosevelt directed that a full investigation be conducted. Ultimately Larkman was unconditionally pardoned. He had served years in prison and almost paid with his life for a crime to which another man confessed.

In the last decade and a half, two men have been executed in England for crimes which they did not commit. In 1949 Mrs. Beryl Evans and her baby daughter were murdered in their squalid flat in London. Timothy Evans, the husband and father of the victims, was charged with the crimes and tried in the Old Bailey. The Crown elected to try him first for the murder of the child, although the evidence was the same for both murders. Much of the testimony offered in court was designed to show that he had killed his wife by strangulation. Evans, who was an illiterate lorry driver, not only vigorously denied his guilt but accused John Christie, the chief witness for the Crown, of the murders. But the jury believed Christie and disbelieved Evans, who was found guilty and on March 9, 1950, hanged while still protesting his innocence.

Three years later Christie was arrested and accused of murdering his own wife. When the police searched his flat and outbuildings they found the bodies of six women. Christie confessed to having strangled all of them. He also confessed to the murder of Beryl Evans. It was conceded by the British Home Secretary in the House of Commons in 1955 that Timothy Evans had been hanged as a consequence of a miscarriage of justice.

The other English case is even more moving, largely because of the eloquent and prophetic words of the condemned man. A prostitute named Olive Balchin was killed with a hammer on a bombed site in Manchester on October 19, 1946, and Walter Graham Rowland was arrested and charged with the murder. Rowland was well known to the police. He had a bad criminal record, admittedly had been sexually intimate with the victim, and had contracted syphilis from her. He had been seen by several witnesses in her company shortly before she was killed.

Rowland was convicted and sentenced to die. At the time of sentencing he was asked the usual question as to whether he had anything to say about why the sentence of death should not be imposed according to law. He answered:

> Yes, I have, my Lord. I have never been a religious man, but as I have sat in this court during these last few hours the teachings of my boyhood have come back to me, and I say in all sincerity and before you and this court that when I stand in the Court of Courts before the Judge of Judges I shall be acquitted of this crime. Somewhere there is a person who knows that I stand here today an innocent man. The killing of this woman was a terrible crime, but there is a worse crime being committed now, my Lord, because someone with the knowledge of this crime is seeing me sentenced today for a crime which I did not commit. I have a firm belief that one day it will be proved in God's own time that I am totally innocent of this charge, and the day will come when this case will be quoted in the courts of this country to show what can happen to a man in a case of mistaken identity. I am going to face what lies before me with the fortitude and calm that only a clear conscience can give. That is all I have got to say, my Lord.

After exhausting his appellate rights Rowland, like Evans, was hanged while still protesting his innocence. Four years later David John Ware walked into a station house in Bristol and told the police he had killed a woman: "I don't know what is the matter with me. I keep on having an urge to hit women on the head." He was found guilty of the attempted murder of a prostitute by battering her with a hammer on the head and face, the exact way that Olive Balchin had died. Ware then confessed to the crime for which Rowland had been convicted. He wrote out a statement describing in detail the murder of Olive Balchin. Everything he said jibed in every detail with the established facts surrounding her death. He is now in Broadmoor, an institution for the criminally insane. And Walter Rowland's case, as he prophesied, is being "quoted in the courts . . . to show what can happen to a man in a case of mistaken identity."

Edwin M. Borchard, in his book *Convicting the Innocent,* quotes a veteran district attorney as saying: "Innocent men are never convicted. Don't worry about it. It never happens in the world. It is a physical impossibility." This would be a most comforting thought if true. But it does happen, and recently it happened with near tragic consequences not far from where that district attorney expressed his total confidence in the infallibility of the judicial system.

Jackson County, Georgia, was the scene. The little country town of Jefferson, located in the Georgia Piedmont, had its biggest trial in 1956, when James Fulton Foster was tried for murder. The indictment charged him with killing Charles Drake, a prominent Jefferson storekeeper, during a robbery on June 19, 1956.

Never in the history of Jackson County had there been such a crowd at a trial. There was no standing room left. Even the balcony was completely filled. The spectators brought their lunch so as not to lose their seats during midday recess. Vendors sold lemonade and sandwiches outside the courthouse and peanuts in the courtroom itself. An evangelist spoke on the courthouse steps. It was a real country carnival.

Inside the courtroom Mrs. Drake, the widow and sole eyewitness, testified in response to the district attorney's questions:

"Is that the man that was in your house?"

"That's the man."

"Is he the man that shot your husband?"

"He is the man that shot my husband."

Foster denied his guilt. He produced alibi witnesses who testified he was on a spree the night of the murder, drinking and carousing with a friend and two women not their wives. Despite his lack of education and limited intelligence, Foster made a stirring plea for his life:

> I hope to God you fellows will believe me—I hope you will. I ain't give up yet, I ain't give up. I know a Man that can do greater things than I can do, or anybody else, and I'm still trusting Him. I know I'm going to git out of this thing, just about know it. . . .
>
> I wish to say this to everybody—that I could have a word of prayer, if it would be pleasing to everybody.
>
> Dear God, as I put my head in their life, God, and approach Thy throne of grace, I want to thank thee, God, for standing by me and giving me the courage, God, to go on through this terrible strain. Heavenly Father, we want to thank Thee, God, for our beautiful day outside, the beautiful sunshine. Heavenly Father, bless each and every one that's in this courthouse today. . . . Father, bless my mother and father, wherever they may be. Bless my children, God, that they may grow up to be fine young men and women, future people of this world. Heavenly Father, we would ask Thee now to be with us all through the remainder

> of this day. If it be Thy will, Father, grant, dear God, that we can all meet in the same place in that home which Thou hast prepared for us. These things we ask in Thy name. Amen. That's all I have to say.

But the jury believed the widow Drake as against Foster and his misbehaving companions. A verdict of guilty was returned. Foster clenched his fists and pleaded, "I didn't do it, I didn't do it." He was sentenced to die in the electric chair. The Georgia Supreme Court affirmed the conviction and the Supreme Court of the United States refused to review it. Everything had failed.

There were still people who had faith in Foster, however, and they kept working. Early in 1957 an ex-convict gave a lead to the South Carolina Law Enforcement Division, headed by J. Preston Strom. He excited Strom's interest in the case by telling him of jailhouse information he had picked up that Foster was innocent. More information came to Strom as he continued his investigation. He learned through the criminal grapevine that one Charles (Rocky) Rothschild had killed Drake and had driven a car belonging to a William Patterson of Greenville, South Carolina.

Patterson gave Strom a statement. He said that Rothschild had borrowed his car on June 19, 1956, and had brought it back that night, saying he had tried to rob a storekeeper and had killed him. Confronted with Patterson's statement, Rothschild confessed. He re-enacted the crime completely and accurately. He was indicted for murder and he pleaded guilty. He is now serving a life sentence, and Foster is free.

Foster almost went to the electric chair on the testimony of a single eyewitness who thought she was testifying truthfully. Now she doesn't know. She is deeply pained by the whole matter. She says, "I thought I was right. Now I just don't know. I certainly don't want to see anyone suffer for anything he didn't do, but I was completely honest. It's a terrible thing to see your husband killed before your eyes and almost be killed yourself."

When Judge Curtis Bok said that the convictions of the innocent still outnumber the acquittals of the guilty he was speaking from long experience on the trial bench. There are several fascinating and fully documented compilations of cases in which defendants were convicted of crimes committed by other men or even of crimes never committed at all. Capital punishment is indefensible if only because it renders irreversible these miscarriages of justice.

The death penalty is also indefensible today because it has become so discriminatory. Lewis E. Lawes served as warden at Sing Sing for many years. He took the last walk with condemned men many times. He later wrote that all of them were poor and most were friendless as well. It was not without some foundation that Clarence Darrow observed, "only the poor are put to death." In 1958, 1959 and 1960 the majority of the defendants executed in this country were indigent Negroes. A penalty which has been virtually abolished for white men with money ought to be abolished for everybody.

Everyone in trouble tries to get the very ablest doctor or lawyer he can afford. It is a fact of life that there are some great trial advocates at the bar who win what appear to be hopeless cases by their eloquence, logic and powers of persuasion. It is a terrifying thought that a poor man may have less chance to save his life because he cannot get the help of the ablest advocate. There are two ways to view this situation. One is to say: "Oh, well, this is just one of the realities of life. It applies to everything. The more money you have, the better the house you can live in, the better the car you drive, the clothes you wear, the food you eat—and the better the doctor and lawyer you can afford."

But there is another answer. We must accept the fact that to the swift goes the race. But in matters of justice we must strive to remove from the course the fatal ditch which the strong may clear in a jump but the weak and the lame cannot. If there is the risk that a man's economic status may affect his ability to defend his life in a court of justice, then capital punishment should go.

Civilized society has made great strides in its concept of crime and punishment. In this decade we must move still further. The gallows, the gas chamber and the electric chair should be relegated to our museums to their appointed places alongside the rack, the thumbscrew, the guillotine and other discarded instruments of primitive injustice.

CHAPTER XV

PUNISHING THE SICK

JACQUES FERRON was charged with the felony of sodomy with a she-ass at Vanvres, France, in 1750. He was haled into court and given a full trial in accordance with the criminal procedures of the times. Witnesses called by the prosecution testified they saw him in the act of coition with the animal. They were vigorously cross-examined by his defense counsel, but remained unshaken in their testimony. Ferron took the stand and swore the accusation was false. His counsel called defense witnesses who either lent support to Ferron's story or testified to Ferron's general good character. After receiving all the testimony the court pronounced Ferron guilty, sentenced him to death by hanging and forfeited all his worldly goods to the state.

With the exception of the punishment meted out, nothing in the trial of Ferron was strange or substantially different from our own procedures. What makes the prosecution noteworthy by our standards is the fact that the animal was tried along with Ferron as a co-conspirator in the crime. This was in accord with the custom of the day. If adjudicated guilty, the animal faced execution by hanging or burning in the public market place. All of the requirements of due process were observed. Defense counsel was appointed and he was permitted to cross-examine the prosecution's witnesses and offer evidence in defense. The theory of defense for the animal was that she had not been a willing participant in the crime, that Ferron had exercised powers of coercion. Witnesses were called to testify. The prior of the convent and some of the leading citizens of Vanvres testified that they had known the she-ass for several years and that she had always shown herself to be virtuous and well behaved at home and abroad. They jointly signed an affidavit that she had never given occasion of scandal to anyone, and that she was "in word and deed and in all her habits of life a most honest creature." The document was executed at Vanvres on September 19, 1750, and signed by Pinteul Prieur Curé and other community leaders. As a piece of exculpatory evidence it must be regarded as unique in the history of modern criminal law. The testimony and the affidavit were persuasive with the court, and after deliberation, a verdict of not guilty was pronounced on the animal. The court found that she had not participated in the crime of her own free will and had been the victim of Ferron.

The trial of Ferron and his co-conspirator is one of the many recorded cases in which an animal was made a defendant in a criminal prosecution. The history of the Middle Ages is replete with accounts of such trials. Animals charged with killing human beings were tried for murder exactly as human beings were. After a full trial in which all of the amenities of due process were observed, the court would make its finding. If guilty, the animal was executed by hanging, burning or being buried alive. E. P. Evans, in his remarkable treatise on *The Criminal Prosecution and Capital Punishment of Animals,* tells of over 200 animal prosecutions from 824 through the early nineteenth century. Horses, bulls, pigs, oxen, goats, dogs, cows, sheep were defendants in such cases.

We find the stories of these trials either shocking or incredible, or both. The concept of putting a dumb animal on trial, adjudicating it guilty of a felony and sentencing it to death makes us recoil. We find execution of an animal after trial more macabre and revolting than the execution of a human. It's not because our standard of values *vis-à-vis* humans and animals is distorted. Rather it's because we reject the idea of punishment for the morally irresponsible. We have recognized the necessity for differentiating in our treatment of the rational and irrational. It is the application of this recognition to rational and irrational humans that has plagued the best minds in the law for the last hundred years.

The late Judge Jerome N. Frank summed up the great dilemma of criminal justice a few years before he died: "Society must be protected against violence and, at the same time, avoid punishing sick men whose violence drives them, beyond their own controls, to brutal deeds. A society that punishes the sick is not wholly civilized. A society that does not restrain the dangerous madman lacks common sense."

But how should society distinguish between those who should be punished for the crimes they have committed and those who should be hospitalized because their crimes are the product of mental illness? The superficial answer is that society should hospitalize those who are insane and punish those who are sane. But that answer merely calls forth the real questions that beset the courts. How does society decide which is which? How does society distinguish, for the purpose of fixing criminal responsibility, between the rational and the irrational, the sane and the insane? What does it do with a man whose mental illness makes him a useless citizen but not a raving maniac?

Down through the years the law has been brushing these questions aside. Men who are mentally ill have been sent to prison, have served their terms and have come back into society, still mentally ill and ready to commit crime again. This has happened because the law has seen fit to send to hospitals only those who are totally deranged, to acquit by reason of insanity only those in whom mental illness has reached its ultimate, destructive form. This is like sending to a hospital only those who have serious cases of typhoid while leaving those with mild cases at home to care for themselves. The mild case, unless properly treated, is a constant threat to society. The milder forms of mental disease, while not making raving maniacs of their victims, can lead them to commit crime time after time. Too often, when a man has committed one crime after another, society has not paused to ask why. Instead, it has sent him to prison again. If it had asked why, it might have found a man who was mentally ill. It's easier not to ask why. It's easier to send to prisons men who should be in hospital wards than it is to face all the problems inherent in squarely confronting mental illness.

For over a hundred years our principal legal test for insanity has been primitive and inept. We have been applying a rule which was archaic at birth—the rule that evolved out of the famous McNaghten case. McNaghten was a madman who labored under the delusion that the Pope, the Jesuits and the head of the Tory Party, Sir Robert Peel, were engaged in a gigantic conspiracy to do him harm. He determined to protect himself and take all means to defend his life. And so he bought a gun and lay in wait for Peel on Downing Street in London. He had never seen a picture of Peel and so could not identify him. By mistake he shot and killed Edward Drummond, Peel's secretary.

Eight doctors testified at his trial—there were no "psychiatrists" at the time. All said McNaghten was suffering from an insane delusion, that he really believed that he was the target of a conspiracy and that Peel, the Pope and the Jesuits were the co-conspirators. Lord Chief Justice Tindal instructed the jury to bring in a verdict of "not guilty by reason of insanity" and McNaghten was sent off to an institution for the insane.

There was a popular outcry at the decision. The crime had attracted much attention and the community wanted a hanging. It wanted vengeance. The House of Lords stepped in. A questionnaire was drawn up and sent to the fifteen High Court judges, in effect asking the judges to formulate definitive rules on the criminal responsibility of persons suffering from insane delusions. The rule enunciated by fourteen of the fifteen judges has come to be known in the law as the McNaghten rule and it has been in effect since 1843. The rule is such that McNaghten himself would not have been adjudicated insane if it could have been made applicable to him. But his case was over and the rule had only future application.

The crucial section of the rule provides that "to establish a defense on the ground of insanity, it must be clearly proved that, at the time of committing the act, the party accused was labouring under such a defect of reason, from disease of the mind, *as not to know the nature and quality of the act he was doing, or, if he did know it, that he did not know he was doing what was wrong.*" Secondly, it provides that if a person has an insane delusion, "he must be considered in the same situation as to responsibility *as if the facts with respect to which the delusion exists were real.*"

Of course, even if McNaghten's delusion had been true in the world of reality, the killing would not have been justified in law. The law does not excuse a homicide because the victim is in a conspiracy to harm the killer. Under the McNaghten rule, a man with a sick mind is held to the same standards as any normal person, save only for the fact that the law, for the purpose of determining his responsibility, treats his delusion as a reality and measures his act in that frame of reference.

The great irony of the McNaghten case was that by the standards of medical science McNaghten was mentally sick. The court which tried him recognized him as mentally ill and as wholly lacking in responsibility for his act. He had no more rationality in the context in which he acted than one of the animals tried in the Middle Ages. Yet there evolved from his case a rule under the application of which he would be held legally sane, for he understood the nature of his act and, even giving reality to his delusion, the homicide was not justifiable in law. The rule was born because society wanted vengeance for the killing of Drummond. When it did not get what it wanted, the agencies of government, responding to the cry, formulated a rule which would ensure social vengeance in the future, even at the price of placing in the prisoner's dock men with no more rationality or responsibility than the she-ass.

For almost a hundred years the McNaghten rule remained the sole test of criminal responsibility in England and in all of the United States except New Hampshire. Gradually some of the states adopted the so-called "irresistible impulse" test as a supplement to the McNaghten rule. This rule recognizes the fact that while a mentally ill person may know the nature of his act and the wrongness of it, he may be irresistibly impelled to do what he knows is wrong, and should be acquitted on the ground of insanity for that reason.

But it has been clear for years that these tests are archaic and that they do not provide answers for one of the most serious problems in the administration of criminal justice today. Not until 1954 did any court in the land really come to terms with the problem and attempt a solution. The case of *Durham* v. *United States* attracted nationwide attention when it was decided by the United States Court of Appeals for the District of Columbia.

Monte Durham belonged to a quiet middle-class family which had neither police entanglements nor any history of mental illness. But at the age of seventeen Durham was discharged from the Navy after a psychiatric board found he had a "profound personality defect which renders him unfit for Naval Service." Two years later, after being arrested for stealing a car, he tried to commit suicide in jail. After a short stay in a mental hospital for observation, he was taken to court, where he pleaded guilty and was placed on probation.

A year later, in 1948, when Durham was twenty, he passed a series of bad checks, violating his probation. As a result, he went to jail to serve out his sentence. While he was in jail this time, his conduct was such that an inquiry into his mental condition was held. He was found to be of unsound mind, and was committed to a mental hospital. There he was treated for fifteen months before he was deemed well enough to return to prison to serve out the last year of his term.

In June, 1950, he was released from jail on parole and promptly broke the terms of his parole by passing more bad checks. He was never tried on those charges because he was again found to be of unsound mind and was returned to a mental hospital. After another nine months in the hospital he was released again in May, 1951, but in less than two months he was arrested a third time—this time for housebreaking.

When Durham's case came on for trial that October, he was found to be mentally incompetent to stand trial. That meant that he did not understand the charges against him and was unable to help prepare his own defense. Back to the hospital he went, where he received subshock insulin treatments for sixteen months until early in 1953 he had recovered sufficiently to stand trial for the 1951 housebreaking. At the trial Durham's attorney argued that he should be acquitted by reason of insanity, but the defense was rejected. Durham was convicted and sentenced to prison.

At this point the Court of Appeals stepped in. It was clear that Durham was mentally ill and that three stays in a mental hospital had not cured him. But it was also clear that a prison term would do even less toward making him a fit citizen of the community. Yet because Durham's mind was not so deranged that he was unable to tell the difference between right and wrong and because he had not broken into that house moved by an impulse he could not resist, the criminal law could do nothing but convict him and send him to prison.

Durham's case squarely posed the problem of the basic aims of the criminal law. Most criminologists, sociologists, judges and lawyers regard rehabilitation and deterrence as the true objectives of criminal justice. The ideal is to rehabilitate the offender for a useful life in society and deter him and others, by his example, from similar conduct. There are those who talk of the protection of society as the real goal of the criminal process. This has always seemed to me to be another way of expressing the deterrence theory with simply a shift in emphasis. Finally, there are those who regard the whole concept of criminal justice as an instrument of social vengeance. They never articulate their beliefs this boldly, but when stripped to the essence, this is the hard core of their convictions.

Prison authorities attempt rehabilitation of the inmates by providing programs of vocational education. By and large these programs have not succeeded in turning the men's thoughts away from crime. The record shows that about two thirds of all the men who are released after serving one term come back to serve a second. Most business establishments will not employ an ex-convict. Even the prisoner who has been "rehabilitated" will find it most difficult to make an honest living. The result all too often is that he returns to crime. Monte Durham had been in prison before—twice before, in fact. Neither term "rehabilitated" him. Most prison and parole personnel would have said the chances of "rehabilitating" him were negligible.

The basic theory of deterrence is that the fear of punishment acts as a brake on the impulse to crime. This theory did not seem to have much validity when applied to Durham. Punishment did not deter him. After two prison terms he had committed a third crime. There was little or no reason to believe that a third term would prevent a fourth crime. His prospects for an honest livelihood diminished with each offense. Most penal authorities would say another term could have little effect on him. He had become an "incorrigible." Would a term of imprisonment have stopped others from breaking into houses? I have grave doubts that it would have prevented housebreakings by men with a mental illness comparable to Durham's.

What of society's need for protection from Monte Durham? It is protected while he is in prison. But when he is released the protection ceases, unless he has been rehabilitated. If he is mentally ill when he goes into prison and receives no therapy, the chances for his recovery at the expiration of a fixed term are *de minimis*. Society has two choices if it wants to feel secure from Durham. Confine him for life, or confine him, treat him for his illness and release him when he is no longer a menace to the social need for a feeling of security.

What of those who would hold that society needs revenge on Durham? *Lex talionis* is the oldest kind of law—

the law of exact retribution in man's dealing with his fellows, the iron rule of doing unto others what they have done unto you. A "life for a life, eye for eye, tooth for tooth, hand for hand, foot for foot, burning for burning, wound for wound, stripe for stripe" was the philosophy of criminal revenge. In its modern garb this philosophy of criminal justice calls for punishment for its own sake. But even the advocates of this theory do not want the sick, the dumb and the irrational punished. They, too, recoil from the concept of trying and punishing animals because where there is no reason, no responsibility, no culpability, there is no place for revenge.

When Monte Durham is placed in the context of the purposes of criminal law and punishment, the problem stands out in bold relief. By the testimony of all, he was mentally ill. Prison terms had neither "rehabilitated" nor deterred him from his way of crime. So long as he was certain to be released at the expiration of a prison term during which he received no treatment, society had no protection. And no one was calling for social revenge against this obviously sick man.

Society found itself with no adequate way of handling Durham when he came to trial because of its reluctance to move forward from the McNaghten test. By this rule and the "irresistible impulse" test he was legally sane, and he was accordingly convicted in the trial court. But his conviction was overturned by the Court of Appeals. In a brilliant opinion written by Judge David L. Bazelon, the court formulated a new test for a jury to use in deciding whether a man is to be acquitted of a crime by reason of insanity. It is, simply: was the crime the product of a mental disease or defect? If it was, the man must be acquitted and sent to a mental hospital. If it was not, he should be convicted and sent to prison.

What this test is designed to do is to allow a jury to be told all the facts known to science as to how a man's mind works. Given all those facts, the jury is then to decide whether society should hold that man responsible for the crime he has committed. Under the McNaghten test, the jury could consider only one basic fact: did the man know that what he did was wrong? Under this new test it can consider all the rest of the things which might be wrong with his mind.

A year after the Durham decision my office handled the case of an eighteen-year-old boy charged with raping a sixty-year-old woman. He had allegedly committed the offense in Maryland, about twenty yards across the line that divides that state from the District of Columbia. He had been a model high-school student and had had no brushes with the law before this time. Eight weeks before his arrest he had married his high-school sweetheart and had been immediately drafted into military service. His adjustment to military life was poor. He had never been away from home before and was filled with homesickness and depression when he was sent to his first post. In a few short weeks he turned from an outgoing, extroverted, happy youth to a lonely, silent recluse.

After his arrest he was examined by two of the outstanding psychiatrists in the area, men known for their complete objectivity and outstanding ability. Each independently found the boy to be so mentally sick that he needed therapy immediately. Each said he was psychotic, but neither could honestly say after hours of examination that he did not understand the nature of the act he had committed or that he did not know it was wrong. This was the sole test of insanity in Maryland, which still clung tenaciously to the old McNaghten rule. Both doctors testified at trial to the boy's psychosis and said he should be in a mental hospital.

But this testimony, under the Maryland concept of insanity, was irrelevant. He was convicted and sentenced to twenty years in prison. Someday he will be released into society without having received any treatment for his illness.

The irony of this case is that twenty yards separated him from help and therapy. I am convinced that both society and the boy would have been better off if he had been acquitted by reason of insanity and sent immediately to a mental institution, where he would have been treated and cured before he was released. If he could not be cured, he would not be released.

Any attempt to treat these men who are sick and who need help instead of punishing them and putting them out of sight in prisons is met with sneers and bitterness in many circles. Not too long after the Court of Appeals announced its decision in the Durham case, a national news magazine wrote of the court system in the District of Columbia under the headline "Easing Up on Murderers." Part of the thesis of that article was that sending a man to a hospital instead of to a prison is "easing" up on him. Yet the United States Attorney for the District of Columbia regularly gets letters from men who have been sent to St. Elizabeth's Hospital in Washington after being acquitted by reason of insanity. They beg to be tried again. They prefer conviction and prison. In prison they know that one day they will get their release whether or not they are well. In the hospital there is no terminal date in sight; they are released only when and if cured.

Those who urge the abolition of the Durham rule on the ground that it's too "soft" and ignores the "rights of the victims" are merely advocating a sophisticated form of the vengeance theory of criminal law. I have never understood how punishing the criminal really helps the victim. The victim of a murder is not helped by the punishment or treatment which society gives the killer. Neither is his family helped, unless the punishment satisfies a desire for vengeance. Only society at large and the perpetrator of the crime can be helped or hurt by the disposition the court makes of the case. The man can be rehabilitated or he cannot. Others may be deterred from committing crimes or they may not. Society may be protected against the man's future crimes or it may not. Those are the issues, and talk about being "soft on criminals" is mere prattling.

There are other reasons, of course, why the law has been so slow to adapt itself to advances in psychiatry and to accept the ideas expressed by the court in the Durham case. We lawyers traditionally have been bastions of the *status quo*. We seem to have a basic distaste for moving the law forward into new areas. Every time the law starts up a new path lawyers must learn new theories and new ways. This my profession has been slow to do. Then, too, there is among lawyers a basic lack of faith in psychiatrists and in the treatment of mental illness. A poll taken a few years ago among 4,000 persons, mostly professional people, showed that only in the legal profession was there a relatively great distrust of psychiatry. More than 40 per cent of all the lawyers polled did not think it worth while to call in a psychiatrist for one whose behavior had become irrational. More than two thirds of the lawyers favored keeping mental illness secret, as if it were a badge of disgrace. As long as we retain this nineteenth-century approach to the problem, few strides can be made in our understanding of criminal responsibility and little progress will be made in the administration of criminal justice. Perhaps this distrust comes from the fact that we expect absolute answers to scientific questions. Psychiatry is unable to state many absolutes about man's mind. But the law, if it is to stay vital and adaptable, must make use of all the knowledge it can get on the subject—not ignore the problem on the ground that it is too difficult of solution.

Another reason for the law's lag behind scientific psychiatric advances is society's nagging fear that any departure from the old right-wrong test augurs a rejection of the theological concept of free will. This danger is consistently cited by those who fear that psychiatrists and criminologists are moving toward a concept of determinism. Such an objection has been raised to the Durham rule and to other proposed changes in the rules on criminal responsibility. It is a legal bogey man that has no foundation in reality. So long as we have a system of criminal justice it will have as its ultimate predicate the acceptance of man's free will. There is nothing in the Durham rule or similar proposals that is in any respect contrary to this premise. The Durham rule is limited in application to sick minds. It does no more than bring the law into closer proximity to the present state of scientific knowledge of mental pathology. It affects in no way the concept of the legal responsibility of normal healthy minds for the consequences of their free acts.

It has always been recognized in law that in every criminal act there is a mental as well as a physical aspect. There must be a criminal intent, or *mens rea,* as it is called in the law. Where the mind is too ill to form a criminal intent, or where the intent is distorted by mental disease, there is no crime because there is no *mens rea.* The mental aspect of the crime is equally as important as the physical. But too often too little heed is paid to the psychic facet of a criminal case as the evidence is developed at trial. A case I handled on appeal a few years ago illustrates effectively the paucity of information that the average jury gets on the mental processes of a defendant even when the defense is insanity. This was the case of Charles W. Douglas, a young man who was arrested and charged in September, 1952, with two robberies.

Within a few weeks after Douglas was arrested, he was sent to a mental hospital for psychiatric examinations. After the doctors examined and studied him for weeks he was taken back to court. On December 19, 1952, the court ruled that he was unable to stand trial because he was of unsound mind. Almost two years later, after extensive hospital treatment, Douglas was found to be mentally competent and was brought to trial. His only defense was that he had been "insane" when he committed the crimes. His sister testified that he had tried to kill himself three times within six months prior to the robberies. In desperation, she had written to the Veterans Administration in an effort to get him committed to a mental hospital, but nothing had been done. The two psychiatrists who had examined Douglas just after he was arrested testified that they thought he was ill when the crimes occurred, and that the crimes were the product of his mental illness. A third psychiatrist testified that he had not seen Douglas until almost a year after the crimes. He said that Douglas' mental illness was serious at that time, but he could not say whether Douglas had been ill a year before. The two policemen who arrested Douglas said he had acted normally when they picked him up and that he looked "sane" to them.

On this evidence the jury found Douglas sane and guilty beyond a reasonable doubt. He was sentenced to from two to seven years in prison. When he appealed the conviction, the Court of Appeals appointed me to represent him because he was indigent. Ultimately the court reversed his conviction, pointing out that if Douglas was to be convicted, the government had to prove beyond a reasonable doubt either that he was not mentally ill when the crimes occurred or that the crimes had no connection with his illness. There was really no evidence in the record from which sanity at the time of the offenses could have been found beyond a reasonable doubt. The prosecution had offered no expert testimony. Two psychiatrists had said that he was insane at the time and one could not decide. These men were all in the employ of the government. Three months after the offense he had been found of unsound mind by the court to the point of being unable even to understand the proceedings against him. His sister had testified to a pattern of irrational behavior antedating the robberies by six months. The sole testimony to the contrary was the observation of the policemen that he acted "normal" at the time of the arrest. Anyone who has ever worked with mentally ill people knows that the most seriously ill act normally upon occasion.

What had happened in Douglas' trial, however, is what happens in too many cases where the only real issue is the mental responsibility of the defendant. Hours were spent eliciting all of the minute physical facts of the case—the color of the defendant's hair, the color of his skin, his height, his weight, the kind of clothes he wore, the way he walked. All of the physical facts concerning the defendant, the surroundings and the robberies themselves were described with concern for minuscule detail. But the jury was told almost nothing of the psychic aspect of the case. The following is the full transcript of the testimony of one of the psychiatrists who was called. The testimony of the others was neither longer nor more detailed:

Q. Doctor, did there come a time when you examined Mr. Charles Douglas?

A. Yes. At the request of His Honor, Judge Laws, I examined Mr. Douglas back in 1952.

Q. Will you give us the place that you examined him?

A. The D.C. jail.

Q. And how many times did you examine him?

A. On two occasions.

Q. And as a result of your examination did you reach a conclusion concerning his mental condition?

A. Yes, I reached a conclusion on the very first examination, December the 7th, 1952, that Mr. Charles W. Douglas was then of unsound mind suffering definitely from a psychosis, that he had definite psychotic symptoms.

Q. And was he suffering from a type of psychosis?

A. Yes, schizophrenia or dementia praecox.

Q. Will you give us some of the symptoms?

A. The symptoms consisted of the presence of delusions, hallucinations, auditory delusions, delusions of persecution, delusions of reference. Also he was confused at that time, and cloudy, depressed, at times appeared to be in a sort of stupor, expressed ideas that he wanted to kill himself, and so on.

Q. Doctor, from your examination can you tell us whether or not that particular type of psychosis is one which would come on a person suddenly or one which develops over a period of time?

A. I believe gradually.

Q. You state, Doctor, that this type of psychosis would have developed over a period of time. Can you state how long a period of time, if you can, give us any estimate whatsoever, over how long a period of time it would take to reach this stage?

A. That cannot be definitely established.

Q. Although it cannot be definitely established, can you give us any idea or any estimate whatsoever?

Would you say that it takes months or a year or a week?

A. I believe that, as far as I can ascertain by reviewing the case, that had been going on for some time, quite a number of months, I thought.

Q. You examined him in December?

A. Yes.

Q. You'd say it went back as far as September?

A. That is right.

The testimony consumed all of five minutes. A jury that must pass on the sanity of a defendant must be told more about his mental condition than that. The jury's job was to decide if Douglas' condition was such that society should not hold him responsible for what he did. Yet, all it was told of his condition was that the doctors thought he was sick, and that the sickness had produced the crime. This is like having a detective testify that he thinks a man committed a crime and not asking him to explain why he thinks so. The jury cannot properly evaluate the condition without knowing all the facts. But evidence of mental illness is seldom spread before a jury as graphically and in as great detail as is the evidence of the crime. Thus, the impact made by the facts of a crime is so great that the jury loses sight of the mental condition of the defendant. When this impact is joined with the attitude of many prosecutors and some judges that almost no one should be acquitted by reason of insanity, that psychiatrists are not to be trusted and that insanity defenses are to be regarded with great skepticism, it is no wonder that there are many miscarriages of justice.

I am often reminded of what Judge Curtis Bok once wrote: "The penology of the future is treatment, not to fit the crime but to fit the prisoner. Someday we will look back upon our criminal and penal process with the same horrified wonder as we now look back upon the Spanish Inquisition."

If we are ever to reach the stage where all men who are sick can be treated and not punished, we must begin to face the problems presented by mental illness and crime. We must realize that society is at its best when it helps a man who has committed crime to understand himself and to stop committing crimes. We must not be afraid to change what is outmoded and what is no longer satisfactory. Even if this means revising many of our ideas and admitting that we do not know all the answers, we must be willing to accept the philosophy that Judge Frank outlined: "A society that punishes the sick is not wholly civilized. A society that does not restrain the dangerous madman lacks common sense."

CHAPTER XVI

"NEITHER SNOW NOR RAIN NOR HEAT . . ."

CENSORSHIP has long been a fighting word. Everybody is against it by name, but too many people are indifferent to it in practice. The problem is that, as with so many other unconstitutional practices, its victims often have no friends. Only occasionally is there a case in which public opinion condemns the censor.

Several years ago I was asked to take a case which squarely raised the whole problem of federal censorship exercised through the Post Office Department. The victim was *Confidential,* an exposé-type magazine which came out bi-monthly and claimed a larger newsstand circulation than any other magazine in the United States. It began publication in September, 1952, and by September, 1955, was selling 4,000,000 copies of each issue. It specialized in exposing skeletons in the closets of celebrities, with emphasis on Hollywood celebrities. Despite its many readers, it had few friends.

In August, 1955, disaster struck the publisher. The magazine was printed by the Kable Printing Company in Mount Morris, Illinois. The Mount Morris postmaster sent the following letter to the head of the Kable Printing Company:

Dear Sir:

We have been instructed by the solicitor not to dispatch any copies of *Confidential* until sample copies have been submitted to that office for examination and advice as to their mailability.

Very truly yours,
V. F. SHAVER
Postmaster

Shaver had written this letter pursuant to instructions from Washington. The Solicitor of the Post Office Department in issuing the order announced that his office had received complaints from members of the public. Since it was impossible to distribute 4,000,000 copies of the magazine without using the mails, the Solicitor's instructions were a death warrant for *Confidential,* and the death warrant was issued without notice, without charges and without a hearing.

As soon as *Confidential*'s editors received the Shaver letter, their general counsel called the Solicitor's office for an explanation. An Assistant Solicitor told them that complaints had been received, but he refused to disclose the identity of the complainants or the nature of the complaints. He further stated that neither he nor anyone else in his office had seen a copy of the forthcoming issue of *Confidential* before issuing the "withhold from dispatch" order to the Mount Morris postmaster. Finally, he said that he would be glad to look the magazine over as soon as a copy reached him and to advise *Confidential*'s counsel whether there was anything "improper" about it.

Several days later *Confidential* was advised that the "withhold from dispatch" order was being suspended as to its forthcoming issue, solely because the bulk of this issue had already gone through the mails. It was further advised, however, that the order would be effective as to all future issues. In other words, no issue of *Confidential* could be deposited in the mail unless and until the Post Office Department had read it and concluded that it contained nothing "improper."

It was at this point that Robert Harrison, the publisher of *Confidential,* and his lawyers came to see me. It seemed to me that the action of the Post Office Department constituted a shocking abridgment of freedom of expression—one that could set a most dangerous precedent. I remembered what Justice Oliver Wendell Holmes had said in *Milwaukee Publishing Co.* v. *Burleson:* "The United States may give up the Post Office when it sees fit, but when it carries it on, the use of the mails is almost as much a part of free speech as the right to use our tongues. . . ."

If the Postmaster General could bar *Confidential* from the mails without notice, without charges and without a hearing he could do the same to any periodical. This took on a more sinister significance to me with the realization that the job of Postmaster General had traditionally gone to the chairman or campaign manager of the victorious political party. I respected Arthur Summerfield, but I didn't think he or anyone else was qualified to be the literary dietitian of America. And so we quickly filed suit against him in the District of Columbia.

The object of our suit was to set aside the "withhold from dispatch" order which was hovering like a specter over *Confidential*'s January, 1956, issue. *Confidential* had already spent $300,000 on this issue. If it did not go through the mails on schedule, moreover, the publisher would become liable to its distributor for crippling damages. Robert Harrison swore in his complaint that he would be forced to discontinue publication if the order remained in effect, and no one contradicted him.

The case came on for hearing before Judge Luther Youngdahl on October 7, 1955. I argued as forcefully as I could that the "withhold from dispatch" order was invalid because it had been issued without giving the publisher a chance to be heard and without any specification of charges. I argued, further, that requiring a publisher to submit his publication for approval before distributing it violated the First Amendment guarantees of freedom of the press. Since the advent of the Bill of Rights no court had ever countenanced any order or edict which required the censor's stamp of approval on words before they were spoken, printed or distributed. This was what the courts had characterized as "unconstitutional prior restraint." If Harrison had transgressed the federal obscenity laws by causing *Confidential* to go through the mails, there was a ready remedy available to the appropriate agency of government. I argued that the matter could be presented to a grand jury and he could be indicted, tried, convicted and imprisoned. I challenged the counsel for the government to take the matter forthwith before the grand jury sitting that day in the very building where the argument was being heard. If government counsel really believed the periodical was "obscene" (and this was the only basis for withholding it from the mails) there could be no reason for not laying the matter before the grand jury once the mails had been used. The government never took up this challenge.

Judge Youngdahl promptly struck down the "withhold from dispatch" order as invalid. He did not reach the question of whether the magazine was mailable or not. He ruled that to withhold it from the mails without notice, charges and a hearing constituted a violation of due process of law.

In his order he provided that no issue could be banned from the mails henceforth without notice, charges and a full hearing, and that if the Post Office Department wanted to deny the use of the mails while the hearing was under way, it would have to get a court order specifically authorizing such a denial. He provided, further, that *Confidential* should submit future issues to the Post Office Department for inspection forty-eight hours before mailing.

In the middle of October *Confidential* submitted its January issue for inspection. The Solicitor's office, after reviewing the issue, did two things. It sent a telegram to the Mount Morris postmaster, telling him that he could accept the issue for mailing. It also issued a press release saying that it had cleared the issue for mailing.

To my mind, these two things were either completely meaningless or completely improper. If the Post Office was complying with Judge Youngdahl's order, there was no necessity for the telegram and the ensuing press release. If, on the other hand, the Post Office still considered that it had authority to withhold the magazine from the mails upon the Solicitor's instructions alone, it was in direct violation of Judge Youngdahl's order. We hastily arranged a conference at the Solicitor's office and asked the lawyers handling the case whether they would agree that their acts were meaningless or whether they were still doing what Judge Youngdahl said they could not do. I advised them that I would ask for a contempt citation if they were still committing the forbidden acts. They agreed with me that their telegram was legally meaningless.

Several months later, after inspecting the March, 1956, issue, the department went before another judge and secured a temporary restraining order barring it from the mails. I have never understood why the Solicitor felt that the January issue was mailable and the March issue non-mailable. The lead stories in the January issue bore the following titles, which give a fair idea of their character:

SURGERY'S NEWEST BUST MIRACLE
GARY COOPER'S LOST WEEKEND WITH ANITA EKBERG
THE LOWDOWN ON KIM NOVAK
COACH "RED" SANDERS VS. THE L.A. COPS
WHY RITA HAYWORTH WALKED OUT ON DICK

The cover stories in the March issue bore equally titillating titles:

DON'T BUY THOSE NEW ABORTION PILLS
HEARD THE LATEST ABOUT SAMMY DAVIS, JR.?
WALTER PIDGEON AND THAT WILD PARTY!
EXCLUSIVE: CLARK GABLE'S FIRST WIFE TALKS BACK!
CAUGHT—GUY MADISON IN BARBARA PAYTON'S BOUDOIR!

Unless exclamation points are obscene, there was no real difference between the two sets of titles and stories. If the morals of the American people could weather the January issue—and the Solicitor's office found that they could—it seemed to me that they could weather the March issue. The court, however, was never compelled to resolve this question, because it dissolved the temporary restraining order on the ground that the Post Office should have filed a new suit instead of filing a new motion in the old suit. The Post Office then sought and obtained an amendment to Judge Youngdahl's original order, obviating the necessity for filing a new suit in the future. By this time, however, the March issue was already on the stands. The Post Office never made another attempt to bar *Confidential* from the mails.

The significance of the *Confidential* case was well summarized by Alan Barth, who editorialized in the Washington *Post:*

> It is easy to understand why Mr. Summerfield might dislike *Confidential;* the publication, composed largely of sex and scandal, maintains no very lofty intellectual standards and is not excessively fastidious in its editorial interests. But to bar it, even tentatively, on a mere suspicion that an issue as yet unprinted is going to be obscene seems highhanded in the extreme. This smacks of preventive arrest and protective custody. . . . Pre-censorship invites arbitrariness and encourages just the sort of disregard for due process displayed by Mr. Summerfield in regard to *Confidential.* If any issue of *Confidential* breaches the law, let the magazine be prosecuted in a court for the specific offense. If any issue contains libelous material, let the aggrieved persons take legal action against the magazine; some have already done so. But let Mr. Summerfield confine himself to getting the mail delivered.

Unfortunately, however, the Post Office Department is still barring publications from the mail while it decides whether or not they are mailable. The Supreme Court has never expressed itself squarely as to the propriety of this practice, and the judges of the lower federal courts are in hopeless disagreement. Of course, it is useless to lock the barn after the horse is gone, and a strong argument can be made for temporary denial of mailing privileges pending determination of mailability. On the other hand, the Postmaster General should not have unlimited discretion to bar any publication from the mail. The answer would seem to be a carefully drawn statute allowing temporary denial of mailing privileges upon court order and for a limited time while a hearing to determine mailability is being conducted. The Supreme Court has upheld a New York statute of similar tenor.

From a lawyer's point of view, I have always been sorry that the Post Office made no further effort to bar *Confidential* from the mails. Judge Youngdahl decided that the Post Office Department could not bar a magazine even temporarily from the mails without notice, without charges and without a hearing. He never reached the question of whether the Post Office Department could bar this magazine from the mails after proper procedural safeguards. In other words, he never reached the question of what is mailable or, more specifically, of what is "obscene." This is one of the most interesting and difficult questions to come before the courts in recent years.

Federal law provides that "obscene" pictures and publications cannot be carried through the mails and cannot be imported into the United States. This law was placed on the books shortly after the Civil War through the efforts of one Anthony Comstock. Even Comstock's admirers admit that he was a fanatic. He proceeded to apply "his" law to such works as Walt Whitman's *Leaves of Grass* and George Bernard Shaw's *Mrs. Warren's Profession*. His successors have seized works by Ernest Hemingway, John O'Hara, James Jones, J. D. Salinger, Erskine Caldwell, Alberto Moravia, John Steinbeck, James T. Farrell, Norman Mailer, Somerset Maugham and others equally well known. The Post Office Department's card index of "obscene" works also includes titles by Voltaire, Maupassant, Zola, Tolstoy and Dumas. Unexpurgated editions of Aristophanes and Ovid are included, as are scholarly works by Sigmund Freud, Margaret Mead and Simone de Beauvoir.

The department has also tried to keep Americans from reading sex-instruction manuals. In one very famous case a woman was criminally prosecuted for mailing a sex-instruction pamphlet which she had originally written for her own children. This "obscene" pamphlet was used by over 400 welfare and religious organizations, as well as by the public schools of Bronxville, New York. In another famous case the department tried to bar a pamphlet called *Preparing for Marriage,* which was published by the eminently respectable American Institute of Family Relations.

Were the Post Office Department able to perceive intelligently and clearly that quality of literature or art called "obscenity," there might be some justification for the existence and use of such censorship powers. But the department's record is as bad as any censor's at any time anywhere. This is not meant as harsh criticism of the Post Office officials charged with responsibility in this area. The absurdities into which they have fallen are of the essence of the very function itself when applied to literature and art.

Everyone agrees that the principal problem with any form of censorship is where to stop. Judge Curtis Bok, who believes that a work cannot be banned as "obscene" unless there is a clear and present danger that it will produce criminal conduct, points out:

> Let us not forget that *Don Quixote* was once banned because of the sentence: "Works of charity negligently performed are of no worth"; that within our lifetime an editor deleted the word "chaste" because it was suggestive; that *Tom Sawyer* and *Huckleberry Finn* were once charged with corrupting the morals of children; that *Jane Eyre* was called too immoral to be ranked with decent literature, *The Scarlet Letter* a

brokerage of lust, *Adam Bede* the vile outpourings of a lewd woman's mind; and that Walt Whitman lost his job because of his *Leaves of Grass*.

The obvious remedy for these absurd abuses is a workable definition of the term "obscenity." In 1868 the English courts formulated a definition which was originally accepted in this country as well. This definition made the test of obscenity whether the questioned passages would deprave and corrupt those whose minds are open to such immoral influences. It obviously was a very broad definition, because it permitted an entire book to be condemned because of a few isolated excerpts and because it used the most weak and susceptible members of the public as its test.

Judge Learned Hand penned a famous protest against this test in 1913, expressing doubt that we should "be content to reduce our treatment of sex to the standard of a child's library in the supposed interest of a salacious few." He urged instead that the term "obscenity" should be defined as "the present critical point in the compromise between candor and shame at which the community may have arrived here and now." Judge Hand was still a trial judge, however, and he felt compelled to follow the old test.

The first case really to free the courts from this test involved James Joyce's *Ulysses*. The courts held that the work must be judged as a whole and must be judged by its effect upon the average reader. Judge Woolsey wrote:

> Whether a particular book would tend to excite such impulses and thoughts must be tested by the court's opinion as to its effect on a person with average sex instincts—what the French would call *"l'homme moyen sensuel"*—who plays, in this branch of legal inquiry, the same role of hypothetical reagent as does

> the "reasonable man" in the law of torts and "the man learned in the art" on questions of invention in patent law. The risk involved in the use of such a reagent arises from the inherent tendency of the trier of facts, however fair he may intend to be, to make his reagent too much subservient to his own idiosyncrasies.

This test is obviously far superior to the old English test. It prevents condemnation of serious literature on the basis of excerpts taken out of context, and it abolishes the standard of a child's library. Judge Woolsey gave clear expression, however, to its inherent weakness. He tells us that, in an effort to avoid the influence of his own idiosyncrasies, he checked his view with two friends who had read *Ulysses* and who in his opinion satisfied the requirements for a hypothetical reagent. The spectacle of a federal judge considering the sex instincts of his friends in an effort to find *l'homme moyen sensuel* with whom he could check his decision demonstrates more forcefully than any argument the need for another criterion. It has all the elements of low comedy.

Judge Thurman Arnold has taken occasion to point out graphically the shortcomings of the "lustful-thoughts" test in judging obscenity. The thrust of his argument is that rigid censorship controls and the application of the lustful-thoughts test tend to create attitudes toward sex bordering on fetishism. Back in 1900, when women were required to swim fully clothed, youths were stimulated by the sight of an ankle or a calf. In 1911 a novel called *Three Weeks* became one of the most popular works of the day. The "obscene" passages consisted of passages of asterisks at appropriate place. These asterisks were branded as "obscene" because they were calculated to arouse lustful thoughts.

Sexual stimulation produced by a row of asterisks can hardly be described as a healthy human reaction.

At the beginning of the century the *Police Gazette* was widely regarded as having pornographic appeal. A dance called the cancan in which a row of chorus girls kicked up their black-stockinged legs was regarded as erotic. Today no one with an appetite for pornography would pay a dime to look at either. A censorship code that has as its objective the reduction of the number of lustful thoughts per capita can produce some pretty ludicrous consequences, a pretty unhealthy psychological approach to sex.

Yet, for lack of a better standard, the Supreme Court gave its tacit benediction to the lustful-thoughts standard when the issue came before it in 1957 in the Roth and Alberts cases. Seven of the justices held that there was nothing unconstitutional about an obscenity statute if it were properly applied. Five of the justices indicated that they believed a work was obscene if it had a "substantial tendency to deprave or corrupt its readers by inciting lascivious thoughts or arousing lustful desires"—if, "applying contemporary community standards, the dominant theme of the material taken as a whole appeals to prurient interest." This was substantially the test applied by Judge Woolsey.

Justice Harlan took vigorous exception to this standard of obscenity approved by the majority of the court. Dissenting in the Roth case, he said:

> The petitioner was convicted under a statute which, under the judge's charge, makes it criminal to sell books which "tend to stir sexual impulses and lead to sexually impure thoughts." I cannot agree that any book which tends to stir sexual impulses and lead to

sexually impure thoughts necessarily is "utterly without redeeming social importance." Not only did this charge fail to measure up to the standards which I understand the Court to approve, but as far as I can see, much of the great literature of the world could lead to conviction under such a view of the statute. Moreover, in no event do I think that the limited federal interest in this area can extend to mere "thoughts." The Federal Government has no business, whether under the postal or commerce power, to bar the sale of books because they might lead to any kind of "thoughts."

It is no answer to say, as the Court does, that obscenity is not protected speech. The point is that this statute, as here construed, defines obscenity so widely that it encompasses matters which might very well be protected speech. *I do not think that the federal statute can be constitutionally construed to reach other than what the Government has termed as "hard-core" pornography.* [Emphasis supplied]

Within a year the high court was confronted with three cases in which lower-court judges had meticulously applied the lustful-thoughts test to allegedly obscene material. In *Sunshine Book Company* v. *Summerfield* Judge James Kirkland had carefully examined nudes in a magazine and determined which ones would cause prurient thoughts. He found that some excited lustful thoughts and some didn't. He held that the magazine as a whole was obscene. I think it is fair to say that the language he had to use in describing the pictures was more repellent than the pictures themselves. The same analytic process was engaged in by two other federal judges in their findings that a motion picture and a book were obscene.

The Supreme Court granted review in all three cases and reversed them without opinion. It was as if the court were telling the federal judges throughout the land that they didn't have to write any more of this unedifying judicial literature comparing one nude to another.

It appears that the court has come to the "hard-core" pornography test advocated by Justice Harlan. By writing no opinions in the cases it avoided the task of defining hard-core pornography. It apparently felt that further definition was useless and simply held that the material it saw in each case was not obscene. It left its actions to speak for themselves—a novel but laudatory judicial approach where pornography is concerned.

To comprehend the full scope of the court's action in these cases it is necessary to know something of the materials before the court in each case. In the Sunshine Book case Judge Kirkland had analyzed a book of nudes put out by an organization advocating and explaining nudism. The material in *Times Film Corp.* v. *Chicago* was described by the Court of Appeals for the Seventh Circuit this way:

> The film, as an exhibit in this case, was projected before and viewed by us. We found that, from beginning to end, the thread of the story is supercharged with a current of lewdness generated by a series of illicit sexual intimacies and acts. In the introductory scenes a flying start is made when a 16-year-old boy is shown completely nude on a bathing beach in the presence of a group of younger girls. On that plane the narrative proceeds to reveal the seduction of this boy by a physically attractive woman old enough to be his mother. Under the influence of this experience and an arrangement to repeat it, the boy thereupon engages in sexual relations with a girl of his own age.

> The erotic thread of the story is carried without deviation toward any wholesome idea, through scene after scene. The narrative is graphically pictured with nothing omitted except those sexual consummations which are plainly suggested but meaningfully omitted and thus, by the very fact of omission, emphasized. The words spoken in French are reproduced in printed English on the lower edge of the moving film. None of it palliates the effect of the scenes portrayed.
>
> We do not hesitate to say that the calculated purpose of the producer of this film, and its dominant effect, are substantially to arouse sexual desires.

The material in *One, Inc.* v. *Olesen* was described by the Court of Appeals for the Ninth Circuit as follows:

> It conveys information to the homosexual or any other reader as to where to get more of the material contained in *One*.
>
> An examination of "The Circle" clearly reveals that it contains obscene and filthy matter which is offensive to the moral senses, morally depraving and debasing, and that it is designed for persons having lecherous and salacious proclivities.
>
> The picture and the sketches are obscene and filthy by prevailing standards. The stories "All This and Heaven Too" and "Not Till the End," pages 32-36, are similar to the story "Sappho Remembered," except that they relate to the activities of the homosexuals rather than lesbians. Such stories are obscene, lewd and lascivious. They are offensive to the moral senses, morally depraving and debasing.

As Judge Desmond of the New York Court of Appeals said of the Sunshine Book and One, Inc., cases, "Presumably, the court having looked at these books simply held them not to be obscene."

The most recent case in this field to attract nation-wide notice involved a Post Office order banning the unexpurgated edition of *Lady Chatterley's Lover.* This edition was published in the United States by a very reputable firm and received favorable reviews in the New York *Times,* the New York *Herald Tribune, Harper's* and *Time.* It had a preface by Archibald MacLeish, former Librarian of Congress and Pulitzer Prize winner, and an introduction by Mark Schorer, professor of English literature at the University of California. The Postmaster General nevertheless concluded that it was "an obscene and filthy work."

The court disagreed, holding that it is an honest and sincere novel of literary merit and that its dominant appeal is not to prurient interest. The court also pointed out that the Postmaster General undoubtedly has special qualifications on many questions involving the administration of the Post Office Department, the handling of the mails, postal rates and other matters. But, the court went on, "he has no special competence to determine what constitutes obscenity within the meaning of Section 1461, or that 'contemporary community standards are not such that this book should be allowed to be transmitted in the mails' or that the literary merit of the book is outweighed by its pornographic features."

Again the Washington *Post* editorialized:

> No one is required to purchase *Lady Chatterley's Lover* as a result of Judge Bryan's decision. No one is obliged to read it or to let his teen-age children read it. All that the Judge has said is that those who want to form their own opinion of a book which has been hailed as an important work of art by many literary

critics may not be forbidden to do so simply because the Postmaster General finds the book distasteful. This seems a thoroughly sensible outcome—the only outcome that could comport with a Bill of Rights the very first article of which guarantees freedom of expression. It is one thing for the Post Office Department to require a stamp for what it carries in the mail; but it is quite another thing to require the stamp of its approval on the contents of what it carries.

Whatever the literary merits of *Confidential* magazine—and I make no brief for them here—it was plainly not obscene under any of the foregoing tests. Its articles were clearly defamatory and actionable if untrue, but they did not tend to excite lustful thoughts and desires in the normal reader. There was certainly no clear and present danger of overt criminal conduct as a result of reading this magazine. It could not by any stretch be regarded as hard-core pornography. And I do not think the dominant appeal of *Confidential* was to prurient interest. It catered to curiosity rather than to concupiscence.

As an aftermath of the *Ulysses* case, the Bureau of Customs retained a recognized expert to advise it on questions of obscenity. The customs authority has adopted a relatively liberal attitude toward works of genuine literary or artistic purpose, and there has been little litigation. I hope that the Post Office Department will see fit to take similar action. If the Post Office would confine its censorship efforts to hard-core pornography or dirt for dirt's sake, almost everybody would be satisfied. D. H. Lawrence himself urged that real pornography should be censored. If any printed page can corrupt the conduct of normal adults and foster juvenile delinquency, it is certainly this kind of commercial pandering. The time and money which went into the *Lady Chatterley* case would have been far better devoted to suppression of such obvious dirt.

It is certainly a fair question to ask what is meant by "hard-core pornography," which has no place within the penumbra of the First Amendment. By this term I mean the depiction or description of sexual acts for reasons unconnected with education, art or literature. Invariably it expresses no ideas and argues no viewpoints. A few examples should bring to mind the kinds of material which are within the comprehension of the term and those which are not. Hard-core pornography includes "stag party" motion pictures, "Parisian" postcards, and cartoons of comic-strip characters or famous personalities involved in sexual acts. Not included within the term are books by Hemingway, John O'Hara, Erskine Caldwell, or James Cain, *Lady Chatterley's Lover* or the motion picture *La Ronde*. Of course there are borderline cases, just as between night and day there is a twilight zone. When does twilight cease being day and become night? This decision in each case is for the judiciary with all of its procedural safeguards and its deep concern for the guarantees of freedom of expression.

It is not for the Postmaster General to decide. When he assumes the role of the arbiter of the literary standards of America, he is arrogating unto himself a position never intended for him. Regardless of his sincerity, his zeal or his identity, he has neither the authority nor the qualifications for such a task. In concluding his opinion in *Esquire, Inc.* v. *Walker*, Judge Thurman Arnold, then of the United States Court of Appeals for the District of Columbia, extended this salutary bit of advice to the Post Office Department:

> We intend no criticism of counsel for the Post Office. They were faced with an impossible task. They under-

took it with sincerity. But their very sincerity makes the record useful as a memorial to commemorate the utter confusion and lack of intelligible standards which can never be escaped when that task is attempted. We believe that the Post Office officials should experience a feeling of relief if they are limited to the more prosaic function of seeing to it that "neither snow nor rain nor heat nor gloom of night stays these couriers from the swift completion of their appointed rounds."

CHAPTER XVII

THE WELL-MEANING MEN OF ZEAL

REFORMATION of postal practices will not mean the end of the censorship problem. Every state except New Mexico has statutes directed toward obscenity, and there are also countless county and municipal regulations. Justice Harlan has expressed the view that this kind of local censorship is far less dangerous than postal censorship, simply because it affects far fewer people. On the other hand, it is more susceptible to abuse and absurdity. Edmund Wilson's *Memoirs of Hecate County,* for example, has been solemnly adjudicated obscene in New York but not obscene in California. I suspect that the principal effect of all this litigation has been to increase the book's circulation. At the time of the adjudication of obscenity the *Saturday Review* carried an advertisement which read: "BANNED in New York—but now on sale in *every other state in America!* Edmund Wilson's controversial novel *Memoirs of Hecate County.*" The expression "banned in Boston" has in certain circles become a synonym for something worth reading.

Experience has shown us that both official censors at the local level and private societies formed to suppress literary vice feel an almost irresistible impulse to stray from the path of moderation and good sense. They tend to become obsessed with the chase and lose perspective in their gratification over finding the objects of their search.

The techniques frequently followed by local censors are demonstrated in several recent cases in which a publisher has filed suit against the officials. The local mayor or chief of police prepares a list of publications considered to be obscene. This list is then furnished to booksellers and news dealers, with the warning that criminal prosecution will follow unless the named publications are withdrawn from sale. Usually no prosecution is necessary.

In Youngstown, Ohio, the chief of police launched a one-man crusade to stamp out the distribution of books offensive to his literary taste. He issued a list of over 400 works which he found objectionable and advised the news dealers to remove these books from their stands. Among the listed books were Ernest Hemingway's *Across the River and Into the Trees,* John Steinbeck's *Cannery Row,* Frederic Wakeman's *The Hucksters,* James T. Farrell's *Studs Lonigan* series and *Gas House McGinty*. Most of the condemned books had not been found by any court in the land to be obscene.

One of the country's largest publishers of pocket-size books brought an injunction suit in federal court against this personal censorship. The court, in a forceful decision written by Judge Charles J. McNamee, put an end to it, and in doing so the judge commented:

> Not only did the defendant exceed his legal powers in suppressing the publications, but the methods he employed in censoring the books were arbitrary and unreasonable. . . . A Chief of Police, like all other public officials, must act within the scope of his express and implied powers under the law. . . . It is

> vital in the interest of public morality that the laws against obscenity be vigorously enforced. But if a free society is to endure, its primary obligation is to protect its "government of laws" from all intrusions of arbitrary power.

But police pre-censorship by warning still flourishes in many cities. Book dealers are generally unwilling to fight in the cause of freedom of expression, and an unlawful suppression of some genuine literary classics survives by default.

Another and more insidious form of local censorship involves removing controversial works from public libraries or restricting their circulation. Recently a children's book called *The Rabbits' Wedding* was banned from the open shelves of Alabama public libraries because of segregationist pressure. The book described a wedding between a white rabbit and a black one. This kind of censorship is difficult to discover and more difficult to defeat.

A few years ago a feminine member of Indiana's State Textbook Commission demanded that the story of Robin Hood be eliminated from all school textbooks and removed from the school libraries of the state, on the ground that Robin Hood followed the Communist line. She declared that there was "a Communist directive in education now to stress the story of Robin Hood. They want to stress it because he robbed the rich and gave to the poor. That's the Communist line."

Of course the news media throughout the country could not restrain their mirth. The hero was referred to as "Robinoff Hoodski," and editors had a field day discussing his membership in the Communist Party. But this did not deter the zealous protector of youth. She next demanded that all references to the Quaker religion be eliminated from the state's textbooks because "Quakers don't believe in fighting wars" and such a policy was helpful to the Communists. Even after these ludicrous demands she was congratulated by the governor of Indiana for her "fine campaign against subversive textbooks."

The consoling factor in the Indiana case was that less hysterical heads prevailed and the "Communist propaganda" in Robin Hood and Quakerism was not removed. Illinois was not so fortunate. In 1953, in Richland County, a schoolgirl borrowed a novel from the Illinois State Library and touched off a storm of controversy. The novel was a story of disillusioned soldiers called *The Boy Came Back,* by Charles H. Knickerbocker. A complaint was registered by the girl's mother that the book was unfit for her daughter to read. Ultimately the complaint found its way up to the State Librarian, who forthwith issued an order to his assistants to remove all books "which are of a salacious, vulgar or obscene character." In the application of this nebulous standard the state librarians boxed and stored almost 8,000 books "relating to sex." Among them were numerous popular literary works of the day by renowned authors. The storm of controversy precipitated by this ill-conceived, intemperate order was so great that the order was ultimately rescinded. But its rescission came only after it was publicized around the world as evidence of our national immaturity.

Finally, there is the problem of censorship by private groups. We all agree that no one should be compelled to read a book which he considers offensive. We all agree that everyone has the right to try to persuade others not to read a book which he considers offensive. This is part of our right of free speech, which is just as important as a free press. The trouble arises when a group goes beyond methods of peaceful persuasion in an effort to impose its literary standards upon others.

The most militant groups organized in the past decade to combat the distribution of "objectionable literature" have been the National Office for Decent Literature (NODL) and the Citizens for Decent Literature (CDL). CDL, although rapidly increasing in size and influence, is still in its infancy. I shall discuss NODL because of its longer history, because of my greater familiarity with it and because it provides the classic illustration relevant to discussion of non-governmental censorship.

In December, 1938, the Catholic bishops of the United States formed the National Organization for Decent Literature, commonly referred to as the NODL. Its avowed purpose was "to set in motion the moral forces of the entire country . . . against the lascivious type of literature which threatens moral, social, and national life." In April, 1955, the bishops set up a National Office for Decent Literature in Chicago to coordinate the work on a nationwide basis. In addition to the negative pledge against the dissemination of objectionable literature, the society pledged positively to "encourage publishing and distribution of good literature" and "to promote plans to develop worth-while reading habits during the formative years."

NODL has serviced all organizations—educational, social, religious and civic—which have sought its aid. It has supplied these groups with information by means of a regularly issued bulletin describing its activities and programs throughout the country. Each month it has printed a list of comic books, magazines and pocket-size books which are branded "objectionable" for youth. NODL claims it has never reviewed a cloth-bound book, and that its concern has been exclusively with paperbacks because of the fact they are available to youth at a modest price.

The publications have been evaluated according to a code. The code makes "objectionable" those publications which:

1) glorify crime or the criminal;
2) describe in detail ways to commit criminal acts;
3) hold lawful authority in disrespect;
4) exploit horror, cruelty or violence;
5) portray sex facts offensively;
6) feature indecent, lewd or suggestive photographs or illustrations;
7) carry advertising which is offensive in content or advertises products which may lead to physical or moral harm;
8) use blasphemous, profane or obscene speech indiscriminately and repeatedly;
9) hold up to ridicule any national, religious or racial group.

Judgment on individual publications has in the past been made by a board composed of five women. They have usually been mothers of grammar-school or teen-age children. The NODL list has carried the names of many mature literary works, some of them award winners, which have come out in paperback editions. Their inclusion on the list has been justified by the statement that, whereas they may be suitable for adult reading, they are objectionable for the youthful mind. The list has included such works as these:

Nelson Algren,
THE MAN WITH THE GOLDEN ARM
Louis Auchincloss,
A LAW FOR THE LION
Vicki Baum,
GRAND HOTEL

Paul Hyde Bonner,
HOTEL TALLEYRAND

Paul Bowles,
THE SHELTERING SKY

John Horne Burns,
A CRY OF CHILDREN

James M. Cain,
THE BUTTERFLY; SERENADE

Erskine Caldwell,
GOD'S LITTLE ACRE; TOBACCO ROAD;
A HOUSE IN THE UPLANDS;
TRAGIC GROUND; TROUBLE IN JULY

Joyce Cary,
HERSELF SURPRISED

James T. Farrell,
FATHER AND SON; MY DAYS OF ANGER;
A WORLD I NEVER MADE

William Faulkner,
SANCTUARY; SOLDIER'S PAY

Radclyffe Hall,
THE WELL OF LONELINESS

Thomas Heggen,
MR. ROBERTS

Ernest Hemingway,
TO HAVE AND HAVE NOT

Aldous Huxley,
ANTIC HAY

Christopher Isherwood,
THE WORLD IN THE EVENING

James Jones,
FROM HERE TO ETERNITY

Arthur Koestler,
THE AGE OF LONGING

D. H. Lawrence,
THE FIRST LADY CHATTERLEY;
WOMEN IN LOVE
Norman Mailer,
BARBARY SHORE
F. Van Wyck Mason,
THREE HARBOURS
John Masters,
BHOWANI JUNCTION;
NIGHTRUNNERS OF BENGAL
Alberto Moravia,
THE TIME OF INDIFFERENCE
John O'Hara,
BUTTERFIELD 8; THE FARMER'S HOTEL;
A RAGE TO LIVE
Will Oursler,
N.Y., N.Y.
John Dos Passos,
1919; THE 42ND PARALLEL
Ann Petry,
THE NARROWS
Harold Robbins,
NEVER LOVE A STRANGER;
A STONE FOR DANNY FISHER
J. D. Salinger,
THE CATCHER IN THE RYE
Budd Schulberg,
WHAT MAKES SAMMY RUN
Margery Sharp,
THE STONE OF CHASTITY
Irwin Shaw,
THE YOUNG LIONS
William Styron,
LIE DOWN IN DARKNESS

Leon Uris,
BATTLE CRY
Gore Vidal,
THE CITY AND THE PILLAR
Nathanael West,
THE DAY OF THE LOCUST
Kathleen Windsor,
FOREVER AMBER
Ira Wolfert,
ACT OF LOVE
Richard Wright,
NATIVE SON
Frank Yerby,
PRIDE'S CASTLE
Emile Zola,
NANA

About 25,000 copies of the list have been sent each month to subscribers throughout the United States. About 5,000 of these have gone to organized groups. Any organization has been allowed to reprint all or part of the list, but there has always been an express disclaimer of responsibility by NODL for any list which has been changed by addition or subtraction.

NODL has distributed instruction sheets for organizing Decent Literature Committees, Citizens Committees and Parish Decency Crusades. Advice has been given on the assigning of definite territories to local organizations so that there "will not be an overlapping of effort." It has recommended that members of the local organizations, armed with identification cards, visit news dealers at two-week intervals to inspect the display of books and magazines and discuss "cooperation" with the organization. It has further suggested that "certificates of cooperation" be given news dealers "after a period of probation (three to six months)" and that stores which cooperate should be mentioned from the pulpit or given a commendation in the parish publication.

Of course there have been many other organizations in a concerted all-out drive against literature which they deem objectionable. But NODL has in the past decade been the largest, the most militant and the most effective and, accordingly, warrants the most attention. Only recently has Citizens for Decent Literature challenged for supremacy in the field. Founded in 1958 by a Cincinnati attorney named Charles H. Keating, Jr., it now has over a hundred units in fifty states. Other large national organizations which have launched such campaigns directly or through their local affiliates are the Daughters of the American Revolution, the Women's Christian Temperance Union, the Daughters of American Colonists, the General Federation of Women's Clubs, the Sons of the American Revolution, and the American Legion.

They all have at least one thing in common. Virtually none of the literature which offends their moral sensibilities, and against which they are carrying their attack, can be lawfully suppressed under the First Amendment test for obscenity laid down by the Supreme Court of the United States. This is true whether you regard the standard as one of "hard-core pornography" or whether you apply the test of the Roth case—i.e., whether the average person, applying contemporary community standards, finds that the dominant theme of the publication taken as a whole appeals to "prurient interest," whether it is material having a tendency toward exciting lustful thoughts. Despite the fact that the distribution of these publications is protected within the constitutional guarantees of free expression, these groups are actively attempting to prevent the sale of the books because they are offensive to the personal standards of the group.

NODL has explicitly stated that its list is not to be used for coercion or purposes of boycott. It has expressly proclaimed that it is just a service organization giving information to those who seek it. The suggestions it has made to some of the groups using its lists, however, have been gravely abused and NODL has perhaps unjustly been made the target of criticism for these abuses. The local groups are the proper and specific targets for criticism for the abuses to which they have put the lists.

There cannot be the slightest question that NODL has the right to advise its subscribers concerning its views on any publication. Nor can there be the slightest question that the NODL has the right to inform the public at large that it regards certain publications as obscene or immoral. Its right to criticize finds the same protection in the First Amendment as the expressions it criticizes. And NODL's right of expression and criticism must always be protected when threatened, so long as it is not exercised by means of coercion.

The uses to which the lists have been put by local groups are many. In some instances public officials have adopted the monthly list *in toto* as the determining factor of what might or might not be sold in their jurisdictions. In Pittsburgh a six-page list of paperbacks and magazines was distributed by policemen to virtually all the dealers in the area. The list was the NODL list, but was not identified as such. Five hundred mimeographed copies had been prepared by the head of the Holy Name Society for distribution by the police. The dealers were asked by the police to "cooperate."

In Michigan a prosecutor sent a letter to all the distributors in his county saying: "This office wishes to inform you that starting on August 15, 1956, all publications on this [NODL] list are to be discontinued."

In September, 1955, the mayor of Baltimore announced that books on the NODL list should no longer be sold in that city. In numerous smaller towns the police have distributed the list to news dealers and informed them they must follow the list or face prosecution. In almost all cases the dealers "cooperated" out of fear, and the edicts were not challenged in court.

More frequently the local groups pursued a different course to secure compliance with their moral views. The threat of boycott was made. Of course, the majority of dealers were cooperative—some out of genuine approval of the program, but many more out of fear of economic reprisal. Usually the suggestion of boycott was privately made and, if necessary, quietly enforced. But there were many open threats of boycott publicly made. For example, a parish bulletin in Orange, New Jersey, advised its readers: "The following stores . . . have agreed to cooperate with the Parish Decency Committee in not displaying or selling literature disapproved by the National Organization for Decent Literature. Please patronize these stores only."

In Newark, New Jersey, the official news organ of the archdiocese carried a lead editorial on the work of the NODL and advised its readers: "In parishes where committees for decent literature have been organized and certificates of approval have been issued to cooperating news dealers, Catholics should buy from these only."

Throughout a large section of New Jersey, Catholics pledged at Sunday Mass not only to refrain from buying "any publication containing articles, illustrations or advertisements of an immoral, indecent or suggestive nature, but also not to patronize those who sell such publications."

In some instances news dealers were advised that the NODL list of publications had been circulated to home owners in the community and that sermons had been delivered about the list in church. They were told that dealers who agreed to cooperate in the program would get recognition on a list given to churchgoers and be given certificates of cooperation for display. Check-ups have been made on a fortnightly basis in many communities. The local groups have named vigilante committees to act as a private morals-police force and inspect newsstands in the area.

This kind of pressure raises grave questions both juridically and prudentially. Especially in a small community, a merchant can't risk the concerted withdrawal of patronage by all the members of an important minority group. Consequently, the listed books and magazines are withdrawn from sale altogether. This means that persons of other religious and moral persuasions can't buy them either. It also means that, insofar as these publications are concerned, the adult population is reduced to the standards of a child's library. As Justice Frankfurter remarked in striking down a Michigan statute which forbade the sale of works deemed injurious to the morals of minors, "Surely, this is to burn the house to roast the pig."

Fortunately, enlightened Catholic opinion does not support such tactics. Father John Courtney Murray, a distinguished Jesuit theologian, had this to say in one of his public statements on the subject of censorship: "Society has an interest in the artist's expression which is not necessarily shared by the family. If adult standards of literature would be dangerous for children, a child's standard is rather appalling to an adult." Declaring that a father or mother is qualified to act as a censor within the family, he said the "ordinary father or mother is not qualified to act as censor within society at large, or to decide what literature and movies may be displayed to the general public."

Father Murray and Professor Vernon Bourke of Marquette University have suggested some basic rules of reason on the over-all subject of censorship. They are four in number, and, substantially, this is the essence of them:

1. Within a pluralist society each minority group has the right to censor for its own members the content of the various media of communication and protect them from materials considered harmful according to its own standards.

2. In a pluralist society no minority group has the right to demand that government impose general censorship upon any medium of communication with a view to prohibiting the communication of materials that are judged to be harmful according to the specific standards of that group.

3. Any minority group has the right to work toward the elevation of standards of public morality by persuasion and pacific argument.

4. In a pluralist society no minority group has the right to impose its religious or moral views on other groups through methods of force, coercion or violence.

I agree with Father Murray and Professor Bourke wholeheartedly as far as they go. I would make one addition: these principles should apply to majority as well as minority groups.

Certainly we must defend the right of NODL and like groups to express their views on any materials that go through the media of communication. They have the clear right to press their opinions on others by argumentation and persuasion. Specifically, they have the clear right to urge people not to buy a book or magazine or see a movie or play they regard as obscene. But, in my view, they transgress the bounds of prudence and justice when they urge people not to patronize a store or purchase even acceptable books from one who sells an objectionable book or not to patronize a theater which exhibits an "objectionable" film along with unobjectionable ones. In both cases their objective is to influence the distributor or exhibitor rather than the reader or the viewer. I cannot defend the right of any group, majority or minority, to force its moral views upon others by coercive methods.

I am a Catholic and the father of four small children. My taste and judgment as to what is good reading for minors are for the most part in harmony with NODL's reviewers. Like all parents, I'm concerned with all the influences at work on my children. And not for a moment do I belittle the possible deleterious effect of books on children. To belittle the influence of the printed page is to beggar the value of the very thing we try to save from censorship. But, in the inevitable choice of risks, I am for avoiding the risks of censorship by pressure and for bearing the risks of freedom.

Between the protectors of community morals and the defenders of free speech, misunderstanding and distrust have long persisted. The churchmen see themselves as the beleaguered defenders of morality against the forces of secularism and materialism. The civil-libertarians see themselves as the harassed guardians of freedom fighting alone against men trying to impose a minority code of morality on the nation. A recognition that on both sides there are men of good will, and that between them there is a noble common cause—the preservation of the essential dignity of the individual—would go far to produce understanding and a desirable community of effort between the two groups.

CHAPTER XVIII

WE ALL DIE EQUAL

THROUGHOUT most of the pages of this book I have been writing about civil liberties. These are a great heritage for Americans. They are immunities against encroachments by government into the rights of privacy that each American enjoys. The founding fathers carefully safeguarded these rights of the people at the time the Republic was born. They protect us against the excesses of totalitarian government and form a vital part of the freedoms to which we urge other nations of the world to aspire. They guarantee Americans freedom of speech, freedom of religion, security against arbitrary police action, a fair trial and other rights which we have too long taken for granted. It is important to remember that they are not rights which the government gives to the people. Rather, they are rights which the people carved out for themselves when they created this government. They are restraints upon the government, not benefits flowing from it.

There are other freedoms which Americans possess—civil rights as contrasted with civil liberties. These are rights guaranteed to the people by the orderly processes of government. The voting franchise is one of the most precious of these. President Kennedy has pointed out the difference between civil rights and civil liberties this way:

By civil rights we mean those claims which the citizen has to the affirmative assistance of government. In an age which insistently and properly demands that government secure the weak from needless dread and needless misery, the catalogue of civil rights is never closed. The obligation of government in the area of civil rights is never wholly discharged.

By civil liberties, I mean an individual's immunity from governmental oppression. A society which respects civil liberty realizes that the freedom of its people is built, in large part, upon their privacy. The Bill of Rights, in the eyes of its framers, was a catalogue of immunities, not a schedule of claims. It was, in other words, a Bill of Liberties. The immunities defined in this Bill of Liberties were set forth in order that the promise of individual freedom might be made explicit. The framers dreamed that if their hope were codified man's energies of mind and spirit might be released from fear.

When civil rights are seen as claims and civil liberties as immunities, the government's differing responsibilities become clear. For the security of rights the energy of government is essential. For the security of liberty restraint is indispensable.

By my lights, the challenge of the new era we have entered is a dual challenge. At the global level we are locked in a struggle with the forces of Communism for the minds of the people of the uncommitted world. At the domestic level we are in the midst of a civil-rights crisis—a disgraceful crisis in race relations.

In the global struggle against Communism we are in possession of the ultimate weapon, a weapon the Soviets can never duplicate. It is the weapon of an unassailable idea.

We tell the world every day that the concept of government by consent must prevail over the concept of government by compulsion, that the concept of government-of-laws must prevail over the concept of government-of-men. We tell the world that ours is a government of laws, a government by consent, and that even those in power are under the law. This we proclaim as the essential difference between us and the Soviets.

In the war of competing ideologies, our victory should be inevitable because we are right. But we shall prevail only if we practice what we preach, if we live as we talk. And in this basic fact lies the relationship of our domestic crisis to our global challenge.

We are in a crisis in race relations precisely because we have not acted like a government of laws. We have allowed the established law of the land to be mocked. We have permitted one sixth of the nation, through its leaders, to ignore, thwart and frustrate the law of the land. And because of this we have suffered humiliation on the world stage.

In 1954 the Supreme Court of the United States in a great, broad-gauged humanitarian decision held that American citizens who are required to pay the same taxes, pledge allegiance to the same flag, give obedience to the same laws, fight the same wars and die in the same battles might go to the same schools. Eight years later the law of the land is still met with arrogant defiance by men in power who regard themselves as above the law. Eight years later 95 per cent of the South's Negro students are still attending segregated classes. This constitutes the most disgraceful act of mass contempt of court in the history of the nation.

I am convinced that we are blessed in the 1960's with the greatest Supreme Court of this century. But it, like any other court, must look to the executive branch of government for the enforcement of its decrees. We too must look to the executive branch of government to prove that ours is a government of laws and that no men are above the law. But real leadership consists of more than the mere execution of the law. It has been gratifying that President Kennedy has shown that he believes, first, that racial segregation is morally as well as legally wrong, and, second, that the time for compliance with the Supreme Court's decision is now. On his leadership and action the Negro must largely depend to gain the already pronounced right to an equal education.

Since 1870 it has been the law of the land, expressed in an amendment to the Constitution of the United States, that no citizen should be denied the right to vote because of race or color. Congress has repeatedly enacted legislation designed to implement this amendment. A new civil-rights bill was passed at the end of the Eisenhower administration. Yet in this regard also the law of the land is thwarted and defied. Except for certain of the larger cities, the Negro in the South is effectively disenfranchised.

Late in 1960 a Negro farmer named Joseph Atlas testified before the Civil Rights Commission. Atlas, who was fifty-six years old at the time, lived on a farm in East Carroll Parish in northeastern Louisiana. He grossed $10,400 on his farm in 1959 and was one of the more prosperous farmers in his area. He told the commission that he thought he was qualified to be a voter, but in his parish none of the 5,330 Negroes of voting age had been permitted even to register to vote.

When asked why he thought he was eligible, Atlas explained that he had attended high school at the Tuskegee Institute in Alabama for three years. He said he had twelve children, five of whom had been graduated from college and two of whom were then in college. He said he had been president of the Negro Parent-Teachers Association for several years and had been treasurer of his church for many years. He added that he had been arrested only once in his life, and that was for a traffic violation.

It seemed to those who heard Atlas' testimony in a crowded courtroom in New Orleans that here surely was a man who was entitled to vote. He spoke articulately and thoughtfully. He was well dressed and obviously prosperous. He had done his best to be a good citizen and to give his children the education he had never had a chance to receive. Surely his intelligence and industriousness, his concern for himself and his family, and his desire to improve himself and his country were equal to that of most voters.

The day after Atlas testified in New Orleans, the sheriff of East Carroll Parish told him that he would no longer be able to get his cotton processed in cotton gins in that parish. Atlas soon found that this was true.

On election day in 1960, six weeks after he had testified, Atlas took a load of cotton to a gin located eighteen miles from his farm. The gin had processed six bales of cotton for him a few weeks earlier, but this time the manager told him that it would no longer take his cotton. There was too much pressure in the community against Atlas, the manager said.

Atlas also discovered that he was unable to buy seeds and equipment for his farm. Those who had sold to him in the past now turned him away. The reason was clear: Joe Atlas wanted to vote, but he was a Negro, and Negroes were not supposed to want to vote in East Carroll Parish.

As he had been told to do if he encountered such problems, Atlas called the Civil Rights Commission and the Department of Justice. Fortunately for him, and for our nation, the Department of Justice stepped in. It asked for a court order aimed at those who refused to deal with him. Within a few weeks the merchants agreed that they would sell to him and gin his cotton as they had done before he testified. But a year later Joe Atlas still had not been registered to vote.

How many times incidents like this have occurred throughout the nation no one can know. How many persons have chosen not to try to vote because of their fear of such action no one can know. But one does know that Americans cannot long tolerate such gross denials of fundamental rights.

It is to no avail to win the argument in court and lose the case, or to win the debate in Congress and lose the cause. It is to no avail to have a government of laws unless they are obeyed. Always it is to the executive branch of government that we must look to enforce compliance and obedience. Fortunately, we have a President who believes that nine decades is long enough for the Negro to wait to vote and that the best way to end Negro disenfranchisement in the South is the quickest way.

Learning and voting are important. Equality for Negroes in these areas has been spelled out by the courts and the Congress, and these rights need only executive enforcement. But just as important as these is economic equality—equality of job opportunity and equality in the enjoyment of the fruits of one's labor. The Negro has none of these. In 1950 his average income in the United States was 54 per cent of the white man's. Since that time it has fallen to 50 per cent. And in the South it is but 44 per cent.

The courts and the Congress are the traditional forums in which Negroes have sought relief from oppressive discrimination. These are avenues which, of course, should be pursued. But history by now must have worn the Negro's patience thin. There is another way. Perhaps my suggestion will be branded as radical. But I believe it to be sound and worthy of expression.

The United States Chamber of Commerce last year reported that American Negroes had a purchasing power of $18,000,000,000. This is equal to the purchasing power of the whole Dominion of Canada. I should think and hope that American Negroes would spend their $18,000,000,000 in places where it is recognized that equal justice, equal respect and equal opportunity are the patrimony of all American citizens. History has shown us quite graphically in the past decade that local customs change dramatically with changing economic conditions.

To those who would say this course is too extreme, that it would mean going too far too fast, it should be pointed out that the Negroes would be doing only what the United States government has announced as its policy. By executive order the United States government deals for goods and services only with contractors who include an anti-discrimination clause in their contracts. On August 13, 1953, by Executive Order No. 10479, President Eisenhower set up the Government Committee on Contracts to report on the effectiveness of this policy and to police its compliance. President Kennedy has revamped the committee, giving it more power and greater potentiality for real impact. The committee has orders which tell it to authorize a boycott by all agencies of the federal government against firms which refuse to give Negroes equal job opportunities. Can it be illegal or radical or immoral if the Negro adopts precisely this same type of boycott in a selective buying campaign?

It seems to me that the policy of selective buying is generally preferable to the "sit-in" demonstrations which have been widely used throughout the South in restaurants and bus stations. The "sit-in" is an affirmative action which time and again has caused the eruption of violence. Negroes may win fair treatment as a result of the "sit-ins," but the violence they breed does America no good, either internally or as it faces the world. Selective buying in most instances can be just as effective without the danger of violence.

It is true that the main impact of selective buying is on the businessmen—the merchants and manufacturers, who may be discriminating only because of community pressure. These men can argue, with some justification, that they are not free to treat Negroes equally. But these men are also the leaders of their communities. They are the men who have it within their power to establish a community climate in which discrimination can be eliminated.

I have been told that I am being inconsistent when I support economic boycotts by Negroes in order that they may obtain their rights, and oppose similar boycotts by groups which want to block the sale of particular books or the showing of a particular motion picture. But there is a considerable difference between the two types of boycott. The Negro is seeking his rights and is refusing to buy until he receives something to which he is morally and legally entitled. Those who boycott bookshops and movies are not seeking anything for themselves to which they are legally and morally entitled. They are seeking to stop others from obtaining something to which they are legally entitled.

If the Negro will use his economic power carefully and wisely to obtain equal job opportunities and equal service, if he will urge the government to help him obtain the right to an equal education and to an equal vote, and if he will use that vote wisely, this country can eliminate its greatest source of embarrassment at the world level.

But in doing these things we as a people must begin to realize that we are ending discrimination not only because it is illegal. We are ending it because it is immoral. As I think of the total picture of discrimination in America—the wrongs which have been done against the Negro in the

South, the wrongs which have been done against the Puerto Rican in New York, the wrongs which have been done against the Japanese in California, the wrongs which have been done against the Mexican in the Southwest, the wrongs which have been done against the immigrant Europeans in Northern cities—I come to agree with what the president of Notre Dame University, the Reverend Theodore M. Hesburgh, C.S.C., said at a symposium there in 1959:

> I think one, after studying and listening to the many approaches to a solution to this problem, sees more and more that the problem needs a total solution. . . . The more one studies it in its concrete aspects, the more one is discouraged and baffled by the shabby rationalizations that come from those who do not want an answer; from the frustration of those who want an answer yesterday—not today and tomorrow; from the extremes on both sides that muddy the waters with their agitation, and somehow lose sight of the personal element of those who are most immediately involved in the problem themselves—those who have been deprived of their civil rights, or, indeed, of their personal dignity.
>
> It seems to me that to come to some solution ultimately, one must within his own soul come to a greater sense of the personal dignity of man and of his spiritual heritage and his God-given rights, than that which is reflected by many of our practices in our present-day society. I would hope that our leaders in the days to come . . . would somehow become more dedicated to what man is—made in the image and likeness of God, something a little less than the angels—and that behind all the accusations and counter-accusations, proposals and counter-proposals, we might see

more deeply into that central core of the problem, the nature and destiny of man, his high dignity, and all those things which man, so treated and so respected, might enable this nation to become.

Some of the most unfortunate incidents our nation has experienced occurred in New Orleans when a handful of Negro children tried to attend two schools which had once been restricted to white children. On each morning in that beautifully haunting city, chimes in the downtown area sound out over the din of traffic as men and women make their way to their jobs. The chimes are usually playing hymns familiar across the South. At the height of the demonstrations over the schools I listened one morning as the chimes played a hymn which little children sing frequently on Sunday morning in the Protestant churches of the South:

Jesus loves the little children,
All the children of the world.
Red and yellow, black and white,
They are precious in His sight.
Jesus loves the little children of the world.

Until we practice what we sing, we must accept it as a fact of history that as a nation, there will be no peace in our conscience. There will be no self-respect in our heart. Until we have broadened the boundaries of democracy at home, we shall daily give the lie to our pious proclamations abroad that ours is a government of laws before which all men are the same. We shall fail to meet our domestic challenge and continue to suffer embarrassment and humiliation before the world.

In the new era into which we pass, "equal" can no longer mean "separate." "Separate" means "unequal." "Equal" must mean "the same."

CHAPTER XIX

THE NEW ERA AND THE NEW ISSUE

FREEDOM for the individual is meaningless outside the framework of law. The same is true for nations. Just as law is the strongest link between the individual and freedom, so too is it the strongest link between nations and freedom. My experience in the Melekh case brought me squarely into confrontation with the concept of rule of law at the world level.

On October 28, 1960, newspapers were filled with a story of espionage. The headlines proclaimed that a Russian spy had been caught by the FBI. Igor Melekh was his name, and he was an official of the United Nations on loan from the Soviet Foreign Ministry. Melekh had been indicted by a federal grand jury in Chicago for conspiring to obtain information concerning the location of military installations in the Chicago area. He had been arrested the night before in his New York apartment during a birthday celebration for one of his children.

Melekh had held the rank of Second Secretary to the Soviet Foreign Ministry in Moscow and he had come here in 1955 as Chief of the Russian Translation Section of the United Nations Secretariat. As such, he was responsible for the translation of all United Nations documents into Russian. He was rated a P-5, a fairly high-ranking position in United Nations hierarchy, carrying an annual salary of about $11,000. He lived with his wife and two children in a residential hotel in the West Eighties near Riverside Drive.

One Willie Hirsch, a free-lance medical illustrator, was named in the indictment as a defendant and co-conspirator with Melekh. According to the grand-jury indictment, Hirsch had made contact with an unnamed United States citizen in Chicago in July, 1958, and again in October of the same year. The day after the second meeting Hirsch had allegedly introduced Melekh to this individual for the purpose of inducing him to collect information for the Soviet Union. The indictment recited that from time to time Melekh had made payments to this unnamed individual for his services and that as a result of this arrangement, Melekh received maps and aerial photographs of Chicago. The grand jury formally charged Melekh and Hirsch with conspiring to obtain information pertaining to the national defense for transmittal to Soviet Russia. It also charged them with conspiring to violate the law which requires agents of foreign governments to register with the Secretary of State. If convicted, both men faced twenty-five years in prison.

The case occupied national headlines for several days after the arrest. On the surface it appeared to be no different from the score or more of Soviet espionage cases that had been uncovered since 1945, most of them involving Russians enjoying some form of diplomatic status. The usual practice had been to send them home after appropriate protests were registered. But this case had broken in the wake of the U-2 incident and the trial of Francis Gary Powers in Moscow. It was the first time in years that our government had secured an indictment and effected the arrest of a Soviet citizen. Coming as it did in juxtaposition to the U-2 case, and offering the prospect of a sensational trial, the Melekh case immediately received international attention and became the subject of debate at the United Nations itself.

Early in November I received a call from the American lawyer for the Soviet Embassy in Washington. He asked me to serve as trial counsel in Melekh's criminal case, explaining that, since Melekh was a citizen and an official of the U.S.S.R., the embassy was assisting him in securing counsel. We did not discuss the merits of Melekh's case at that time. I said that if I were to undertake his defense I would have to have a prior commitment giving me total control over the conduct of the litigation and an assurance of total candor from the defendant himself. Without such a commitment I would not consider entering the case. I also said that if the commitment, in my judgment, was broken after I took the case, I would feel free to withdraw. It was decided at this preliminary conference that I should meet with Melekh to discuss these and other conditions of representation. To do this it was necessary for me to go to New York, because Melekh's terms of bail would not permit him to leave Manhattan.

Before my scheduled meeting with Melekh, I had lengthy discussions with my associates. We all recognized that there would be wide misunderstanding if we entered the case. The usual brickbats would be hurled. We would be called Commiesymps, and worse. But this is not what troubled us. The important question was whether we could really expect control and candor from someone who certainly was under Communist discipline. As we discussed the case around the conference table, new vistas opened before us. Already the U.S.S.R., through its ambassador and its United Nations delegates, was asserting that Melekh enjoyed diplomatic immunity. This was being claimed on two grounds: first, that Melekh was an official of the Soviet Foreign Ministry and, second, that he enjoyed, as a result of his assignment at the United Nations, an immunity conferred by treaty on all United Nations officials.

It is an elementary proposition of international law that one who enjoys diplomatic status is not subject to the jurisdiction of the courts in the country to which he is assigned. Thus, if X, a diplomat from England, commits a criminal offense in the United States while serving his country here, he may not be tried in our criminal courts unless his government waives diplomatic immunity. This is rarely done. What is often overlooked is that the immunity may not be asserted or waived by the individual involved in the criminal charges. This must be done by his government, for the immunity does not belong to the individual. It belongs to the sovereign power which he serves. This, of course, opened up fascinating possibilities in the Melekh case. If we were truly to have control over the course of his litigation, we would have to have not only control over the conduct of the case so far as Melekh could give it, but also control of the legal aspects of the case involving diplomatic immunity. This meant that the Soviet government would have to agree to put the disposition of this question in the hands of Melekh's American counsel.

This would be the test. If I could get such an agreement, I would try the case. Otherwise I would not have the kind of control that a trial lawyer in a major criminal case must have, and I would decline the representation.

Already I had an idea about this case which excited my imagination as nothing had excited it in all my previous practice. I had long had an obsessive interest in the concept of world rule of law. I had spent hours in discussion of the American Bar Association's "World Peace Through Law" program with Charles Rhyne, former President of the ABA.

Rhyne has been the spearhead of this project and has given it much of his life over the past three years. Whatever success the program has had to date has been due to his tremendous dedication and ability.

The whole concept of world rule of law and the whole project of "World Peace Through Law" are premised on some fairly basic facts of modern life. We are told almost daily by our national leaders that the continued existence of our system of government is imperiled as never before in its history by the spread of global Communism. Most of our national resources are going into a tremendous effort to contain the diffusion of Communism. The concept of government by consent is locked in struggle for the minds and hearts of the uncommitted world with the concept of government by compulsion. But it is not just a struggle of ideologies. We are furiously contesting in a deadly arms race. We are told that the flight of a single intercontinental bomber today can deliver an explosive load greater than the total of all the bombs exploded, including those at Hiroshima and Nagasaki, and all the guns fired every day on every front throughout all of World War II. The warning time for an intercontinental-ballistic-missile attack on the United States is now down to fifteen minutes. We are told that defense against such a disaster can no longer be entrusted to earthbound creatures. Rather it must be left to hundreds of bombers armed with our mightiest weapons in perpetual flight in the skies above nations and to the missile power of fleets of nuclear submarines prowling silently under the seas. We are told that the explosion of a hydrogen bomb at a sufficiently high altitude can, from a distance of a thousand miles, strike our pilots blind as they deliver a retaliatory blow.

The cost of these weapons of death is paid in the hopes

and wants and needs of all mankind. Emmet Hughes in his great book *America the Vincible* graphically translates the cost for us. He points out that one nuclear submarine costs schools for 150,000 children. One fighter plane costs 500,000 bushels of wheat. Every intercontinental bomber costs one large, fully equipped modern hospital. Hughes calls these "equations balanced in madness." They are balanced in a madness born of realization that thirty hours of nuclear war can wreak a havoc that dwarfs into minuscule insignificance that wrought by thirty years of religious wars three centuries ago in Europe. Yet we are racing on at an ever accelerating pace to maintain a peace through mutual terror, a peace that is no peace at all.

In the history of the world, mankind has found only two ways to settle individual or collective disputes when no agreement can be reached: (1) by violence, and (2) by submission of the dispute to a third party whose decision is binding.

Violence has now become unthinkable because violence means annihilation. During his last days in Princeton, New Jersey, Dr. Albert Einstein was visited by some college students who asked him how he thought World War III would be fought. The great scientist replied that his mind could no longer race fast enough to keep pace with the advances in the weapons of destruction that were being devised by science. He said that he would not want to predict how World War III would be fought. And then he added, "But I can tell you how World War IV will be fought—with stones."

I have long been convinced that the time has come to make a bold, dramatic new try at realizing man's ancient hope of world peace through law. Idealistic folly? What is the alternative? A rocket to the moon was the metaphor for folly for 100 years. To go around the world in eighty minutes was an opium-smoker's dream. Now both are facts of history.

Dr. Albert Schweitzer in his primitive jungle hospital in French Equatorial Africa has said this is the most dangerous period in history—not just modern history but all human history. Why? Because heretofore nature has controlled man, but now man has learned to control the elemental forces before he has learned to control himself.

We must have a program as large, as resolute, as dynamic and as passionate as world Communism—a program that has for its spiritual fuel the belief that certain universal concepts can be brought together into the fabric of law. We must have a program that has as its essence the belief that broad basic rules of reason and decency can be incorporated into a world system of justice and applied by an international judiciary. As never before in history, mankind aches for a challenge to exalt him. World peace through law is a challenge worthy of his greatest collective effort.

Sober and practical lawyers throughout the world have been marshaling forces for almost five years to provide the challenge. Meetings have been held in Europe, Asia and South America looking toward the realization of this concept. A great World Rule of Law Center has been created at Duke University under the direction of Arthur Larson, former assistant to President Eisenhower. In quiet research centers around the country—Harvard, Cornell, New York University, Columbia, Michigan, Southern Methodist, Chicago, Yale and elsewhere—students are considering the codifications of the great systems of law and the new problems with which international law has not yet dealt. The program has found support from former President Eisenhower and President Kennedy, from the late Secretary of

State John Foster Dulles, from Secretary of State Dean Rusk, from former Vice President Nixon, from the Chief Justice of the United States and from bar-association heads across the land.

These lawyers are not advocating unilateral disarmament, world government, world federalism or the abandonment of the conventional uses of diplomacy. They are for building and strengthening a world judiciary for resolution under law of conflicts between nations.

Back in 1945 the International Court of Justice was created as an adjunct to the United Nations. It meets amid majestic splendor in a beautiful building at The Hague. Fifteen black-robed justices with lace-curtain throat pieces sit in a magnificent oak-paneled courtroom. Outside, a great Gothic clock tower points skyward, tapering to a cone; it has been described as a picture of time preparing to soar into space. But the court has been a failure. It has virtually no business. What few cases it has decided have been of minor importance.

The United States must assume major responsibility for the court's failure, because we have refused to submit unqualifiedly to its jurisdiction. By virtue of the so-called Connally Amendment we have reserved unto ourselves the right to decide which controversies fall within the court's jurisdiction and which do not. Specifically, we have reserved the right to decide whether complaints filed against us in the International Court of Justice are within the domestic jurisdiction of the United States. This stultifying provision says to the world that we decline to trust the court to rule correctly on such an issue. This lack of respect by us, the most vocal advocates of "rule of law" in the world, has largely destroyed the prestige and usefulness of the court. Of all the nations which submit to the jurisdiction of the court only six have the so-called self-judging clauses. We find ourselves in the company of Liberia, Pakistan, Mexico, Sudan and the Union of South Africa.

We violate the basic maxim of all jurisprudence: no one should sit as a judge in his own case. Our moral position is wholly unsound for a nation which is daily telling the world through its propaganda organs that the force of law must be substituted for the law of force. What would have happened to the Supreme Court of the United States if the founding fathers had decided that all the litigants before the court had it in their power to say whether the court had jurisdiction over them? The Supreme Court would have been wrecked in one decade.

By virtue of the Connally Amendment, we cannot use the World Court when it is in our deep national interest to do so. Because we reserve the right to refuse to submit to its jurisdiction when we choose, any nation we sue may likewise invoke the self-judging clause against us. France for a time had a self-judging reservation until it found out through sad experience that the clause was detrimental to the nation's interests. France went into the World Court with a case against Norway. The Norwegian government had borrowed large sums of money from investors in France. When the French government undertook to present the claims of these investors against Norway, the court pointed out that France, in originally accepting the court's jurisdiction, had excluded disputes within the domestic jurisdiction of the French courts "as determined by the government of the French Republic." The court ruled that since France had such a reservation in its original submission to the court, Norway could reciprocally make a similar reservation. Norway did, and France was left without a remedy to gain redress for its citizens.

For a nation such as ours, with $28,000,000,000 of

private capital invested abroad, with 500,000 citizens living permanently in foreign countries, and with 750,000 citizens traveling outside the territorial limits of the United States each year, it is the height of folly to permit any nation to defeat our just claims by taking advantage of the Connally Amendment.

The United States and Russia have been involved in four cases before the World Court. We sued Russia in 1954 for damages to a United States airplane and its crew in Hungary. In 1955 we sued Russia for damages for shooting down one of our aircraft over the sea near Japan. In 1958 we again sued Russia for shooting down another of our airplanes in the same area. Still another such case was brought in 1959. All the cases were dismissed because Russia would not consent to be sued. It was impossible for us to make a valid complaint about this. The Soviet Union, in asserting its unwillingness to be sued, was saying in effect that these incidents were within its domestic jurisdiction "as determined by itself." They were doing no more nor less than we have claimed is our right *vis-à-vis* the court.

This is the court before which all the questions arising out of the U-2 incident should properly have been submitted. How far up is a nation sovereign? Was the U-2 flight justified as an act of self-defense, a right conferred upon nations by Section 51 of the United Nations Charter? Can overflight by an unarmed plane constitute an act of aggression? These are questions for the International Court applying principles of international law to new facts of world history. This is the court for resolution of treaty disputes on the whole muddled problem of Berlin. Perhaps it is folly to think that the Soviets would submit these questions to any tribunal. Even if we repealed the Connally Amendment the Soviets might well continue to scoff at the court. But at least we could then demonstrate that they are the outlaws who recognize no law and no court, and our position as the world leader of "government of laws" would be consistent. We are stopped from preaching effectively the concept of rule of law because we are not practicing it. We are steadfastly refusing to submit our collective disputes in a meaningful way to a third party whose decision is binding.

It has long been my conviction that our offer to the world should be a meaningful proposal of peace through law. It has been my conviction that we should repeal the Connally Amendment, advocate the strengthening of the World Court and seek to bring all international disputes involving questions of international law to this court for resolution. Even if the Soviets refuse to follow suit, we should then have the propaganda initiative and have the better case in the court of world opinion. We should have the virtues of being consistent and constructive. The democratic concept would once again be dynamic and mobile. We would be offering the world in the true tradition of the democratic ideal a fresh concept, a new hope and an uncommon example.

These were thoughts that had long occupied my mind before I met Igor Melekh or heard of his case. And now I saw a chance, a wonderfully exciting chance, to do something about them. I met Melekh in late November at a hotel in New York just off Madison Avenue. We talked for several hours. While we talked, FBI agents sat downstairs in a car and watched the entrance to the building. Melekh was a highly intelligent man, soft-spoken and articulate. He seemed frightened and confused. He readily agreed that if I accepted his case I should have total control over its conduct and promised that I would get total candor from him. I pointed out to representatives of the embassy that legal questions involving the immunity of international employees were involved and that I wanted the power to dispose of these questions in accordance with my judgment as to what was in the interest of the best over-all disposition of the case. They agreed.

When I left the hotel several hours later, the FBI agents were still sitting unobtrusively in a car across the street. I couldn't help smiling at their obvious curiosity about my identity and the reason for my visit. They had seen me enter earlier with the attachés of the Soviet Embassy. I walked to the nearest intersection, turned down Madison Avenue and paused at a shop window. One of the agents emerged from the car to begin the "tail." He hurried to Madison Avenue and turned the corner, almost bumping into me. I could not resist the temptation to introduce myself and explain that I had just conferred with Igor Melekh about representing him at trial. The agent was nonplused at first. Then he grinned sheepishly. His sense of humor overrode his embarrassment. We shook hands pleasantly and he walked slowly back to his car.

When I got back to Washington, I called Robert Kennedy for an appointment. He had already been designated Attorney General by the President elect, but of course he would not take office until after January 20, 1961. He had been given an office by Attorney General Rogers in the Department of Justice to help him get the feel of the department and to facilitate an orderly transition of business. Strictly speaking, I should have called Mr. Rogers, but this seemed a useless subservience to protocol. He was leaving office in a month and certainly would make no major decision that would tie the hands of his successor. What I wanted to see Robert Kennedy about would require a major decision.

The Attorney General designate was not familiar with the Melekh case. There was no reason he should have been.

I gave him the background of the case and briefed him on some of the legal questions involved. The main question at issue was whether Melekh, as an official of the United Nations, enjoyed diplomatic immunity from criminal prosecution. I told Mr. Kennedy that if he would agree on behalf of the United States government that this question, which turned on the interpretation of the treaty creating the United Nations, could be decided by the International Court of Justice, I would so agree on behalf of my client. I said to him that I thought rarely, if ever, were two lawyers given the chance to make such a contribution to the cause of world peace. If my idea could be implemented, it would mark the first time in history that the U.S.S.R. had ever submitted to the jurisdiction of the World Court. I told him that I thought it would be a dramatic new precedent for the settling of some of the disputes that were plaguing the peace of the world on so many fronts. It seemed to me a constructive, worth-while experiment by which nothing could be lost. It seemed to me also an especially appropriate experiment for a new administration.

Robert Kennedy quickly saw the possibilities of the idea, and I think he was intrigued by them. He saw the whole case in its true perspective. Merely convicting another spy would be insignificant in the course of international events. But getting the Soviets into court would open up horizons unlimited. It was not my idea to participate personally in the argument before the World Court. Our government would probably be represented by its United Nations ambassador and the Soviets by their top legal representative at the United Nations, Mr. Platon D. Morozov. Mr. Kennedy said that the whole proposal would have to be taken up with other officials of government and that he would be in touch with me.

Time was important. Motions challenging the federal

court's jurisdiction to try Melekh had to be filed. The whole question of immunity had to be raised in the federal court in Chicago and it would come on quickly for hearing. Several weeks went by. Additional conferences were held with the Attorney General, who had by this time assumed office. Arguments in the case were adjourned "in the national interest" while the proposal which I had made was considered.

Finally the answer came. The Attorney General told me my proposal was rejected. No explanation was given. I had a strong feeling that the decision was not one with which he was in full accord. I was heartsick over the outcome of our discussions. It seemed to me that as lawyers we had missed a chance to effect the most constructive disposition of a criminal case that had been made in many years. I felt the government was being myopic and narrow-gauged. To exalt in importance the conviction of a spy over the Soviet Union's submission to the World Court made no sense to me. But there was nothing for me to do except to go back and begin preparation for what was now just another criminal case.

Early in March I argued defense motions for a full day before Judge Edwin Robson in Chicago. He reserved decision. On March 20, two weeks later, he read an opinion rejecting all of our arguments and ordered that Melekh go to trial. He directed that we appear on March 24 in Chicago for arraignment and for the setting of a trial date.

I went to New York on Wednesday, March 22, for a day of work. At the end of the day I received a telephone call from the Attorney General, who told me that on Friday the government would voluntarily dismiss the Melekh case. I was to tell no one except the defendant himself. I asked no questions. No reasons were volunteered. I called Melekh and told him the news. Needless to say, he was overjoyed.

We flew to Chicago and on Friday, March 24, the government prosecutor, in accordance with the Attorney General's instructions, dismissed the case. It was announced through a departmental press release that Secretary Rusk had recommended the dismissal in the hope of winning better treatment of American prisoners in Russia.

I claim no expertise in the esoteric ways of diplomacy, nor am I privy to any secrets concerning this matter. The cogency of my observations must be diluted accordingly. But I have never understood why, when the United States government decided to give up the prosecution, it did not agree to my original proposal. No one ever suggested any harmful effect that could have flowed except for the fact that the prosecution might have been delayed a matter of months. In the light of what transpired this argument certainly had no validity.

Melekh was, of course, ordered out of the country. He felt that I had wrought a miracle for him. I could not convince him that I had accomplished nothing—and that what was a great result from his point of view had come wholly apart from my efforts.

Before Melekh left the United States I had a long conversation with him and some of the members of the Soviet delegation. We talked far into the night, covering a myriad of subjects. I explored the whole question of the World Court with Platon D. Morozov, a noted Soviet lawyer, who is a delegate to the United Nations and is the Soviet representative in the General Assembly's Legal Committee. I told him of my hopes that both my country and his would one day make unqualified declarations recognizing the compulsory jurisdiction of the court. Morozov joined in this expression. He pointed out with eloquent clarity, although in halting English, that in the beginning of social order disputes between man and man were settled under the rule of the jungle, by brute strength. Then sticks and stones were used. Then spears and arrows. Then guns and powder. Now in all civilized countries disputes between man and man are resolved in courts of law. But brute force is still the final mechanism for settling disputes between nations.

I told the group of my hope that the United States would take leadership in enhancing the prestige of the World Court by removing our reservation of jurisdiction, and that the court would make its processes more available and efficacious by sitting at the seat of the United Nations in New York. We discussed the great advantage to be gained from the court's announcing its willingness to sit all over the world in bancs of three judges. It is now authorized to do this, but has never used the authority. I expressed my conviction that we need to go beyond the present structure of the court and create a world-wide network of courts to make law an instrument of peace available to all the peoples of the world. We need a system of trial courts and circuit courts on a regional basis with a final appeal to the International Court of Justice, a system comparable to the present federal system in the United States. The cost of such a system would be about $10,000,000 a year. The nations of the world are now spending $100,000,000,000 a year on arms.

We talked of the splendid record of objectivity that the judges on the court have made in passing on issues to which their own countries have been parties. Time and again judges on the court have voted against their own countries when they believed them wrong. There are now two judges on the court from Communist countries. Winiarski of Poland has voted thirty-five times with the majority and four times with the minority. Combining the votes of the two successive judges from the Soviet Union, Krylov and Kojevnikov, the record shows that the Soviet judges have voted eighteen times with the majority and ten times with the minority. Zoricic of Yugoslavia, whose term expired in 1958, voted twenty-nine times with the majority and four times with the minority. In the famous Interhandel case (*Switzerland* v. *United States*) the Soviet judge voted in favor of the United States position on three of five issues decided by the court. On one of these issues the United States judge, Hackworth, voted against the United States while Kojevnikov of the U.S.S.R. voted for the United States. Morozov agreed that the strengthening and expanding of a world judiciary would offer the best hope of world peace.

The Soviet lawyers were generally astounded that I, as an American lawyer, could voluntarily stand beside a Soviet citizen as an advocate in an American courtroom and not be ruined socially, financially and professionally. Time and again one of them would make an observation, the substance of which was: "But the newspapers didn't even use any bad adjectives about you." "What will happen to you now?" they asked.

It is difficult to reach a common denominator on which to base discussions with dedicated Communists on law, morals, peace and war. There is almost no community of words or ideas between us and them. There is no common denominator in economics, because our systems are anti-polar. There is no common denominator in politics, because we mean different things by the term. There is no common denominator in morals because they reject God, and God is the essence of our moral code.

It seemed to me that there was only one common touchstone between us, one predicate on which to build a real hope for peace and security. It may be branded as sentimentality, but I am convinced it has validity. Like all people, the Russians share with us the greatest love in all the world—the love of parents for their children. With that, they have cognizance that total war means total destruction of civilization as we know it. They know it means that we shall leave to any children who survive us a legacy of ruin, disease, poverty and despair. From this we recoil. So do they. On this emotion and on this knowledge must be built the hope of peace through law in our time.

Constructing the peace is the most important task that confronts mankind in this era. It can never be built with arms. It can only be built with law, for peace is the tranquillity of order and without law there can be no order. The design for peace must be accomplished by sober and practical idealists who can translate the best of humanity's impulses into an effective world judicial system. Abraham Lincoln articulated the loftiest aspiration of my profession when he said: "It is as the peacemaker that the lawyer has the superior opportunity to be a great man."

BIBLIOGRAPHY

Barnes, Joseph, *Willkie,* New York, Simon and Schuster, Inc., 1952.

Barth, Alan, *The Price of Liberty,* New York, The Viking Press, Inc., 1961.

Bennett, James V., "Statement on the Abolition of Capital Punishment in Delaware," *Nat'l Probation and Parole Jnl.,* vol. 4 (1958), and *The American Bar Association Journal,* November, 1958.

Borchard, Edwin M., *Convicting the Innocent,* New Haven, Conn., Yale University Press, 1932.

Bowen, Catherine Drinker, *John Adams and the American Revolution,* Boston, Little, Brown & Co., 1950.

Brown, Peter Megargee, and Peer, Richard S., "The Wiretapping Entanglement: How to Strengthen Law Enforcement and Preserve Privacy," *Cornell Law Quarterly,* Vol. 44, No. 2 (Winter, 1959).

Brown, Ralph S., Jr., *Loyalty and Security,* New Haven, Conn., Yale University Press, 1958.

Brownell, Herbert, Jr., "The Public Security and Wire Tapping," *Cornell Law Quarterly,* Vol. 39, No. 2 (Winter, 1954).

Camus, Albert, "Reflections on the Guillotine," *Evergreen Review,* Vol. 1, No. 3 (1957).

Chafee, Zechariah, Jr., *Freedom of Speech and Press,* New York, Carrie Chapman Catt Memorial Fund Inc., 1955.

Cushman, Robert E., *Civil Liberties in the United States,* Ithaca, N.Y., Cornell University Press, 1956.

Dash, Samuel, *The Eavesdroppers,* New Brunswick, N.J., Rutgers University Press, 1959.

DeGrazia, Edward, "Obscenity and the Mail: A Study of Administrative Restraint," *Law and Contemporary Problems,* Durham, N.C., Duke University School of Law, Vol. 20 (1955), p. 608.

Douglas, William O., *An Almanac of Liberty,* Garden City, N.Y., Doubleday & Co., Inc., 1954.

———, *America Challenged,* Princeton, N.J., Princeton University Press, 1960.

———, *The Right of the People,* Garden City, N.Y., Doubleday & Co., Inc., 1958.

Eavesdropping and Wiretapping, Report of the New York State Joint Legislative Committee to Study Illegal Interception of Communications, Albany, N.Y., Williams Press, Inc., 1956.

Eavesdropping, Wiretapping and Licensed Private Detectives, Report of the New York State Joint Legislative Committee to Study Illegal Interception of Communications, Albany, N.Y., Williams Press, Inc., 1957.

Ernst, Morris L., and Schwartz, Alan U., "The Right to Counsel and the Unpopular Cause," Symposium, *University of Pittsburgh Law Review,* Vol. 20, No. 4 (June, 1959).

Fellman, David, *The Defendant's Rights,* New York, Rinehart & Company, Inc., 1958.

Fortas, Abe, "The Fifth Amendment: *Nemo tenetur prodere seipsum,*" *Cleveland Bar Association Jnl.,* Vol. 25 (1954), p. 91.

Frank, Jerome, *Courts on Trial,* Princeton, N.J., Princeton University Press, 1949.

Frank, Jerome and Barbara, *Not Guilty,* Garden City, N.Y., Doubleday & Company, Inc., 1957.

Frank, John P., *Marble Palace,* New York, Alfred A. Knopf, Inc., 1958.

Frankfurter, Felix, *The Problem of Capital Punishment,* New York, Harcourt, Brace and World, 1956.

Glover, Edward, "Notes on the M'Naghten Rules," *British Jnl. Delinquency,* Vol. 1 (1950).

Goldstein, Abraham S., "The State and the Accused: Balance of Advantage in Criminal Procedure," *Yale Law Journal,* June, 1960.

Grant, Father John, "Is the Electric Chair Condemned?" *The Ave Maria,* Vol. 85 (1957).

Griswold, Erwin, *The Fifth Amendment Today,* Cambridge, Mass., Harvard University Press, 1955.

Haight, A. L., *Banned Books,* New York, R. R. Bowker Company, 1955.

Hand, Learned, *Bill of Rights,* Cambridge, Mass., Harvard University Press, 1958.

Harvey, C. P., *The Advocate's Devil,* London, Stevens & Sons Limited, 1958.

Hempel, William J., and Wall, Patrick M., "Extralegal Censorship of Literature," *New York University Law Review,* Vol. 33, No. 7 (November, 1958).

Hook, Sydney, *Common Sense and the Fifth Amendment,* New York, Criterion Books, Inc., 1957.

Kamisar, Yale, "Illegal Searches or Seizures and Contemporaneous Incriminating Statements: A Dialogue on a Neglected Area of Criminal Procedure," *University of Illinois Law Forum,* Spring, 1961.

Koch, Adrienne, and Peden, William, *The Life and Selected Writings of Thomas Jefferson,* New York, Random House, Inc., 1944.

Koestler, Arthur, *Reflections on Hanging,* New York, The Macmillan Company, 1957.

Larson, Arthur, "Arms Control Through World Law," *Daedalus, Journal of the American Academy of Arts and Sciences,* Fall, 1960.

———, *On the World Court and the United States,* Durham, N.C., Duke University Law School.

———, *When Nations Disagree,* Baton Rouge, La., Louisiana State University Press, 1961.

Lawes, Lewis E., *Life and Death in Sing Sing,* New York, Garden City Publishing Company, 1928.

Lindman, Frank T., and McIntyre, Donald M., Jr., *The Mentally Disabled and the Law,* Chicago, University of Chicago Press, 1961.

Lustgarten, Edgar, *Verdict in Dispute,* New York, Charles Scribner's Sons, 1950.

McKay, Robert B., "The Right of Confrontation," *Washington University Law Quarterly,* No. 2 (1959).

Maslow, Will, "Fair Procedure in Congressional Investigations: A Proposed Code," *Columbia Law Review,* Vol. 54, p. 839.

Mason, Alpheus Thomas, *Brandeis, A Free Man's Life,* New York, The Viking Press, Inc., 1946.

———, *The Supreme Court from Taft to Warren,* Baton Rouge, La., Louisiana State University Press, 1958.

Mayers, Louis, *Shall We Amend the Fifth Amendment?,* New York, Harper & Brothers, 1959.

Medina, Harold, *Anatomy of Freedom,* New York, Matthew Bender & Co., 1954.

Millis, Walter, *Permanent Peace,* Santa Barbara, Calif., Center for the Study of Democratic Institutions, 1961.

Murray, John Courtney, S.J., "Literature and Censorship," an address.

Neal, Fred Warner, *U.S. Foreign Policy and the Soviet Union,* Santa Barbara, Calif., Center for the Study of Democratic Institutions, 1961.

Pfeffer, Leo, *The Liberties of an American,* Boston, Beacon Press, 1956.

Phillips, Harlan B., *Felix Frankfurter Reminisces,* New York, Reynal & Co., 1960.

Prettyman, Barrett, Jr., *Death and the Supreme Court,* New York, Harcourt, Brace and World, 1961.

Quincy, Josiah, *Memoirs of Josiah Quincy Jr.,* Boston, 1874.

Report of the Special Committee on the Federal Loyalty-Security Program of the Association of the Bar of the City of New York, New York, Dodd, Mead & Company, Inc., 1956.

Reports on Wiretapping and Eavesdropping Legislation in the State of New York (Special Committee on Wiretapping and Eavesdropping Legislation and Committee on the Bill of Rights), New York, Association of the Bar of the City of New York, 1958.

Rogat, Yosal, *The Eichmann Trial and the Rule of Law,* Santa Barbara, Calif., Center for the Study of Democratic Institutions, 1961.

Rogers, William P., "The Case for Wire Tapping," *Yale Law Journal,* Vol. 63 (1954), p. 792.

Rutherford, Livingston, *John Peter Zenger,* New York, Peter Smith, 1941.

Schlesinger, Arthur M., *Prelude to Independence,* New York, Alfred A. Knopf, Inc., 1958.

Schwartz, Louis B., "On Current Proposals to Legalize Wire Tapping," University of Pennsylvania Law Review, Vol. 103 (1954), p. 157.

Seward, William H., *Frederick W. Seward: An Autobiography from 1801-1834,* New York, Derby and Miller, 1891.

Shientag, Bernard L., *Moulders of Legal Thought,* New York, The Viking Press, Inc., 1943.

St. John-Stevas, Norman, "Obscenity, Literature and the Law," *Cath. Lawyer,* Vol. 3, p. 301.

Steinberg, Harris B., "A Re-examination of the Fifth Amendment," *New York State Bar Bulletin,* July, 1959.

Stone, Irving, *Clarence Darrow for the Defense,* New York, Peter Smith, 1941.

Weihofen, Henry, *Mental Disorder as a Criminal Defense,* Buffalo, Denis & Co., 1954.

———, *The Urge to Punish,* New York, Farrar, Straus and Cudahy, 1956.

Wellman, Francis L., *The Art of Cross-Examination,* New York, The Macmillan Company, 1903.

Wertham, Frederick, *The Circle of Guilt,* New York, Rinehart & Company, Inc., 1956.

———, *The Show of Violence,* Garden City, N.Y., Doubleday & Company, Inc., 1940.

Westin, Alan F., "The Wire-Tapping Problem: An Analysis and a Legislative Proposal," *Columbia Law Review,* Vol. 52 (1952), p. 165.

White, William S., *Citadel, The Story of the United States Senate,* New York, Harper & Brothers, 1957.

Williams, Glanville, *The Proof of Guilt,* London, Stevens & Sons Limited, 1955.

———, "The Royal Commission and the Defense of Insanity," *Current Legal Problems,* Vol. 7 (1954).

"Wiretapping, Congress and the Department of Justice," *International Juridical Association Monthly Bulletin,* Vol. 9, No. 9 (March, 1941).

"The Wiretapping-Eavesdropping Problem: Reflections on the Eavesdroppers. A Symposium," *Minnesota Law Review,* Vol. 44, No. 5 (April, 1960).

INDEX

EDWARD BENNETT WILLIAMS

Edward Bennett Williams, who is forty-one, grew up in Hartford, Connecticut. He earned a scholarship to Holy Cross College and was graduated summa cum laude *in 1941. After serving in the Air Force he completed his law studies at Georgetown University Law School and on graduation was appointed professor of criminal law and procedure. He remained on the faculty at Georgetown until 1956. In 1954 he lectured in Europe on American criminal law as a guest professor at the University of Frankfurt.*

9 781439 19686